Get the eBook FREE!

(PDF, ePub, Kindle, and liveBook all included)

We believe that once you buy a book from us, you should be able to read it in any format we have available. To get electronic versions of this book at no additional cost to you, purchase and then register this book at the Manning website.

Go to https://www.manning.com/freebook and follow the instructions to complete your pBook registration.

That's it!
Thanks from Manning!

Zero to AI

THE NONTECHNICAL, HYPE-FREE MANUAL
ON HOW TO PROSPER IN THE AI ERA

GIANLUCA MAURO AND NICOLÒ VALIGI

MANNING

SHELTER ISLAND

For online information and ordering of this and other Manning books, please visit www.manning.com. The publisher offers discounts on this book when ordered in quantity. For more information, please contact

> Special Sales Department
> Manning Publications Co.
> 20 Baldwin Road
> PO Box 761
> Shelter Island, NY 11964
> Email: orders@manning.com

Manning Publications Co.
20 Baldwin Road
PO Box 761
Shelter Island, NY 11964

Development editor:	Lesley Trites
Technical development editor:	Danny Vinson
Review editor:	Ivan Martinović
Production editor:	Deirdre Hiam
Copy editor:	Sharon Wilkey
Proofreader:	Melody Dolab
Technical proofreader:	Andrew Harmor
Typesetter:	Gordan Salinovic
Cover designer:	Marija Tudor

ISBN 9781617296062

Printed and bound by CPI Group (UK) Ltd, Croydon, CR0 4YY

"The future is already here—it's just not very evenly distributed."

—William Gibson

brief contents

1 ▪ An introduction to artificial intelligence   1

PART 1   UNDERSTANDING AI 11

2 ▪ Artificial intelligence for core business data   13
3 ▪ AI for sales and marketing   36
4 ▪ AI for media   68
5 ▪ AI for natural language   91
6 ▪ AI for content curation and community building   119

PART 2   BUILDING AI 137

7 ▪ Ready—finding AI opportunities   139
8 ▪ Set—preparing data, technology, and people   167
9 ▪ Go—AI implementation strategy   185
10 ▪ What lies ahead   210

contents

preface   *vii*
acknowledgments   *xv*
about this book   *xvii*
about the authors   *xxi*

1 An introduction to artificial intelligence   1

1.1   The path to modern AI   2

1.2   The engine of the AI revolution: machine learning   4

1.3   What is artificial intelligence, after all?   6

1.4   Our teaching method   8

PART 1   UNDERSTANDING AI...............................11

2 Artificial intelligence for core business data   13

2.1   Unleashing AI on core business data   14

2.2   Using AI with core business data   15

The real estate marketplace example   16 ▪ *Adding AI capabilities to FutureHouse   18* ▪ *The machine learning advantage   22*
Applying AI to general core business data   24

2.3   Case studies   25

How Google used AI to cut its energy bill   25 ▪ How Square used AI to lend billions to small businesses   29 ▪ Case studies lessons   32

2.4   Evaluating performance and risk   33

3 *AI for sales and marketing   36*

3.1   Why AI for sales and marketing   37

3.2   Predicting churning customers   38

3.3   Using AI to boost conversion rates and upselling   42

3.4   Performing automated customer segmentation   44

Unsupervised learning (or clustering)   45 ▪ Unsupervised learning for customer segmentation   49

3.5   Measuring performance   52

Classification algorithms   52 ▪ Clustering algorithms   55

3.6   Tying ML metrics to business outcomes and risks   56

3.7   Case studies   58

AI to refine targeting and positioning: Opower   58 ▪ AI to anticipate customer needs: Target   64

4 *AI for media   68*

4.1   Improving products with computer vision   69

4.2   Using AI for image classification: deep learning?   73

4.3   Using transfer learning with small datasets   76

4.4   Face recognition: teaching computers to recognize people   78

4.5   Using content generation and style transfer   81

4.6   What to watch out for   83

4.7   AI for audio   84

4.8   Case study: optimizing agriculture with deep learning   85

Case questions   88 ▪ Case discussion   88

5 *AI for natural language   91*

5.1   The allure of natural language understanding   92

5.2   Breaking down NLP: measuring complexity   93

5.3 Adding NLP capabilities to your organization 96

*Sentiment analysis 99 ▪ From sentiment analysis to text
classification 102 ▪ Scoping a NLP classification project 105
Document search 106 ▪ Natural conversation 108
Designing products that overcome technology limitations 111*

5.4 Case study: Translated 113

Case questions 116 ▪ Case discussion 116

6 ***AI for content curation and community building 119***

6.1 The curse of choice 120

6.2 Driving engagement with recommender systems 120

*Content-based systems beyond simple features 124 ▪ The
limitations of features and similarity 126*

6.3 The wisdom of crowds: collaborative filtering 127

6.4 Recommendations gone wrong 129

The recommender system dream 130

6.5 Case study: Netflix saves $1 billion a year 131

*Netflix's recommender system 131 ▪ Recommendations and user
experience 133 ▪ The business value of recommendations 134
Case questions 135 ▪ Case discussion 135*

PART 2 BUILDING AI 137

7 ***Ready—finding AI opportunities 139***

7.1 Don't fall for the hype: Business-driven
AI innovation 140

7.2 Invention: Scouting for AI opportunities 144

7.3 Prioritization: Evaluating AI projects 146

7.4 Validation: Analyzing risks 150

7.5 Deconstructing an AI product 152

7.6 Translating an AI project into ML-friendly terms 157

7.7 Exercises 161

*Improving customer targeting 161 ▪ Automating industrial
processes 163 ▪ Helping customers choose content 164*

8 Set—preparing data, technology, and people 167

8.1   Data strategy   168

Where do I get data?   169 ▪ *How much data do I need?   173*

8.2   Data quality   177

8.3   Recruiting an AI team   180

9 Go—AI implementation strategy   185

9.1   Buying or building AI   186

The Buy option: Turnkey solutions   186 ▪ *The Borrow option: ML platforms   188* ▪ *The Build option: Roll up your sleeves   190*

9.2   Using the Lean Strategy   192

Starting from Buy solutions   193 ▪ *Moving up to Borrow solutions   195* ▪ *Doing things yourself: Build solutions   195*

9.3   Understanding the virtuous cycle of AI   197

9.4   Managing AI projects   202

9.5   When AI fails   204

Anki   204 ▪ *Lighthouse AI   205* ▪ *IBM Watson in Oncology   205* ▪ *Emotional diary   207* ▪ *Angry phone calls   208* ▪ *Underperforming sales   208*

10 What lies ahead   210

10.1   How AI threatens society   211

Bias and fairness   211 ▪ *AI and jobs   214* ▪ *The AI filter bubble   215* ▪ *When AI fails: Corner cases and adversarial attacks   217* ▪ *When the artificial looks real: AI-generated fake content   219*

10.2   Opportunities for AI in society   220

Democratization of technology   220 ▪ *Massive scale   221*

10.3   Opportunities for AI in industries   222

Social media networks   223 ▪ *Health care   224* ▪ *Energy   226 Manufacturing   228* ▪ *Finance   229* ▪ *Education   230*

10.4   What about general AI?   231

10.5   Closing thoughts   232

index   235

preface

In 2014, we opened an email that changed our lives. We had received a scholarship to study and work in the cradle of technology: Silicon Valley. It turned out to be the perfect moment and the perfect place to witness the rebirth of modern artificial intelligence. The technologies that would be powering the AI revolution of the 2010s were taking their first steps outside academic labs. In Silicon Valley, it was easy to peek behind the curtains, as excited geeks shared their knowledge at open events.

For the two of us, and for Silicon Valley companies, it was clear that AI was set to shake industries left and right. And yet, we returned home to Europe to realize that the rest of the business world had not caught up with this reality. Business leaders, professionals, and entrepreneurs knew little about the potential of AI. Even the few enlightened people who did have a vision struggled to find the tools and skills needed to make it a reality.

Once again, it looked like the fruits of a new wave of technological innovation would be the exclusive playground of a handful of companies in Silicon Valley, and Europe would be once more left behind. This time, we decided we wouldn't stand for that. We set out on a mission to spread the awareness, skills, and vision needed to create value with AI. We did it by founding AI Academy: a company focused on education and strategic consulting on artificial intelligence. Over the past few years, we've had the great honor of coaching hundreds of people, ranging from entrepreneurs to decision makers in large corporations in health care, energy, consumer goods, and fashion. We helped them filter through the noise and the hype and guided them toward their own vision of how AI could grow their organization.

In the summer of 2018, we realized that, no matter how successful our business had become, we were drifting away from our mission of democratizing AI. In fact, our knowledge was useful to only the small group of companies that we could reach with workshops and coaching. Outside this circle, many talented and inspired individuals from all over the world still wanted to understand more about AI and do exciting things with it. And yet, all they had was either super-technical material from academia or hype-heavy stories shared by mass media. Excited by the latter and confused by the former, they dreamed up ambitious AI projects for their organizations without really knowing how to make them successful.

This book is our attempt to distill all our coaching and consulting experience to help these visionaries. While journalists focus on clickbait articles and corporate PR, we'll expose you to the less flashy, but incredibly effective applications of AI that helped Google cut its energy bill by 40%, Amazon boost its sales by 35%, Pinterest increase user engagement by 30%, Netflix save more than a billion dollars per year, and Square offer small business loans within 24 hours. This book will teach you how they did it. We'll give you a clear understanding of AI's principles, strengths, and current limitations. This new knowledge will complement the experience you already have in your domain and make you a leader in the AI era.

You'll understand that AI isn't a silver bullet, and using it in a product (or claiming to do so) is not a free pass for success. We'll share with you our hard-earned lessons about how to design, build, and manage successful AI products. Before you even finish the book, you'll already start thinking about the *actual* role of this technology in your organization.

Understanding AI is not just about being up-to-date on technology. It's also the key to fundamentally changing what organizations can achieve. The prize is huge: a blue ocean of opportunities is still waiting for enlightened AI leaders. Tech companies are already making their fortunes with AI. This book is our invitation for you to join the party.

acknowledgments

Writing this book has been hard. Very hard. In a world where the internet encourages people to favor quantity over quality and push content fast and often, we decided to take the opposite route. We invested thousands of hours to put together what we believe is the best nontechnical guide for people to understand and start using AI.

It was a gigantic effort, and we'd like to thank the people who helped us in this journey.

Thanks to the Fulbright BEST commission, which offered both of us the scholarship that allowed us to meet and spend six unforgettable months in Silicon Valley.

We'd like to thank everyone at Manning who provided invaluable guidance (and sometimes just plain hand holding) during our first adventure as authors. Specifically, thanks to development editor Lesley Trites, review editor Ivan Martinović, technical development editor Danny Vinson, technical proofreader Andrew Harmor, project editor Deirdre Hiam, copy editor Sharon Wilkey, and proofreader Melody Dolab.

Thanks also to all our reviewers: Alain Couniot, Alan Matcham, Antonio Moro, Arun Pavuri, Clemens Baader, Davide Cadamuro, Francesco Catarinozzi, Harro Lissenberg, James Gray, John Montgomery, Lisa Örtegren, Marc Falk, Marianna Ricci, Mario Grassi, Michael B Marcus, Michael Modenese, Neil Croll, Nelson Wong, Nick Vazquez, Peter Hampton, Peter Trydeman, Peter White, Ravi Sajnani, Ritwik Dubey, Shiloh Morris, Sune Lomholt, Todd Wade, Tomasz Struminski, and Vitosh Doynov. Your feedback has been of immense help. We sincerely believe that without you, we wouldn't be as proud of this work as we are now. And apologies if our first drafts left something to be desired.

From Gianluca: Thank you, Sofia, for being my partner and my friend. Your relentless passion for life inspires me to live mine to its fullest, joyful and humbled by knowing I have a special place in your heart. Grazie alla mia famiglia. Sapere di poter contare sul vostro supporto e amore incondizionato è il mio porto sicuro dalla quale far partire ogni mia avventura, passata, presente e futura.

From Nicolò: Thank you, Angela, for being the complementary half of my personality. Your energy, passion, and dedication have filled my life with optimism and challenge, inspiring me to become a better person than I could ever hope to be. Grazie alla mia famiglia per essere stata una roccaforte di stabilità, un esempio di amore, e un fuoriclasse di pazienza con il sottoscritto.

about this book

Zero to AI is designed to help you understand how you can use AI in organizations small and large, for-profit and nonprofit. We want this to be a one-stop solution and leave you with the confidence you need to start using AI in your organization. To help you get there, we divided the book into two parts with two different goals:

- Part 1 of the book is about the technology, its core principles, and how companies have used it to build amazing products. At the end of this part, you'll understand what AI can and can't do, and know the vocabulary to communicate effectively with technical people.
- Part 2 focuses on organizations and value creation. We'll share with you the strategies we use in our consulting practice to select, design, and build successful AI products.

Who should read this book

Three groups of people benefited from the recent spate of improvements in AI: tech entrepreneurs, the venture capitalists who showered them with money, and the few sought-after AI experts who saw their salaries balloon to seven figures. If we had started writing five years ago, we would have written a technical handbook with these people in mind.

Today, we think that techies have had their share of success, and it's time to let the next class of professionals join the AI revolution. The protagonists of the upcoming chapter of the AI era won't be interested in building AI applications for the sake of technological progress. They're not computer science or mathematics gurus.

They're experts in a specific industry who want to use AI as a tool for solving real-world problems.

Some of these future protagonists work for large corporations. It doesn't matter if their business card says *CEO, manager,* or *intern.* What matters is their drive to strengthen their careers by helping their organization be competitive in these fast-changing times. Others work for smaller companies and want to see them grow and create new products and services. Yet others are entrepreneurs, looking for the "next big thing" to build. And let's not forget about students and fresh graduates who want to develop unique skills.

In our experience as consultants and engineers, we met many such people who aspired to be AI leaders (see figure 1). We did our best to give them what they needed: a clear understanding of what AI is, what it can do, and how it can be used to bring value to their organizations. We wrote this book because we want you to join the crew of revolutionaries.

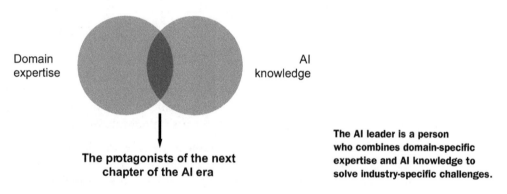

The AI leader is a person who combines domain-specific expertise and AI knowledge to solve industry-specific challenges.

How this book is organized

Because you'll need two fundamental sets of skills to bring AI into your organization, this book is also divided into two parts covering 10 chapters.

Part 1 is about *understanding* AI. Because modern AI is built on data, each chapter in this section introduces you to different types of data and the AI tools best suited for each:

- Chapter 1 is a brief introduction to the history of AI and the innovations that sparked the AI revolution of the 2010s.
- Chapter 2 is about the data produced by core business operations, and how AI can be used to build unique products and services on top of it.
- Chapter 3 takes a deeper look at AI applications for sales and marketing.
- Chapter 4 introduces AI models that can understand, produce, and transform media such as images, video, and audio.
- Chapter 5 presents AI algorithms for understanding and producing written text.
- Chapter 6 demonstrates models for recommending personalized content to humans.

Part 2 is about *building* AI. This part is meant to be your guide to design and build new projects within your organization:

- Chapter 7 describes a framework for identifying opportunities for AI in your organization and selecting the best ones.
- Chapter 8 discusses the challenges involved in building AI projects, from collecting the right data to recruiting an effective team.
- Chapter 9 is about implementation strategy. It presents the trade-off involved in building or buying technologies and a lean approach to minimizing risk. It also covers strategies for managing AI projects and incrementally improving them.
- The book ends with chapter 10, which offers a final broad view of how AI can impact society.

We recommend reading the chapters in order, as they all build on each other to offer you a full understanding.

liveBook discussion forum

Purchase of *Zero to AI* includes free access to a private web forum run by Manning Publications, where you can make comments about the book, ask technical questions, and receive help from the author and from other users. To access the forum, go to https://livebook.manning.com/book/zero-to-ai/discussion. You can also learn more about Manning's forums and the rules of conduct at https://livebook.manning.com/#!/discussion.

Manning's commitment to our readers is to provide a venue where a meaningful dialogue between individual readers, and between readers and the authors, can take place. It is not a commitment to any specific amount of participation on the part of the authors, whose contribution to the forum remains voluntary (and unpaid). We suggest you try asking the authors some challenging questions lest their interest stray! The forum and the archives of previous discussions will be accessible from the publisher's website as long as the book is in print.

Other online resources

After finishing this book, you might want to continue learning about two main areas. You may want to deepen your knowledge about the technical aspects of AI that we cover in part 1 and start building some AI projects. In this case, you can choose from a variety of online courses and materials. Two of the most widely known are Andrew Ng's Machine Learning and Deep Learning courses, available on Coursera. Both include programming assignments and will give you a strong foundation in the math and implementation issues behind many well-known algorithms. Several universities also offer some of their ML courses online, complete with video lectures and homework assignments. We can recommend Stanford's CS231 course about Deep Learning for Computer Vision applications (covered in chapter 4) and CS224N about Deep

Learning for Natural Language Processing (covered in chapter 5). Compared to online-first material, university courses generally tend to cover theory more in depth.

Recommendations are sparser if you're interested in learning more about the business aspects of AI implementation, which we cover in part 2. Indeed, that's one of the main reasons we wrote this book in the first place. However, some good books can give you a much deeper overview of best practices you want to follow when building innovative products. For example, *The Lean Startup* by Eric Ries (Crown Business, 2011) covers many of the experimentation and incremental development techniques we present in part 2. *The Startup Owner's Manual* by Steve Blank and Bob Dorf (K&S Ranch Publishing, 2012) offers a great step-by-step blueprint that can be used for anything that has to with innovation, within AI and beyond. For a more seamless continuation on the topics of this book, please forgive us for a shameless plug and sign up for our newsletter at https://ai-academy.com, where we cover themes at the intersection of AI and business.

about the authors

Gianluca Mauro and **Nicolò Valigi** cofounded AI Academy, a company that advises on AI strategy and runs workshops teaching the concepts covered in this book. Through AI Academy, Gianluca and Nicolò have helped companies, ranging from idea-phase startups to multinational corporations, kick-start their AI journeys.

Gianluca has a background in engineering and entrepreneurship. His passion is to use human creativity to explore how technology can build better products and a better society. He thrives to inspire people to do the same by speaking at universities, corporations, and industry conferences. In his free time, he enjoys playing music, practicing martial arts, and lifting weights.

Nicolò likes tinkering with code, robots, and (seemingly) intelligent software. He has worked on the brains of drones, the gears of NASA spacecraft, and helped push bits in self-driving cars. He also regularly presents at international conferences and even more regularly tries to take apart any electronic gadget around him.

An introduction to
artificial intelligence

1

This chapter covers

- Gaining perspective about the history of artificial intelligence
- Understanding machine learning and its relationship to AI
- Exploring the drivers of the explosion in AI applications

Artificial intelligence (AI) is not a new technology. For decades, computer scientists have tried different approaches to reach the holy grail of computing: intelligent machines. While we are still far away from replicating the wonders of the human brain, AI applications have started to fill our daily lives and power our electronic devices, from smartphones to home alarm systems.

Why this seemingly sudden explosion? This chapter will answer this question by teaching you about modern AI—including the core principles behind it, and how and why we got to where we are now.

1

1.1   *The path to modern AI*

As humans, we've always tried to find ways to understand the world around us and bend nature to meet our goals. To do so, we have always relied on external tools that amplify our brain's capabilities.

The abacus was probably the first such tool, invented about 5,000 to 6,000 years ago to help people make calculations. Although it's still used in schools to help children visualize simple mathematical operations, it doesn't really save us from the labor of actually performing them. We had to wait until the 1960s for the first machines that could add and subtract numbers automatically. Computers have come a long way since then, but deep down their capability has still been pretty simple: executing calculations exactly as some (expert) human has instructed them to do. There's little "intelligence" in them.

The two words *artificial* and *intelligence* were first put together on August 31, 1955, when professor John McCarthy from Dartmouth College, together with M.L Minsky from Harvard University, N. Rochester from IBM, and C. E. Shannon from Bell Telephone Laboratories, asked the Rockefeller Foundation to fund a summer of research on artificial intelligence. Their proposal stated the following:

> *We propose that a 2 month, 10 man study of artificial intelligence be carried out during the summer of 1956 at Dartmouth College in Hanover, New Hampshire. . . . An attempt will be made to find how to make machines use language, form abstractions and concepts, solve kinds of problems now reserved for humans, and improve themselves. We think that a significant advance can be made in one or more of these problems if a carefully selected group of scientists work on it together for a summer.*

The researchers knew that tackling intelligence as a whole was too tough of a challenge, both because of technical limitations *and* the inherent complexity of the task. Instead of solving the broad concept of intelligence, they decided to focus on subproblems, like language. Later, these applications would be called *narrow AI*. An artificial intelligence capable of matching or surpassing human capabilities would instead be called *general AI*. In other words:

- *General AI* (or *strong AI*)—An artificial intelligence program capable of tackling every kind of task it's presented. This is similar to an extremely resourceful human, and you can think of it as the robot from *The Terminator* (or, hopefully, a more peaceful version of it).
- *Narrow AI*—An artificial intelligence program capable of solving a single, well-defined task. It can be broad (recognizing objects from pictures) or extremely specific (predicting which customers who bought product A are more likely to purchase product B as well). This means one task at a time, and not any other: an AI that recognizes cats in images can't translate English to Italian, and vice versa.

General AI is still far away: researchers still don't know when we'll finally get it. Some argue that we'll never get there. Even though general AI is still a distant, fuzzy dream, this is what many people have in mind when AI is mentioned in the news. If you were one of those people, and are now disappointed that general AI is not here yet, don't despair. Narrow AI applications are still capable of creating immense value. For example, AI that can detect lung cancer is a narrow application but nevertheless extremely useful.

The results of the Dartmouth research summer of 1956 were so interesting that they sparked a wave of excitement and hope among the participants. The enthusiasm of the scientists spread to the US government, which started heavily funding research on a specific application: English/Russian translation. Finding trustworthy Russian translators must not have been easy in the midst of the Cold War.

After the first few years of work, a government committee produced the infamous 1966 Automatic Language Processing Advisory Committee (ALPAC) report. The document featured the opinions of many researchers about the state of AI research. Most were not very positive:

> *Early machine translations of simple or selected text . . . were as deceptively encouraging as "machine translations" of general scientific text have been uniformly discouraging. . . . No one can guarantee, of course, that we will not suddenly or at least quickly attain machine translation, but we feel that this is very unlikely.*

> *. . . there is no immediate or predictable prospect of useful machine translation.*

The ALPAC report marks the beginning of a period called the *first AI winter*: public funding for AI research stopped, excitement cooled, and researchers focused their work on other fields.

Interest in AI faded until the 1980s, when private companies such as IBM and Xerox started investing in a new AI spring. New hopes were fueled by a technology called *expert systems*: computer programs that encode the knowledge of a human expert in a certain field in the form of precise, *if-then* rules. An example will help you understand how expert systems were designed to work.

Suppose you want to build an AI system that can stand in for a gastroenterologist. This is how you do it with an expert system: you ask a doctor to describe with extreme precision how they make decisions about patients. You then ask a programmer to painstakingly transform the doctor's knowledge and diagnosis flow to if-then rules that can be understood and executed by a computer. An extremely simplified version would look something like this:

> *If the patient has a stomachache and the body temperature is high, then the patient has the flu.*

> *If the patient has a stomachache and has eaten expired food, then the patient has food poisoning.*

And so on. Once the doctor's knowledge is encoded into the software and a patient comes in, the software follows the same decision path as the doctor and (hopefully) comes up with the same diagnosis. This approach has several problems:

- *Poor adaptability*—The only way for the software to improve is to go back to the drawing board with a computer scientist and the expert (in this case, the doctor).
- *Extreme brittleness*—The system will fail in situations that weren't part of the original design. What if a patient has a stomachache but normal body temperature, and hasn't eaten spoiled food?
- *Tough to maintain*—The complexity of such a system is huge. When thousands of rules are put together, improving it or changing it is incredibly complicated, slow, and expensive. Have you ever worked with a huge Microsoft Excel sheet and struggled to find the root cause of a mistake? Imagine an Excel sheet 100 times bigger.

Expert systems were a commercial failure. By the end of the 1980s, many of the companies that were developing them went out of business, marking the beginning of the *second AI winter*. It wasn't until the early 2000s that the next generation of AI successes came along, fueled by an old idea that became new again: machine learning.

1.2   *The engine of the AI revolution: machine learning*

The first definition of *machine learning* dates back to 1959, from American AI pioneer Arthur Samuel:

> *Machine learning is the field of study that gives computers the ability to learn without being explicitly programmed.*

The key elements here are *learning* and *without being explicitly programmed*. Let's focus on the latter first. Explicitly programming a computer means defining the rules and instructions it must follow to perform a specific task. This is what software engineers do when they write software that handles your everyday tasks like doing taxes or filling out spreadsheets.

People without programming experience often feel like software engineers are powerful creatures who can bend machines to their will. Unfortunately, things are not always that easy. Try to think about the various decisions you make as you perform some trivial actions: can you explain the process you follow to recognize your friends when you see them? All the split-second decisions you make while driving? Can you list all the English grammar rules you apply as you talk? If you can't precisely explain how you do something, there's no chance that you can instruct a computer to do it.

Samuel proposed to replace "instructing computers" with "giving them the ability to learn." If you think about it, learning instead of following instructions is (coincidentally?) what human beings do all the time. Our mothers and fathers don't teach us their native tongue by giving us grammar books at the tender age of one. They just speak to us naturally, and we learn from their example, applying thousands of grammar rules without even knowing it. In fact, our brain is capable of automatically extracting rules way before it becomes capable of rationally understanding grammar at school! Even for us humans, it looks like learning rules from examples can be easier than being told about them.

In the same way we learn from experience, machine learning (ML) techniques allow computers to learn from data. Let's make it more concrete with a classic toy example: teaching a computer to tell dogs from cats in pictures. If you had to teach a kid to perform this task, you wouldn't pick up a veterinary book and start reading about the differences in ear shape or fur color. Instead, you'd probably just point them to a few pictures and let their brain do its magic.

An ML solution to the "dog or cat" problem is similar to our childhood learning experiences. We feed the computer thousands of images of cats and tell it "these are cats," and then thousands of images of dogs and tell it "these are dogs." Finally, we let it figure out the difference between the two pets automatically. We don't have to explain the key elements that distinguish dogs from cats. A good ML application learns to figure that out from the examples it receives. Figure 1.1 shows the difference between traditional programming and machine learning.

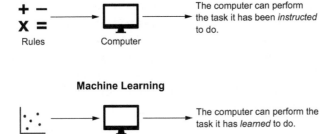

Traditional Programming

Rules → Computer → The computer can perform the task it has been *instructed* to do.

Machine Learning

Data → Computer → The computer can perform the task it has *learned* to do.

Figure 1.1 The difference between the traditional programming approach and machine learning: the first relies on precise rules and instructions, the latter on data and learning.

You may start to sense why ML couldn't possibly have blossomed before the 2000s. The main ingredient of this set of techniques is *data*, and the internet has made collecting data much easier. The other crucial ingredient for ML is *computing power*: learning from data doesn't happen for free, and computers need fast processors to perform this task. Thanks to cloud computing and increases in processing power, access to powerful computers has never been so easy and cheap.

To give you a sense of how much things have changed in just a few years, we asked Alex Waibel, one of the pioneers of AI in speech recognition and among the first hires of Facebook's AI team, how different it was to work on ML 20 years ago. The most powerful computer he could use in the early 2000s was as big as an apartment, cost a few million, and he needed to rent it to train his models. Today, he has much more computing power sitting on his desk for a few thousand dollars. Your phone is probably more powerful than what top researchers had available just 20 years ago.

Availability of data and cheap computing power created the perfect environment for machine learning to bloom. Indeed, many (most) of the coolest consumer-facing applications of what we call AI today rely heavily on ML: the Siri voice virtual assistant, Google Translate, self-driving cars, and many more.

Going back to the history of AI, it seems that ML is the engine that powered today's AI explosion, finally bringing some hope after the last AI winter of the 1980s. In fact, the success of modern AI has been so dependent on ML techniques that people are often confused about the difference between the two. What is artificial intelligence, then? Let's find out.

1.3   What is artificial intelligence, after all?

In our experience as technologists, consultants, and public speakers, we are constantly meeting people with different opinions about the definitions of *AI*, *data science*, and *ML*. Although many are quite opinionated, few can defend their position. Indeed, finding a universal definition of AI is not as trivial as it might look.

Going by its name, we might try to define *artificial intelligence* by finding the human traits that we associate with intelligence. Once we agree on what makes humans intelligent, we can say that any computer that does the same thing is AI. It makes sense, right? Although this is a common approach, it falls apart even with simple scenarios. For instance, a human who can divide 13.856 by 13 down to the tenth decimal number in a split second would definitely be called intelligent, yet its artificial counterpart is a $2 pocket calculator that nobody would dare call AI. At the same time, we would never call someone intelligent just because they're able to drive in heavy traffic, yet a self-driving car is generally considered one of the toughest forms of AI the tech industry is working on today. We shouldn't be surprised by how hard defining *intelligence* is; after all, philosophers and scientists have been debating about it for centuries.

Not only do we have different weights to measure human and machine intelligence, but we also seem to be changing our mind pretty fast about what is AI and what isn't. Let's take an example from Paul Graham, founder of Y Combinator, the most successful Silicon Valley startup accelerator, and arguably one of the most forward-looking people in tech. In 2002, Graham wrote an essay proposing a new solution to detect spam emails. Back then, email was just getting off the ground, and spam (unwanted email) was one of the most serious threats to widespread use of the internet by nontechies. It seems hard to imagine now, but the best computer scientists were busy trying to write complex rules to let computers automatically sort through Viagra advertisements.

In his essay, Graham thought about a new ML-based approach that would learn to classify an email by processing thousands of "good" and spam emails. Paul's simple software learned to recognize spam better than the complex rules concocted by engineers. Fast-forward 20 years, and automatic spam detectors are such a boring technology that we would be laughed out of the room if we dared call it AI.

In fact, it seems like AI is about mastering tasks that our imagination suggests computers shouldn't be able to do. Once we get used to a technology in our daily life, we remove the AI badge of honor and start calling it just computer software. This is a well-studied phenomenon called the *AI effect*.

Because of the AI effect, the goalposts for what we call AI keep moving just as quickly as technology improves. The definition of AI we draw from these considerations is "a temporary label to a piece of software that does something cool and surprising, until we get used to it." We don't know about you, but that just doesn't feel like a satisfying definition.

We hope we have convinced you that it is extremely hard to find a definition that makes everyone happy and can be valid as technology evolves. With the AI effect in mind, we decided to avoid a narrow definition of AI that rewards "flashy" applications just to ditch them once the hype is gone. We embrace a broader definition that includes less flashy applications. This is our definition of AI:

Software that solves a problem without explicit human instruction.

As you can see, our definition focuses on the outcome of the technology rather than the specific techniques used to build it. Some people will not agree with it, because it's almost equivalent to what we said about machine learning earlier in the chapter. The truth is, learning *is* an intelligent trait, and while ML is just a tool, it is *the* tool behind 99% of the successful applications we happen to call AI today. This may change in the future, but we don't see any new approaches on the horizon that hold the same promise as ML. This is why every AI application we'll cover in this book is based on ML: it's simply the most accurate picture of the AI landscape of today and the near future.

We now have a clear view of what ML is, a working definition of modern AI, and some perspective about how these terms evolved. We are just missing the third buzzword you've probably heard about: data science.

Data science (*DS*) is a broad, multidisciplinary field that uses scientific methods and processes to analyze data and extract insights. ML techniques are some of the tools in the DS toolbox. In practice, when people refer to a *data science project*, they often mean something *static*: extracting insights from data and presenting them as a presentation or report. On the other hand, AI is more commonly used in the context of live software.

For instance, analyzing traffic data to design a new urban plan for a city to minimize congestion likely falls into the realm of data science. However, if you use the same data to control traffic in real time and direct cars through less-congested routes, most people would say the project is about AI. In the first case, the output of your project is a report, and in the second, it's "live" software that runs 24/7. Keep in mind that this division is mostly conventional: there really are no hard-and-fast rules about what's AI and what's data science. Table 1.1 summarizes the differences as we see them.

Table 1.1 The main differences between AI and data science

Artificial intelligence	Data science
Automates tasks or predicts future events based on data.	Produces insights based on data.
Is commonly used "live": it continuously elaborates new data and produces answers.	Is commonly "one-off": it produces some insights that inform decisions.
It commonly has the form of software.	It commonly has the form of a presentation or report.

Hopefully, these sections helped demystify some commonly misunderstood terms and created context for these technologies. Now you can start learning the core principles of AI, what you can potentially do with it, and how to bring this transformative technology into your organization. In the next section, we'll explain the steps of this journey and how this book guides you through them.

1.4 *Our teaching method*

If you want to productively use AI in your work life, it's paramount that you understand its nuts and bolts first. We noticed that nontechnical people who approach AI without a solid understanding of its principles often end up dreaming about projects that are simply impossible to build, or miss low-hanging fruit that could be easily tackled. After the first part of the book, you'll know all the AI principles you need to avoid these dead ends and get the best out of the technology.

Even after just this first chapter, you already understand that virtually all modern AI applications rely on machine learning, and machine learning is all about learning from data. This is why we used data as your guide to understanding AI. Each chapter of the first part of the book focuses on one specific kind of data, showing you how to spot it in your organization, what you can do with it, and how it fits into the world of AI.

Each chapter in part 1 uses a toy example to introduce the ML concepts you need. We found this to be the most efficient way to teach ML concepts that would otherwise be too dry and abstract. We didn't dig deep into technological aspects for two simple reasons:

- Technology changes so rapidly that implementation details would soon become obsolete.
- Simply put, you don't need it. Unless you want to pivot your career to writing code, we believe there's more value in adding AI to your wealth of knowledge and letting someone else practically implement your vision in computer terms.

This doesn't mean that we'll completely spare you from technicalities. From our experience as engineers, we know that it can be difficult for your technical team to communicate with people without the smallest bit of technical understanding. We don't want them to have trouble talking to *you*, so we made sure that you'll be learning the most important technical aspects of AI tools. Even as you leave them in the hands of your team, knowing about them will help you plan and manage the efforts.

Each chapter includes one or more real-world business cases about companies that achieved extraordinary results. To the extent that we mention specific companies, products, or services, keep in mind that we do so because we want you to develop awareness, but you shouldn't feel limited to them in any way. We have no affiliation or stake in any of the companies in the case studies; it just so happens that they're building great products we can all learn from.

When presenting cases, we followed a methodology inspired by the Harvard Business School case method: we'll first present the case in the most neutral way possible, and ask you open-ended questions at the end. Right after that, we include our thoughts about these questions and prompts for further discussion. We recommend you don't read these answers right away, but rather try thinking about how *you* would answer based on your knowledge and what you've read in the case, and only then read our take. Be aware that there's no unique solution to the questions we asked: if you found an interesting take on the cases that we didn't include in the answers, good job! This means you've learned what you needed and are able to extract insights on your own (so if that happens, we reached our goal with this book as well).

Summary

- AI has had a long history of successes and failures that dates back to the 1950s.
- General AI is the pipe dream of having an all-knowing machine. All AI applications we have today are instead narrow; they focus on specific tasks.
- Machine learning is the prevalent way to implement AI today, and is based on letting machines learn autonomously from data.
- Data science is related to AI and ML, but focuses more on extracting insights than persistent intelligence.

Part 1

Understanding AI

This part of the book focuses on the core principles of modern artificial intelligence. By the end of part 1, you'll know what AI can do for the different kinds of data your organization deals with. Perhaps more important, you'll also become familiar with what AI cannot do yet.

Today's AI revolution is based on training computers to learn from data, and that's why we have decided to organize this book based on the various shapes and forms that data can take. Every chapter focuses on a specific kind of data and uses a simplified example to help you learn key concepts about AI. At the end of each chapter, you'll find case studies from real companies that have used the technologies and data we talked about to achieve astonishing results.

Artificial intelligence
for core business data

2

This chapter covers

- Looking at business data in terms of dollar density and business impact
- Using supervised learning to predict key information
- Comparing machine learning to conventional software engineering
- Case studies: Using AI to create new business lines and optimize processes

This chapter covers *core business data,* the type of data that's closest to the value proposition of your business. Core business data is the secret sauce that makes your organization tick. It's the order data collected by commercial operations, the human interactions tracked by social networks, and the blood-pressure measurements tracked by a health-care startup. Because core business data is at the heart of the organization, it's also a prime candidate for your first AI applications. Doing AI on core business data is like cheating: the data is so close to the value-generating engine of the organization that successful projects are almost guaranteed to make a dramatic impact.

To whet your appetite, let's briefly mention the two case studies you'll find at the end of this chapter. The first one is about an initiative of Jim Gao, an ex-Google employee in charge of operations at its data centers. He looked at the data collected from the large air-conditioning systems used to cool Google's gigantic computers and thought about using machine learning to optimize their consumption. The result was a 40% bill cut for the tech giant. The second case is about Square, a payment services company based in San Francisco. Square had been processing credit card payments for small businesses and realized that all the data it was collecting could be used to offer customized and low-risk loans to small businesses. By using machine learning models, Square created an entirely new business line and tackled the blue ocean of small business loans. The quality of its service is unmatched: by automating the lender-vetting process, Square can deposit loans to a customer's bank account just one business day after the request is submitted. As a result, Square loaned more than $3 billion in four years, with exceptionally low delinquency rates of 4%. By the end of this chapter, you'll know how these companies made these changes possible.

2.1 Unleashing AI on core business data

We define *core business data* as "data with a direct impact on the top or bottom line of the organization." Core data looks very different depending on what your organization does: cart history for an e-commerce operation, physical measurements for an engineering organization, and patient behavior for a health-care company. Regardless of its form, core data is valuable because it describes events and patterns that have a direct impact on the organization's performance, and it's easy to attach a monetary value to it.

We already mentioned the two case studies that await you at the end of this chapter. Let's look at why the data used by the two companies is core business data:

- A company like Google relies on massive data centers to offer its services (process web searches, store photos, route emails, and so forth). Probably the only variable cost for Google is the energy spent to keep the data centers' computers cool. Therefore, data about its cooling plants is core to Google's business, as it correlates directly to one of its main costs.
- Square's core product is its point-of-sale (POS) solution. Through that product, Square processes all the payments going to its customers. Because Square's mission is empowering small businesses, its transaction data is strictly linked to that vision and is valuable for its customers.

A good way to look at the value of data is to think about a metric we'll call the *dollar density of data*: how much the data influences the top or bottom line of the organization. Core business data has a high dollar density: each e-commerce order, job lead, or financial transaction has a direct impact on your top or bottom line. As you move away from the core value proposition of your organization, the dollar density of the data you collect decreases accordingly. Recording visits to your website can be valuable, but not nearly as much as tracking orders coming in. For a hospital, the call center data could be useful, but not nearly as much as patient records. This is why we have decided to start the book with the highest-dollar-density data of all: your core business data.

Often we see that the core business data takes a structured form, just like the tidy rows and columns of a Microsoft Excel spreadsheet. In engineering terms, we call this type of data *structured*. Other examples of structured data are weather reports, measurements of physical processes, financial transactions, most markets, and supply chain and warehousing metrics. As a rule of thumb, anything that you can load in Excel is likely to fall within the structured data umbrella. Other types of data are harder to fit into neat Excel columns: think about pictures, voice recordings, or text in a book.

It's important to understand that the same information can exist in both structured and unstructured forms. For example, consider the following way of recording a medical diagnosis:

> *The patient Gianluca Mauro has a severe inflammation of the shoulder joint; the therapy is to take two pills of Cortisone per day for five days.*

The same information can be recorded in a structured way, as in table 2.1.

Table 2.1   A medical diagnosis in structured form

Patient	Diagnosis	Area	Medication	Frequency (times/day)	Therapy length (days)
Gianluca Mauro	Severe inflammation	Shoulder joint	Cortisone	2	5

The information is the same—but in the first case, it's represented in an unstructured way (text), whereas in the second, it's structured. Structured data is much easier for computers to process than unstructured data. Later chapters cover AI techniques for unstructured data, including images and written language. For now, let's stick to structured data, happily knowing that most core business data falls into this category.

2.2   Using AI with core business data

Now that you know how to find and recognize core business data, let's look at what AI can do with it. Because we believe in the teaching power of stories, we developed a simplified example that's going to keep you company throughout this first part of the book.

FutureHouse is a fictional business that operates an online real estate marketplace where homeowners can advertise their homes for sale and hopefully attract interested buyers. FutureHouse has always prioritized customer service and employs agents who can offer their support to help sellers assess their house price. Buyers use the site to look for the house of their dreams.

We chose this example because it will be familiar to many readers, while giving us the opportunity to explore many aspects of the AI landscape. A nice bonus is that the housing market is a typical example in the ML literature. Should you decide to delve deeper into the technicalities of ML and maybe write your own code, you'll find plenty of references on the web.

We'll start by explaining a bit about how housing markets work, and then we'll introduce an application of ML to this business. We're going to use this description as an excuse to introduce key terminology and concepts, and conclude by extending these concepts to other, more general applications.

2.2.1   *The real estate marketplace example*

Real estate agents are at the center of housing markets. They connect sellers and buyers and help them figure out the right price for their property. Figure 2.1 shows how the typical home-sale transaction unfolds under the careful watch of a realtor:

1   A customer comes in looking to sell their house. Before they put it on the market, they want a professional opinion about how much it's worth.
2   The realtor checks out the house and sets a price based on its square footage, age, included appliances, other offers in the neighborhood, and so on.
3   The house gets listed.
4   Potential buyers find the listing and come in for an open house event. One lucky buyer eventually gets to buy the property.

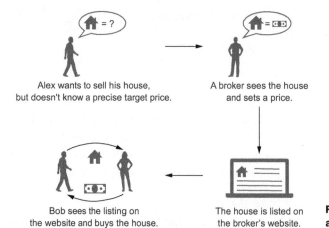

Alex wants to sell his house,
but doesn't know a precise target price.

A broker sees the house
and sets a price.

Bob sees the listing on
the website and buys the house.

The house is listed on
the broker's website.

**Figure 2.1   The process of listing
and selling a home on the market**

FutureHouse gets to collect data at each step of this process. These are its main data assets:

- Pictures of all homes for sale
- Descriptions of the homes (square footage, location, and so forth)
- Web visit and click history for all users of the website

- Historical records of properties sold in the region
- Reviews of the homes left by people who visited them
- Transcripts of negotiations between agent and buyer
- Newspaper articles about upcoming construction in the region

All these data sources don't hold the same value; their dollar density is different. For instance, the newspaper articles are a very general dataset that every other company has access to. Therefore, while it might be valuable, it's not core to FutureHouse. Website visits, images, and reviews may be important because they're specific and unique to the business, and therefore their dollar density is higher than that of newspaper articles. Still, they don't have a direct impact on the success of the business. The historical records of houses sold is much more connected to the business's performance than all the other data sources, as the traditional business model of realtors is a success fee per house sold: this is your core business data.

Let's assume we want to leverage this data to build an AI-powered property evaluation tool that automatically predicts the best price for homes listed on the platform. Price estimation is usually performed by an agent who has experience with the area and similar homes. They'll have overseen the sale of many properties in the past, developing deep intuition about what the fair price of the property would be. This is the task that we want AI to take over.

Let's try to come up with a more exhaustive list of the factors an agent might consider before suggesting a sale price:

- Square footage
- Number of floors
- Number of bedrooms
- Number of bathrooms
- Year of construction
- Does it have a pool?
- Does it have a garage?
- Energy efficiency
- Location
- Quality of the neighborhood
- Public transportation

If you ask how the agent came up with the price, they'll probably say something like "by experience." They might refer to standard guidelines like the average price per square foot in that neighborhood, but it's hard for them to articulate how other factors affected their decision. If you can't explain your thought process, you can't even code it into a computer program.

An agent learns how to value homes by looking at the selling price of many properties over time. The main idea behind ML is that a computer can do the same: it can learn how to value a home from the historical data of previously sold ones, feeding it with both their characteristics (size, neighborhood, and so forth) and the final sale price.

This AI would allow you to have the same expertise as an experienced broker, at the same speed, scale, availability, and cost of software, allowing any home seller to get an estimate of their property's value in a split second. This marriage of data availability and business value is the holy grail of AI-based innovation. We have identified a clear value proposition, backed by the right type of data to build it.

2.2.2 Adding AI capabilities to FutureHouse

One of the goals of this book is for you to learn how to talk to data scientists and engineers, so this is the paragraph where you become familiar with the lingo and technical details. At this stage in the ideation process, we have decided that we want to build an automated house-price-prediction engine. We believe it will help optimize our internal processes and offer value to our customers, as they'll be able to get a quote for their home directly online. We also have a record of transactions in the region, including some important features of the house (for example, square footage) and the sales price. If you brought all of this to an engineer, here's how the hypothetical conversation would go (keywords are highlighted in italics):

> You: We'd like to add an automatic price predictor to our real estate listings website. Can you help us with that?
>
> Engineer: Nice—this is a standard problem in machine learning. There are some well-known *machine learning algorithms* that I'm pretty confident can produce a good *model*. What *inputs* do we have?
>
> You: We spoke with the agents, and they usually factor in the square footage, number of bathrooms, distance to public transport, and things like that. Here's a complete list.
>
> Engineer: Sure, the list of *features* seems like a good start. And what *target* do you need from the model? Just the expected property price?
>
> You: Correct, that's all we need. The price will help us offer real-time quotes on our website for free.
>
> Engineer: Cool. What data do you have available for this?
>
> You: We have records for all house transactions in the region for the past decade.
>
> Engineer: Great! Do those records include all the *features* you mentioned earlier?
>
> You: Yes, most of them. We surely have the square footage and stuff like that, but you might have to figure out something for the public transport.
>
> Engineer: OK, I can work with that. Do you also have *labels* for all of them?
>
> You: Yes, the records include the final sale price of each property.
>
> Engineer: Amazing. How many *examples* are we talking about?
>
> You: We have around 200,000 transactions for the past five years.
>
> Engineer: Fantastic! That should be enough to *train our model*.

Let's rewind a bit and rephrase what you just went through. First of all, the engineer referred to your project as a *machine learning problem*. The word *problem* in a field like ML doesn't hold a negative connotation; it's used to refer to well-defined tasks that have a specific objective and known conditions. The objective of this project is to build a *model*: an automated computer program that can estimate property values for our specific area. Even if its inner workings are infinitely more complex, a model is just like a pocket calculator: it has a set of *inputs*, processes them through a *machine learning algorithm*, and then produces the *target* that we care about. Many people also like to say that the model *predicts* the target, or makes a *prediction* (for example, you'll often read about the *quality of predictions* of a model). In our case, the input is the set of *features* that describe each home: square footage, number of rooms, and so forth.

The engineer also asks about the number of *examples*, meaning the number of past home sales we have in our records. When we talk about the expected value of the output for a specific example (home), we usually call it a *label*, as if we're labeling each example with the correct value of the output. It's easy to visualize this in terms of an Excel sheet like the one in figure 2.2.

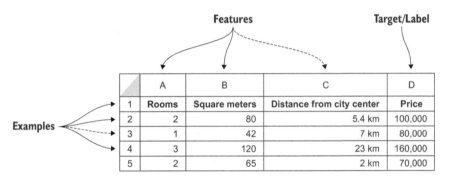

	A	B	C	D
1	Rooms	Square meters	Distance from city center	Price
2	2	80	5.4 km	100,000
3	1	42	7 km	80,000
4	3	120	23 km	160,000
5	2	65	2 km	70,000

Figure 2.2   An Excel sheet with features and labels for several examples

Our ML engineer asked for historical data because they have to instruct the computer to go through a process called *training*.

Just as an experienced realtor can guess the price of a new home based on their experience of homes sold in the past, a machine learning algorithm can learn how to predict the price of a house based on past examples in a phase called *training*. In this initial phase, engineers write code to feed the model with the thousands of examples we have. Each example contains both the features (the house characteristics to learn from) and their corresponding label (sale price), so that the algorithm can *learn* from these past experiences. Once training is complete, we have a self-contained computer program (the *model*) that packs all the predictive power of house-price prediction. Because the model now embeds the knowledge contained in the training dataset, we can start using it independently of the training data.

Anytime we want to evaluate a new home, we can feed its features to the model and get an answer about its likely price on the market. This second step, which is called *inference*, makes the model useful for the organization because it's producing estimates on new houses being listed on our platform. Once the model is trained, we can ask engineers to plug it into FutureHouse's website and start answering customers' requests as they come in.

It's normal if the boundary between training and inference is still a bit fuzzy for you. After all, humans go about their lives training on new knowledge and inferencing on past beliefs at the same time: our real estate agent friend has been evaluating properties and learning from each one sold at the same time since the beginning of their career. However, it's important that you realize that those are two very separate steps in the world of machine learning. Once the dataset is ready, training is little more than mechanical plumbing between the data and the different models that an engineer may decide to test. The real value is generated during *inference*, when we can use all that past experience to make new predictions. This distinction between training and inference is expressed graphically in figure 2.3.

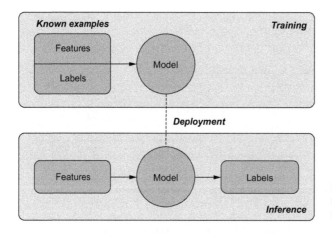

Figure 2.3 **The two phases of machine learning: training and inference**

So far, we've managed to rephrase our property-price-prediction problem in general terms, which is going to come in handy when we tackle other problems. We're asking engineers to build a model that can map inputs (aka *features*) to the *target* value (the price of the home). We're also going to hand in some data, in the form of a long list of *examples* (past sales), each with some *features* (square footage and other numbers) and a *label* (the sale price). We want the model to be able to predict the price of new homes that are coming onto the market, and do so in a way that's consistent with the examples that we provided. In other words, we expect the model to price a new two-bedroom flat in New York's Tribeca neighborhood similarly to other two-bedrooms that have been sold nearby in the past year.

We've introduced quite a few abstractions so far, so let's stop for a second and recap:

- *Machine learning algorithm*—A technology that allows computers to learn from data
- *Features*—A set of characteristics of an object that the algorithm can learn from
- *Label*—The output or target we want the algorithm to predict
- *Training*—A phase in which the machine learning algorithm is fed with past examples and learns from them
- *Model*—The output of the training phase—a self-contained computer program that can predict a label, given a set of features
- *Inference*—The phase in which the model is used with new examples

The great thing about all these abstractions is that we can now apply them to other problems. For example, say we want to predict the price of used cars rather than homes. Can you think of what features you would use? Car model and mileage probably are good guesses, as is the maintenance history. But you can have even more imagination: think about government subsidies for low-pollution vehicles, the number of Google searches for those models, and more. More generally, all problems for which we want to predict a value (which we don't know yet) based on a set of information we do have are examples of *supervised learning*.

Supervised learning is the area of machine learning that has the most applications in industry and research today. Our example so far belongs to this subset: it uses a set of techniques that allow machines to learn a mapping between a set of information called *features* and a target value called a *label*. The beauty of supervised learning, and of machine learning in general, is that the computer will automatically find this formula, no matter how complex it is. A successful model will make predictions that are consistent with the labels, thus transferring the experience embedded in the dataset to new cases. Figure 2.4 shows how features and labels interact in supervised learning applications.

By now, you have learned the basic concept behind supervised learning. As you can see, it's not rocket science. It's actually simple to grasp. The complexity is in the inner workings: the *machine learning algorithms*, the engines that allow computers to perform the learning. In this book, we won't dig deep into these algorithms unless we think it

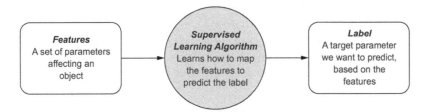

Figure 2.4   The core concept of supervised learning: finding a mapping between a set of features and a label

can be interesting and useful for you. With today's tools and services, we believe that you can generate value for your organization by knowing just enough to come up with AI products or services and passing the ball to ML engineers when it's time. Now you're starting to know how to do both, so high five!

Even if the previous concepts seem simple, don't underestimate your newfound knowledge: billions of dollars have been produced by companies that used the simple techniques you just learned. Why is machine learning so powerful, then? This is the topic of the next section.

2.2.3 *The machine learning advantage*

In the previous section, we had a pleasant conversation with an imaginary engineer, and we parted ways knowing that they would be building a model to predict house prices based on some of its features, such as the square footage. Scrap the price-prediction problem for a second, and imagine that we want a calculator for the property tax that the buyer would have to pay. If that were the case, our conversation with the engineer would have been much shorter:

> *You: We'd like to add a property tax calculator to our website. Can you help?*
>
> *Engineer: Cool. What's the relevant section in the tax code?*
>
> *You: You can refer to 4123 and 564b.*
>
> *Engineer: Great, that's all I need.*

The main difference between building a price predictor and a tax calculator is that the latter is governed by precise rules already expressed in mathematical form. Even the most junior of accountants can apply the mathematical formulas that determine property tax and apply them to new properties, with little need for experience. The same goes for physics: ever since Isaac Newton discovered the laws of dynamics in the 1600s, we have been able to predict the motions of bodies and build rockets to send people to the moon. Anytime we have situations like these, mathematics and conventional computer science will do just fine: we can just translate the rules and formulas into computer code, and the result will be 100% accurate.

This is not the case for the price-prediction example: the relationship between the features of the house and its sale price is fuzzy, unclear, and definitely not written down in a rule book. There's no way even the most experienced agent can write down computer-friendly rules for valuing properties, and no way a programmer can translate them into software.

In the past century, humanity used computers to realize amazing goals, even going as far as launching rockets into space and orchestrating billions of financial transactions every day. And yet, our most sophisticated robots still can't cross a road as safely as a six-year-old kid can.

In fact, computer science has been stuck on many important problems for a long time because they were just too complex to be understood analytically. Translating poetry into foreign languages, driving cars, or answering the phone are all tasks that humans learn to perform through experience rather than by following instructions. Machine learning has finally enabled computers to do the same, sidestepping mathematical rules altogether and therefore enabling whole new domains of application.

The fundamental insight is that we can use *experience* to make up for the lack of rules and mathematical relationships. In other words, the model is developed by learning relevant information from past examples. This is in contrast to traditional programming, in which the model is developed by a person and laboriously encoded into a computer (that is, *programmed*).

Figure 2.5 represents this fundamental difference. The core idea of machine learning is that we can use the features and the labels in the data to have the computer autonomously learn the relationship between them. Having stored this information, the goal is for the model to replicate the same relationship on unseen examples (new homes), predicting a label (the house price), given a set of features (the house characteristics). The general concept is not unlike what humans usually do: kids need to be taught the difference between horses and ponies only a few times before they "get it" and internalize the difference.

Compared to conventional software engineering, machine learning has two aces up its sleeve. We already discussed the first: there are some problems that we just can't solve with a computer in any other way. The second reason for using machine learning is that software is static: even if engineers can come up with complex logical rules, these can't change after the product is shipped. With machine learning, adding new training data can both improve performance and solve entirely new situations, without the need for additional engineering effort. For example, as a wave of new condos is sold, we can simply repeat the training with the new data, and the predictions will be adjusted.

These two advantages have been the key to generating value with machine learning in the last decade. Now that you understand them, let's see other cases to which they can be applied and real-world examples of companies making fortunes thanks to them.

Traditional programming—problems with known rules and relationships

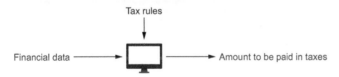

Machine learning—problems that can't be explained analytically but can be learned from experience

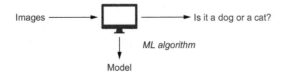

Figure 2.5 Difference between traditional programming and machine learning methods

2.2.4   *Applying AI to general core business data*

You can probably guess that AI can be applied to more industries than real estate. AI can be applied to countless domains. This section will help you broaden your horizons by generalizing the basic tools introduced in this chapter.

Our price-predictor algorithm belongs to a branch of machine learning called supervised learning, as we noted previously. Supervised learning algorithms are obviously not limited to spotting relationships between house features and their selling price. The beautiful attribute of these algorithms is that they are general learning machines that can be adapted to virtually any phenomenon for which features influence the value of a label.

Switching labels is the most immediate way to appreciate the flexibility of supervised learning algorithms. Say we replace our current label (sale price) with the time it took for the house to be sold. This metric would be equally easy to get from our historical records, and would be useful to customers and agents so that they could gauge demand for a home and act accordingly. It seems reasonable that large, luxury homes would sell slower than two-bedroom apartments. Even with different labels, we could likely reuse the same set of features we identified for price prediction to end up with a new algorithm that, instead of predicting the best price for a house, will predict the time it'll take to find a buyer.

If every time you open an Excel spreadsheet you look at the columns in terms of potential features and labels for a machine learning problem, a world of opportunities will open up for you. For instance, if you work for a bank and are used to seeing Excel sheets with customer data, you may now see how you could use that data as features and labels. Banks famously use supervised learning to predict the credit risk of their customers before handing out a loan, using features such as income, age, and marital status. If you work for a maintenance firm and have some data on equipment failures, you shouldn't be surprised that some firms can predict the likelihood of equipment breaking down within the new month by using features such as its age and the amount of time that has passed since its last overhaul. You now have all the knowledge needed to understand and formulate problems like these, and you'll also get more practice with the case studies at the end of the chapter.

In the next chapters within part 1, we'll expand on this technology in two main ways: looking at either the *inputs* or the *outputs* of the model. When it comes to inputs, we're going to teach you about AI techniques that can use images or text as inputs, greatly expanding the types of problems we can tackle. Regarding outputs, we're going to discuss families of models that don't just predict labels matching the training data, but do other useful things such as grouping similar items together, or helping customers find interesting content.

It's now time to wrap up the technical portion of this chapter, so let's recap the most important concepts. You have learned that the magic of machine learning lies in replacing an analytical understanding of complex processes (such as the real estate market) with a model that has learned automatically from data points. As long as the examples are a good representation of the behavior of the system, we can use the knowledge embedded in the model to predict unseen events (such as new homes coming on the market). You have seen that there is some work that we have to do beforehand, in defining the business vision and identifying the data. We're then ready to ask the engineers to train the model. After training is done, we get a finished model that we can use for inference, finally getting some business value.

While this and the other chapters in part 1 focus on what you can do with AI, we'll have much more to say about how to make it real in part 2. It's now time to circle back to the two case studies.

2.3 Case studies

This section presents two case studies from two companies that worked on two very different AI applications, but with many points in common: they both used core business data and supervised learning to gain an incredible competitive advantage.

The first one is from Google, which used core business data from its data centers' energy consumption to cut its energy bill by 40%. The protagonist of the second case is Square, which used the core business data of its customers' POS transactions to win the blue ocean of small business loans.

2.3.1 How Google used AI to cut its energy bill

In 2014, Jim Gao was an engineer at Google. He was responsible for making the massive air-conditioning systems of the tech giant's data centers (DCs) run as smoothly and efficiently as possible. With a background in mechanical engineering, Gao was following established best practices in the energy industry and obtaining great results.

After the most commonly adopted energy-saving measures were implemented, the performance of Google's DCs started to plateau, uncovering the limitations of the traditional approach to energy saving. It was clear that a new approach was needed. Gao decided to pursue an unbeaten path, taking advantage of Google's 20% policy—an initiative that allows employees to spend 20% of their time working on what they think will most benefit Google. Being a data center engineer, he was well aware of the sensors deployed in the DCs and of the large amount of data collected from them for operational purposes. Gao decided to study up on machine learning and tried to build models to predict and improve the DC performance.

THE DATA CENTER ENERGY CONSUMPTION PROBLEM

A *data center* is a building that houses networked servers. In the case of Google, these machines serve Search and Maps queries, store photos and documents, and perform all the other tasks that Google needs in order to offer its services to users.

Energy consumption is a major driver of cost for DCs because of the large number of power-hungry computers they house. High costs are not the only factor to take into account when weighing a DC's energy consumption; the environmental impact is also important. DCs nowadays consume 2% of the world's electricity, a number that's bound to increase as the need for networked services increases. The amount of energy used to power computers can't readily be optimized by an operations team because it depends on the computing workload and the efficiency of the chips. For this reason, data center engineers strive to reduce all extra consumption.

The efficiency of data centers is usually measured by tracking a metric called *power usage effectiveness* (*PUE*). This metric reflects how much energy is used on anything other than the actual computers that make the data center:

$$PUE = \frac{Total\ Facility\ Energy}{IT\ Equipment\ Energy}$$

A perfect data center has a PUE of 1: all the energy is spent to power the computers. The higher the PUE, the more energy is spent on other systems, among which cooling is the most important. For example, a PUE of 1.5 means that for every kilowatt-hour (kWh) of energy consumed to power computers, an additional 0.5 kWh of energy is needed for cooling and other minor needs.

Google has always been a leader in PUE efficiency. According to a 2018 survey of 900 DC operators by the Uptime Institute, the average PUE in the industry was 1.58. Google continuously improved its PUE until it reached 1.12 in 2013. Unfortunately, this value didn't improve until 2017.

THE ML APPROACH TO DATA CENTER EFFICIENCY

Gao realized that one of the obstacles to lowering the PUE further was that it's extremely complex to predict it correctly in different scenarios using a traditional engineering approach, because of the complex interactions between factors (for instance, wind can help cool the plant and reduce the need for artificial cooling). On the other hand, he was well aware of the large datasets collected by his team as part of day-to-day operations, thanks to thousands of sensors deployed across components that collect millions of data points.

Gao foresaw the potential of using this data to train an ML model capable of overcoming the limitations of traditional thermodynamics. His first approach was to build a simple neural network (a classic algorithm used to build supervised learning models) that was trained to predict the PUE, given a list of features that affect it. Gao used a total of 19 features, including these:

- Total server IT load
- Total number of process water pumps running
- Mean cooling tower leaving-water-temperature set point
- Total number of chillers running
- Mean heat exchanger approach temperature
- Outside air wet-bulb and dry-bulb temperatures
- Outside air relative humidity, wind speed, and direction

The label of this supervised learning problem is the PUE. As you can see in figure 2.6, to train his model, Gao used 184,435 time samples at five-minute resolution (approximately two years of operational data). The final model was able to predict DC PUE

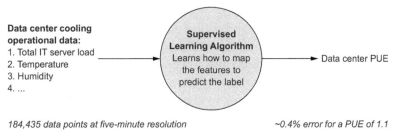

Data center cooling operational data:
1. Total IT server load
2. Temperature
3. Humidity
4. ...

Supervised Learning Algorithm
Learns how to map the features to predict the label

Data center PUE

184,435 data points at five-minute resolution   *~0.4% error for a PUE of 1.1*

Figure 2.6   Gao's machine learning model

within 0.004 +/– 0.0005, an approximately 0.4% error, for a PUE of 1.1. Gao was able to build the first proof-of-concept (POC) model quickly using open source coding frameworks.

The final resulting model has been used for three main applications:

- Automatic performance alerting and troubleshooting, by comparing actual versus predicted DC performance for any given set of conditions
- Evaluating PUE sensitivity to operational parameters
- Running digital simulations with different configurations without making physical changes

The results of Gao's work had a large impact on the company and was recognized publicly by the VP of the data center, Joe Kava, who described the work and results in an Google official blog post. "Better Data Centers Through Machine Learning" highlighted how Gao's models were able to identify patterns in the data that are impossible for a person to spot, leading to a model capable of predicting the PUE with a 99.6% accuracy.

Gao and his team started using the model to come up with new ways to improve efficiency. When servers were taken offline, that was known to cause lower performance in the data center, for example. Thanks to Gao's models, the Google DC's team was able to run simulations of the data center's behavior and find new ways to contain the performance loss, saving energy and money.

ML APPLIED TO DATA CENTER OPTIMIZATION GAINS MOMENTUM

Gao's single-handed work attracted attention at higher levels of the company. He was promoted to lead a cross-functional team of machine learning, software, electrical, mechanical, controls and operations engineers to develop an end-to-end data center intelligence solution.

The ML expertise in the new team was brought in by DeepMind, a British company specializing in cutting-edge AI algorithms that was acquired by Google in 2014 for $500 million. The additional ML expertise turned out to be a key asset in reaching performance never seen before in the company's history, reducing the PUE's overhead by 15% and resulting in a 40% overall reduction in the energy bill.

Even if DeepMind's model was more complex and accurate than Gao's approach and allowed Google to cut its energy bill by 40%, it was still producing recommendations that needed to be vetted and implemented by a human. The next logical step of the project was to completely offload the DC power management to an AI solution, keeping human experts as supervisors.

DeepMind's models were deployed in August 2017, and were already delivering an energy savings of 10%. While the new models were running, they were producing additional data that was used to retrain the models and improve their performance further. In a year, the energy savings of 10% improved to 30%.

The AI control system used novel ways to manage cooling that delivered top-notch performance in ways that were unexpected and unexplored by expert DC operators. For instance, Dan Fuenffinger, one of Google's data center operators, remarked about being surprised when the AI system was able to autonomously take advantage of winter conditions and produce water at a lower temperature, reducing energy usage.

CASE QUESTIONS

1 Improving the PUE of a data center is a challenging problem, and Gao intuited that ML could be a solution to tackle it. What are the characteristics of this challenge that make it a good fit for ML?

2 What are the key elements that allowed Gao to build the first POC by himself?

3 How did Google turn the initiative of a single engineer into a company-wide success?

CASE DISCUSSION

Google's data center project is a classic case of optimization for which ML is a perfect fit. It starts with key performance indicators (KPIs) that we have a business interest in predicting (PUE), and a large set of parameters that affect it (temperatures, pressures, load, and so forth). Engineers have tried to build a model that can map these parameters to the PUE, but traditional methods that rely on thermodynamics have severe shortcomings that have prevented them from delivering results over a certain threshold.

This is what a machine learning business problem should look like: a complex, unknown relationship between a set of variables that affect a metric that has a direct business impact. Gao did a great job in spotting these characteristics and realizing that ML could be the right hammer to hit this needle.

A few elements allowed Gao to succeed. The first one is the availability of data, without which it would have been impossible to pursue an ML solution. Gao knew from his work experience about the existence of this dataset, and was able, thanks to agile data governance of his company, to easily retrieve the data he needed to start conducting experiments. We'll talk about data governance later in greater detail, but it's clear that availability and access to data is paramount to starting work on an ML project like this. Notice that this data had been available for years, but no one had seen past its mere operational purpose.

Another factor that helped Gao get started was the availability of open source tools that enabled him to quickly build a POC. This allowed him to gain the attention and corporate support he needed to bring his approach to the next level, bringing onboard skilled ML engineers from DeepMind and building on top of his first intuition.

Finally, the way that this project was carried out is a perfect case of great ML strategy. We'll cover this topic in more detail in the second part of the book, but notice that the project didn't start with a grandiose mission and a complex solution. The first step was simple enough to be built by a single engineer in 20% of his time, but also powerful enough to prove the potential of the approach. The second step was more complex, and achieving higher performance required gaining new knowledge, performing tests, gaining momentum, and moving to the next step of completely automated AI control. Google planned the project to be built in steps, each one with a tangible return on investment (ROI) and building on the previous, until reaching state-of-the-art performance and having a great impact on the bottom line.

To sum up, this case study has the following main takeaways:

- A problem that has the potential of being a good fit for ML must have certain characteristics:
  - An important KPI exists.
  - The KPI is impacted by a series of measurable parameters.
  - The parameters influence the KPI through a complex and unknown relationship.
- Operational datasets can have tremendous hidden value.
- Open source technologies can allow small teams of engineers to build POCs that bring tangible results to the business, and prove that the concept can be scaled and further improved.
- When building ML projects, it's always a good idea to start small, identifying the smallest task that can give immediate business impact, to build the foundation for more-complex projects.

2.3.2 *How Square used AI to lend billions to small businesses*

This case study is about how a fintech startup challenged the big banks by lending capital to traditionally underserved small businesses. Using machine learning on its retail transactions dataset, Square Capital can proactively offer small loans to businesses before they even ask for them. Square's delinquency rate is half of the industry average.

SQUARE AND SQUARE CAPITAL

Square is a financial services company focused on the needs of small businesses. It was founded by Twitter founder Jack Dorsey in 2009, and went public in 2015. Based in San Francisco, it had a $26 billion market cap in 2019 and employs 2,300 people. Square's first product was a credit card reader that plugged directly into a smartphone to allow small retailers and professionals to accept credit card payments. The reader hardware was distributed for free without the need for a monthly subscription, kick-starting

Square's reputation among small retailers. The hardware's iconic design and steady flow of referrals also contributed to cement Square's reputation (international expansion has been limited so far).

In its first years of operation, Square was focusing on a niche of small businesses with less than $125,000 in turnover; these businesses were badly served by banks and conventional payment processors. Square's low fees and easy-to-use website helped drag entrepreneurs into what was growing into a complete financial ecosystem. In the years leading up to its public listing, Square complemented its services by launching a peer-to-peer payment app, a customer relationship management (CRM) and marketing platform, and point-of-sale hardware for larger merchants.

In 2014, Square launched Square Capital, another component of its financial ecosystem. As small businesses expand, they often develop cash-flow issues that could be relieved with additional working capital. However, conventional banks are often not sensitive to the needs of these customers, as the small amounts don't justify the overhead involved in marketing and processing the loan. Square Capital uses its point-of-sale transaction data to proactively offer small loans to its customers. For customers, the experience is seamless, as they can accept and manage the loan directly from the same management website that they use for the other services in the ecosystem. Loans don't have a specific repayment schedule: funds are automatically withheld from the credit card transactions processed by Square. The combination of frictionless experience and existing customer base has allowed Square Capital to expand rapidly: 200,000 merchants have borrowed more than $3.1 billion through the platform in the years 2014–2018 alone.

While credit-risk models have been a staple of the financial industry for many decades, Square has access to a much more extensive dataset, including seasonality and timing of each individual purchase. This allows Square to build models with great visibility into the cash-flow position of each business and appropriately size the offered loan. Together with straightforward repayment options, this pushes the loan delinquency rate down to 4%, half of the industry average.

CRITICISM AND COMPETITION

From a financial standpoint, the loans offered by Square Capital are nothing new. Lenders have been offering merchant cash advances (MCAs) to cover businesses' short-term cash needs since time immemorial. Compared to MCAs, which don't have a prescribed time limit, Square Capital loans must be paid back within 18 months. This makes it possible for Square to pass off the loans to a wider array of financial institutions, which have a harder time dealing with MCAs without a known repayment date. Square operates only as an originator of loans, rather than a lender, maintaining an attractive balance sheet that's comparable to other tech companies.

While most financial institutions use machine learning to evaluate credit risk, the current crop of fintech companies like Square have also been criticized for removing too much human oversight from their credit application processes. For example, peer-to-peer lending startup Prosper came under scrutiny in 2015 after lending

$25,000 to the terrorist couple behind the San Bernardino (California) shooting, which left 24 people dead.

While the technology community is excited about fintech being able to disrupt and scale traditional banking through the use of machine learning, some communities are not as optimistic. For example, the very same small businesses that enjoy fast turn-around time for Square Capital loans are also vocal about perceived unfairness and lack of transparency when their loan applications end up rejected. Because Square does not publish any details about its risk-evaluation models, some merchants are left to reverse-engineer algorithmic decisions. From a technical standpoint, this is linked to issues of both accuracy (expressed in terms of true/false positives) and bias of the model.

Thanks to its integration with the Square ecosystem, Square Capital can offer attractive features compared to traditional banks and MCAs, which have less direct access to a merchant's transaction flow. However, other services such as PayPal Working Capital also have access to this source of data, making it harder for Square Capital to stand out. Surveys conducted on small business owners have suggested that they usually choose a lender based on the perceived chance of being approved, rather than on loan amounts or terms. This means that Square Capital might have to focus on user experience and integration with the rest of the ecosystem, rather than optimizing risk-evaluation models.

CASE QUESTIONS

1 Credit risk is a well-explored application of machine learning. What do you think Square did well compared to past history and its present competition?

2 What lessons can you take away from the interaction between machine learning and regulatory organizations (banking, in this case)?

3 Can you develop a strategy to collect training data for this application? How would you measure the performance of the resulting models?

CASE DISCUSSION

We presented this case study about Square Capital because it is a success story about integrating an AI-based business model into an existing ecosystem of services. Furthermore, it also explores the issues around introducing ML-based features into a heavily regulated industry like banking.

Square's core product has historically been a point-of-sale system for small businesses. Its perceived strong points were design, user experience, and customer service, rather than cutting-edge technology. However, data was effectively at the core of Square's business, since fraud detection and prevention are foundational aspects of any financial services company. This goes to show that once an organization has established a powerful culture around data (including collecting, storing, and making it available to employees), it's only natural to introduce new products based on it. When there's a well-designed data infrastructure, credit-risk models can be integrated into the same platform that had been scouring real-time transaction feeds for fraud, adding value to those investments in core technology.

From the point of view of the user experience, Square Capital is a good example of seamlessly bringing AI-based features into an existing platform in a way that's completely transparent and natural for end users. Building upon the trust that merchants already place in Square, Square Capital's offerings are low-key and appropriate for its audience. There's no needless boasting of "AI-based risk evaluation" or obscure tech-first marketing. All that is left is to focus on the customer experience.

When it comes to corporate finance, it's interesting to see how the flexibility that Square got by using ML for credit-risk evaluation allowed it to experiment with new business models. Offering fixed-term loans, rather than traditional MCAs, enabled Square to focus on its core mission rather than taking on the loans itself. This enables Square to create explosive (about 50% yearly) growth that uses its strong points without piling additional risk onto its balance sheet.

An interesting element of this case is the drawbacks of ML in specific corner cases. We've considered the autonomous learning of ML algorithms as a strength, but sometimes we struggle to peek into the logic followed by the algorithms when making a decision. If the loan application of a small business is rejected by an ML algorithm, explaining why can be hard or impossible. We'll cover this aspect of ML more in detail in the last chapter.

Square started from a position of strength as its business model allowed the company to collect core business data about all its customers: their transaction history. This data asset is the pillar upon which Square Capital is built. Notice that this data was collected naturally to offer the standard POS service by Square, and became an incredible asset later when Square Capital was introduced.

2.3.3   *Case studies lessons*

Both Google and Square created AI applications that gave them a large advantage over their competition, while being different at their core. Google used AI to reduce costs and improve operations, while Square used it to launch an entirely new service. The underlying principle stays the same: both Square and Google used AI on core business data, creating immense value from what most other companies see as a sunk cost.

Notice that both Google and Square used data that was originally not collected with AI in mind. In the case of Google, it's common practice to store operational data from the air-conditioning plants of a data center, mostly for reporting and to monitor that the systems are operating as expected. Jim Gao's idea of using ML to improve the system's performance was novel and shows great intuition by a Google engineer.

The same is true for Square: it was collecting data on customer transactions in order to offer services like sales analytics, but offering loans wasn't the original reason for collecting this data. Square wasn't even offering a business loan service in the first place: it's an entirely new service enabled by ML and by this rich dataset it owned. This enabled Square to enter a new market that was completely underserved, as traditional banks don't have the resources to evaluate the loan eligibility of small businesses.

Another aspect you should keep in mind from these two case studies is that both used supervised learning methods. Google learned to predict a cooling plant's PUE from its operational parameters, and Square determined the eligibility of a small business based on its transaction history. The similarities in terms of problem setting are shown in figure 2.7. In Google's case, supervised learning was particularly useful in overcoming the limitations of traditional solutions to the energy-efficiency problem. Square's application was used to automate a process that would have been too time-consuming if made by humans.

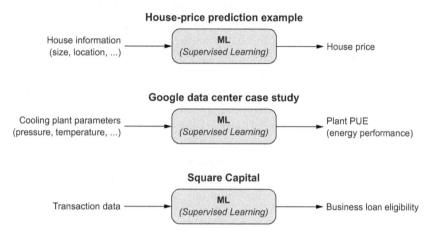

Figure 2.7   How the house-prediction example and the Square and Google case studies used supervised learning

2.4   *Evaluating performance and risk*

It's now time for a meeting with FutureHouse's leadership, to sit down and talk about the risks and concerns of the project we have delivered. We have identified a great business case for the property-value-prediction algorithm, collected the right data, and built it. Now, you just need to push the red button that makes the feature appear in the website for users. You're about to go ahead; everyone in the office is looking at you. Your hands are sweaty and jittery. You take a leap of faith, push the button, close your eyes, and hope the algorithm will work. Luckily, this is not how things happen in the real world. Deploying models without thoroughly measuring their performance is irresponsible.

First things first: machine learning is based on data and statistics, and thus its predictions will likely never be 100% accurate. But we do want predictions to be *valuable* to the business, while respecting all standards of safety and ethics. The overall systems that we build must be tolerant to this margin of error for the same reason that we're using machine learning in the first place: some of these problems are so complex that no amount of data could possibly capture them all. Companies using ML in life-or-death situations (like self-driving cars) must be much more careful and conservative than marketers using it to optimize their messaging to customers. Luckily, all of the applications we talk about in this book belong to the latter category.

Evaluating the performance of a model has two main aspects. A good way to think about them might be familiar to you from management literature: *known unknowns* and *unknown unknowns*.

The main *known unknown* is *accuracy*: a measurement of how good the model is at matching features to labels. In the home-value-prediction problem, this translates to how close the predicted price is to the actual price after the home is sold. For supervised learning problems, there is a smart way to measure the accuracy of the model. Engineers usually randomly split the training data into two parts (say, 70% and 30% of the data), as you can see in figure 2.8. They train the model on only the first part, and use the second part as a *test set* to simulate the real-world scenario of the model running on unknown data. Because the test set was also part of the initial dataset, we do have labels for it. Therefore, we can compare the predicted labels with the actual ones and measure the accuracy of the model in a situation that matches the real world reasonably well. Setting aside a test set is important, because testing on data that was used for training is a bit like giving students an exam with questions they have already seen the solutions to. In the case of home-price prediction, you could imagine selecting one or two homes in each block, removing them from the dataset used for training, and adding them to the test set. This will give us a good idea about how well the model performs.

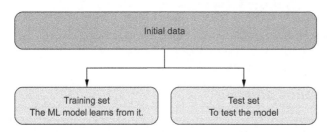

Figure 2.8   The available data is split into training and test sets. The first is used to make the model learn, and the second is used to test the model on unknown data, simulating the real-world application.

When it comes to AI use in organizations, accuracy is not the yardstick by which to measure success. An inaccurate model applied to the right problem can be way more valuable to the business than a very accurate model that solves an insignificant problem. The golden rule to keep in mind is by statistician George Box:

> *All models are wrong, but some are useful.*

If accuracy is a good metric to measure the known unknowns, what about the (scarier) *unknown unknowns*? In these situations, the model gives a flat-out incorrect or nonsensical answer. More often than not, this is because the training data was incomplete, and we're trying to predict the target in a situation (a combination of features) that was never seen before in training. Even if inference in unseen situations is the whole point of using machine learning, wholly unpredictable queries can still throw off the model. For example, incorrect data entry might lead to the model trying to guess the price of a home with 50 bathrooms in the case where no mansion like that was present in the training dataset at all. Most families of models don't raise a red flag in situations like this, so engineers have to implement some sanity checking into the inputs and outputs to ensure safety.

Another important risk factor revolves around the core of what makes machine learning so great: the automatic extraction of a mapping between target and features. This is a powerful ability, but also means that engineers can't easily understand why the model makes a specific prediction, given a set of features. This is why machine learning is often called a *black box*: you know what comes in (the features) and what comes out (the target), but it's hard to understand *why* the model has chosen that output. While some families of models are better than others, the truth is that this is one of the most worrisome facets connected to large-scale use of AI. Fear not, because we devote a substantial amount of material to this issue in the second part of the book.

We've covered a lot in this chapter. We introduced you to the main concepts of supervised learning by working through the design of a customer-facing AI feature: property-value prediction for a fictional real estate brokerage firm. You learned the value of data and how it's used to build a machine learning model. The case studies have helped you apply this knowledge to industry situations, so you'll start to be able to recognize similar opportunities in your own organization.

In closing, a fun fact. Zillow is the leading online real estate marketplace in the United States. Predicting property values was so important to Zillow, and machine learning such an obvious solution, that it hosted a competition for the best algorithm. The winning prize? One million dollars.

Summary

- Core business data is the kind of data with the strongest ties to the value-generating engine of an organization. Therefore, it also holds the highest potential for impact by AI.
- Supervised learning is a family of machine learning algorithms that allows computers to learn how to map inputs (features) and outputs (labels), given enough examples.
- Machine learning can tackle many hard problems where conventional software engineering fails, because it's based on historical data rather than mathematical understanding.
- Even if ML-based models can never be 100% accurate, numerical metrics (such as accuracy) can help track their performance.

AI for sales and marketing

This chapter covers

- Identifying which customers are most likely to abandon a service (churn)
- Targeting customers who are most interested in buying more (upselling)
- Using unsupervised learning for data-driven customer segmentation
- Case studies: using AI on electric grid data and mining retail analytics

In the previous chapter, we explored the role of structured data in a variety of business applications. Even if sales and marketing can sometimes fit into the core business data category, they're so important and peculiar that they deserve their own chapter. We'll cover various marketing problems and explore how you can use artificial intelligence and data science to strengthen and improve the relationship between your organization and its customers.

3.1 Why AI for sales and marketing

One of the main goals of marketers is finding the best way to offer the right product to the right customer at the right time. But even with billions of dollars at stake, marketers have suffered from various limitations. The first one was a lack of data. When the world wasn't as connected as it is now, the only way to get one's questions answered was to talk to people. The internet largely solved this problem: it's now easier than ever to reach broad audiences, expose them to a message, and measure their reaction. The flip side of the coin is that it's easy to end up with data that is so large and granular that it's too much for humans to understand and extract insights.

We want to start this chapter by giving you a little insight into why AI changes everything. Every marketer knows that not all customers are alike, and that they respond best when they're engaged with a personalized message. A common marketing strategy is to divide customers into *segments* according to demographics or similar aspects. A simple segment can be "wealthy women between 25 and 30 years old who spend more than $1,000 per year on entertainment." A marketer can come up with a custom message to reach this category of people, which is different from what will be done for other segments. While this technique is as old as the marketplace, it really was the best we could do before AI came on the scene.

The problem with this approach is that no matter how specific you get with your segmentation (marketers talk about *microsegmentation*), you'll always end up in a situation where two customers get treated exactly the same even if they're fundamentally different, just because they fall into the same category. There is a limit to the number of categories a human brain can manage. Just think about how many of your friends have similar characteristics to you on paper (same age, neighborhood, education) but have completely different tastes.

As you can see in figure 3.1, the traditional marketing segmentation approach can't target Marc for being Marc. It will always target him as a "male between 25 and 30 years old who lives in a large city." AI changes the rules of the game because it can process much more information. With AI, you can reach personalization at scale, learning about people from their specific actions and characteristics and targeting them for who they really are, and not for the handcrafted bucket they fall into.

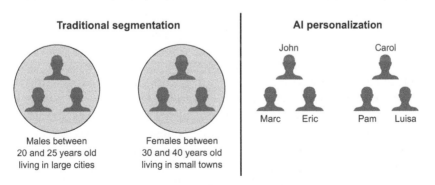

Figure 3.1 AI personalization versus traditional marketing segmentation

What does the ability of such fine-grained personalization mean for a business? Well, companies specializing in AI for marketing can show some eye-popping metrics that would be every marketer's dream. An example is Amplero, a US company specializing in AI-driven marketing. Here are some of the results it reports in its marketing material:

- It helped a major European telco increase the first 30-day average revenue per user from 0.32% to 2.8%, an almost 800% increase.
- It reduced the customer acquisition cost (CAC) of one of the top five North American mobile carriers by over 97%: from $40 per customer to just $1.
- It managed to retarget the unhappiest customers of a major European mobile carrier three weeks before they were canceling their plans, created a more meaningful customer experience for reengaging them, and increased retention rates from 2% to 10%.

These numbers aren't meant to boast about the results of a specific marketing company. You'll find many startups and larger organizations that can achieve similar results. If the idea of reaching this kind of performance in your organization gives you goosebumps, you're not alone. Let's see how this can be made possible.

Marketing is a complex function, so instead of listing all the possible applications, we'll focus on three general problems that apply to most businesses:

- Identifying which customers are likely to leave your service (churn)
- Identifying which customers are likely to buy a new service (upselling)
- Identifying similar customer groups (customer segmentation)

3.2   *Predicting churning customers*

One of the most important marketing metrics is the customer *churn* (also known as *attrition* or *customer turnover*). The churn is defined as the percentage of customers leaving a business over a period of time. Wouldn't it be amazing to know beforehand which customers are unhappiest and most likely to abandon a product or service in the near future? This is exactly how AI can help you solve the problem of customer churn: using machine learning and the data assets of the organization, we can find the customers who are most likely to leave your service and reach out to them with personalized messages to bring their engagement up again. Next we'll show how a churn predictor works, giving you the confidence to see opportunities for this application in your organization.

In this machine learning problem, we have two classes of customers: the ones who are likely to churn and the ones who are not. Therefore, the label that our ML model will have to learn to predict is whether the customer belongs to one class or the other (let's say that customers who are about to churn belong to class 1, and the others belong to class 0). For instance, a telephone company may label with "churned" all the customers who dropped out of its phone plan, while with "not churned" all the others who are still on their plan.

Now that we have defined a label that our algorithm has to predict, let's look into what features we can use. Remember that *features* in an ML problem are the parameters that the model will look at to discriminate between classes. These can be an attribute of the user (for example, demographics) or its interaction with your product (for example, the number of uses of a specific service in the last month).

What we have just described has the form of a *supervised learning* problem: an ML algorithm is asked to learn a mapping between a set of features (customer characteristics) and a label (churned/not churned) based on historical data. Let's recap the necessary steps to solve it, as visualized in figure 3.2:

1 Define an ML task starting from a business one (identifying customers who are likely to leave our service).
2 Clearly identify a label: churned or not churned.
3 Identify the features: elements of a customer that are likely to influence the likelihood of churning. You can come up with possible examples by thinking about what you would look at if you had to do this job by yourself:
   – Age
   – How long the customer has used the service
   – Money spent on the service
   – Time spent using the service in the last two months
4 Gather historical data of churned and active customers.
5 Train the model: the ML model will learn how to predict the label, given the features.
6 Perform inference: use the model on new data to identify which of your current customers are likely to churn.

Notice that the label must be found retroactively by looking at past customer records. Let's consider the easiest situation first. Assume you have a subscription-based business model, like Netflix or Spotify. Subscriptions are usually renewed automatically, so

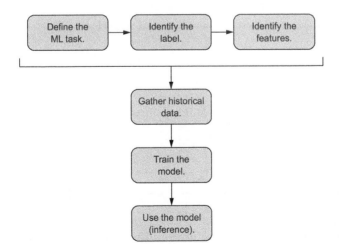

Figure 3.2 The process of creating and using an ML model, from its definition to its usage in the inference phase

customers have to actively pursue an action in order to cancel the subscription: call the customer service in case of a phone company, or go to the website and turn off automatic renewal in the case of Netflix or Spotify. In these situations, finding your label is easy: there's no doubt about whether a customer is still on board or not, and a clear database table exists that can tell you exactly when that happened.

Other business models are more complex to deal with. Let's assume you are the marketing manager of a supermarket, and you use fidelity cards to track your customers every time they come in and shop. Most likely, a customer who found a better supermarket won't call you and say, "By the way, I just want to let you know that I won't be back again shopping at your supermarket." Instead, this person likely won't show up anymore, and that's it! No traces left, no Unsubscribed column in your database, no easy label. Can you still find a way to assign labels to these kinds of customers? Sure you can. As you can see in figure 3.3, a common and simple way to do it is to look at purchase patterns and see when they change suddenly. Let's assume that a very loyal family comes in to buy groceries every Sunday. However, in the last month, you haven't seen them. You may assume that they've decided not to come anymore, and therefore label them as "churned."

Is one month the right threshold? It's hard to say without additional context, but luckily, that's not your job: leave the task of figuring it out to your data scientists. What's important is that you understand that no matter the business, if you have returning customers—and have collected data on their interactions—there's likely a way to define churn and identify who has left and who is still active.

Once you come up with some labels to distinguish "happy customers" from churned ones, the situation becomes similar to the example of house-price prediction we've seen before. Luckily, the training data for churn prediction can easily be extracted from a company's customer relationship management system (CRM). More specifically, we can extract CRM data from up to, say, 18 months ago, and then label whether customers have churned in the past 6 months.

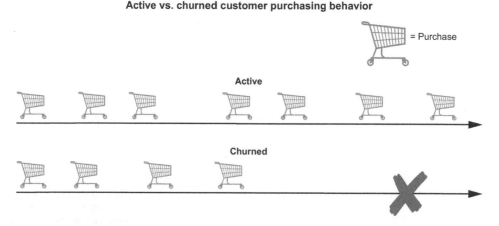

Figure 3.3   A graphical representation of the buying pattern behavior of churned and active customers

By now, you are already much more confident and effective in defining a label for a churn-prediction project than most business managers. Every data scientist will be thankful for that, but if you really want to help them, you need to put in extra effort: help them selecting features.

If this sounds to you like a technical detail, you're missing out on a great opportunity to let your experience and domain knowledge shine. In an ML problem, remember that a feature is an attribute of the phenomenon we're trying to model that affects its outcome. Assuming you're a marketing expert, no one in the world has better insights about the relevant features, and your expertise can help your data science team follow a path that leads to successful results.

To give you an idea of what your contribution may look like, ask yourself, "If I had to guess the likelihood of churn of just one customer, what parameters would I look at?" This can inform the conversation with an engineer:

> *Engineer: Do you know what is affecting the customer churn? I need to come up with some relevant features.*

> *Marketer: Sure, we know that the payment setup is highly relevant to churn. Usually, someone who has a contract instead of a prepaid card is less likely to abandon the service because they have more lock-in. It's also true that when we're close to the expiration date of a contract, customers start looking at competitors, so that's another factor.*

> *Engineer: Interesting. For sure, I'll use a feature in the model that expresses "contract" or "prepaid." Another feature will be the number of days to the expiration of the contract. Anything else?*

> *Marketer: Sure, we know that age plays a big role. These young millennials change companies all the time, while older people are more loyal. Also, if someone has been our client for a long time, that's a good indicator of loyalty.*

> *Engineer: Nice; we can look in the CRM and include a feature for "days since sign-up" and one for age. Is age the only interesting demographic attribute?*

> *Marketer: I don't think gender is; we never noticed any impact. The occupation is important: we know that the self-employed are less eager to change plans.*

> *Engineer: OK, I'll try to double-check whether gender has any correlation with churn. Regarding the occupation, that's a good hint. Thanks!*

A conversation like this can go on for days, usually with a constant back-and-forth between the engineers and you. You'll provide your experience and domain knowledge, and the engineer will translate that into something readable by a machine. Eventually, the engineer will come back with some insight or questions that came out of the data analysis and that require your help to interpret. As you can see, it's not a nerd exercise: it's a team effort between the business and the nerds.

3.3   *Using AI to boost conversion rates and upselling*

You've seen how churn prediction can be a powerful application of classification algorithms. In this case, the classes we are labeling the customers with are "churned" or "not churned." In other situations, you can label customers with a class that is relevant to your marketing department and use ML algorithms to make predictions. A natural one is whether a customer will buy a service based on past sales.

Let's imagine you have a classic marketing funnel: customers subscribe to a free service, and then eventually some of them upgrade to a premium one. You therefore have two classes of customers:

- *Converted*—Customers who bought the premium service after trying the free version
- *Not converted*—Customers who kept using the free service

Web companies may end up investing millions to maximize the number of users who convert to a paid product. This metric is holy to software companies that have a Software as a Service (SaaS) business model: companies that offer services purchased with a subscription. Depending on the conversion rate, a web-based subscription business can live or die.

The most naive way to try increasing the paying users' conversion rate is to massively target the entire user base with marketing activities: newsletters, offers, free trials, and so on. More-sophisticated marketers may think about setting up elaborate strategies to assess the likelihood of a conversion and invest the marketing budget more wisely. For instance, we may believe that a user who opened a newsletter is more interested in buying the premium service than one who never opened any, and target them with Facebook ads (have you ever been spammed on Facebook after you visited a website or opened a newsletter?).

Given the importance of the topic and the amount of money that rides on it, let's see if we can use ML to classify users by their conversion likelihood, optimizing our marketing costs and achieving better results. If you look at the problem, you'll see it's a perfect fit for machine learning. You've already seen that you have a clearly defined task: identifying users who can upgrade from a free to a paid service. This is a supervised learning classification task, and you have the labels ready: let's say 1 for users who bought the paid service, and 0 for users who didn't. You now need to think of what features you would use to train your classifier. Remember that a good starting point for identifying features is to ask yourself this question: "If I had to guess the likelihood of a conversion myself, what information would I need?" This information might include the following:

- Usage of the free product. Remember this has to be an actual number, so you have to come up with a useful way to describe this. If you're selling a service like Dropbox, usage may be described with a bunch of parameters:
  - Number of files stored

- – Number of devices the users logged in from (gives a hint about how useful the service is for the user)
- – Number of accesses per day/week/month (indicates how frequently the user relies on it)
- Newsletter open rates (How interested is the user in our message?)
- How long ago the user subscribed
- Acquisition channel (Someone who subscribed after a friend's referral may be more valuable than someone who clicked on a Facebook ad.)

These variables may vary based on the kind of business you own, but the concept is generally simple: think of what factors can hint at a likelihood of conversion and then feed your ML algorithm with them. It's worth pointing out that some businesses have more data than others: for instance, internet services that use a Facebook login will be able to know all their users' interests as features for such classifiers.

Assuming you have historical data on past customers who converted as well as those who didn't convert, you can train your algorithm to identify how the features you select affect the user's likelihood to buy your premium service. Once the training phase is done, your algorithm is finally ready to apply what it has learned from previous customers to your existing customers, ranking them from the most likely to convert to the least likely. As you may recall from the preceding chapter, this phase is called *inference* (making predictions on new data after an algorithm has been trained on a past one). Figure 3.4 illustrates this process of learning from past customers' behavior and making predictions about new customers.

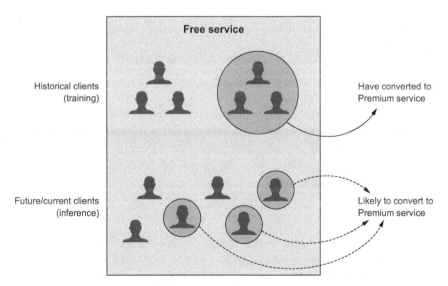

Figure 3.4 To boost conversion rates, an ML algorithm is trained with data of customers who have purchased a premium service in the past. Later, this algorithm identifies which customers are most likely to do the same.

Notice that we applied this methodology to the case of an internet-based system that uses a *freemium* model (a free service and a paid upgrade), but it can be applied to any other case in which you have a group of customers performing one action and another group doing something else (or nothing). This scenario is common, and we'd like to encourage you to look for such situations and think about whether there's space to build an ML classifier for it.

To give you some inspiration, here are some other cases where you can apply this methodology:

- You have a basic product and some upsells (accessories or additional services, which are common for telco companies). You can label customers with "has bought upsell X" or "hasn't bought upsell X" and use their basic product usage to assess whether it may be worth proposing the upsell to your customer.
- You have a newsletter and want to optimize its open rates. Your labels are "has opened the newsletter" or "hasn't opened the newsletter." The features you use for the classifier may be the time you sent the email (day of the week, hour, and so forth) and some user-related features, and you may also tag emails by their content (for example, "informative," "product news," or "whitepaper").
- You have a physical store with a fidelity card (to track which customer buys what). You can run marketing initiatives (newsletters again or also physical ads) and classify your users based on what brought them into your store and what didn't.

As you can see, the method we just described of dividing users into two separate classes and building an ML classifier that can recognize the two is pretty flexible and can be used on a lot of problems. Pretty powerful, isn't it?

3.4 Performing automated customer segmentation

In this chapter's introduction, we referenced one of the key activities that marketers have to perform when developing a marketing plan: customer segmentation. *Segmenting* a market means dividing customers who share similar characteristics and behaviors into groups. The core idea behind this effort is that customers in the same group will be responsive to similar marketing actions. For example, a fashion retailer would likely benefit from having separate market segments for men versus women, and teenagers versus young adults versus professionals.

Segments can be more or less specific, and therefore more or less granular. Here are two examples:

- *Broad segment*—Young males between 20 and 25 years old
- *Highly specific segment*—Young males between 20 and 25 years old, studying in college, living in one of the top five largest US cities, and with a passion for first-person-shooter video games

Many marketers can intuitively perform this segmentation task in their brains as long as the amount of data is limited, both in terms of examples (number of customers) and features. This usually produces generic customer segments like the first one, which can be limiting considering the amount of variation that exists among these groups. A marketer could attempt to define a more specific segment like the second one, but how do they come up with it? Here are the questions that could be raised during a typical brainstorming session:

- Is it a good idea to use the 20- to 25-year-old threshold, or is it better to use 20 to 28?
- Are we sure that the college students living in large cities are fundamentally different from the ones living in smaller ones? Can't we put all of them into a single cluster?
- Is there a fundamental difference between males and females? Do we really need to create two segments, or is this just a cliché?

Answering these questions can be done in three ways:

- Go by your gut feeling. We're not in 1980, so don't do that.
- Look at the data, and use the marketer's instinct to interpret it. This is better than a gut feeling, but marketers will likely project their biases into their analysis and see what they want to see. So avoid this as well.
- Let AI come up with customer segments by itself, keeping a marketer in the loop to use their creativity and context knowledge.

Option 3 is most likely to outperform the others. Let's see why and how.

3.4.1 Unsupervised learning (or clustering)

Let's look at the problem we just described:

- What we start with: a pool of customers, with a bunch of elements that characterize them (age, location, interests, and so forth)
- What we want: a certain number of segments we can use to divide our customers

You can imagine this problem as having a bunch of customers and needing to place each one into a bucket, which we'll call a *cluster* (figure 3.5).

The customers' characteristics that we'll use resemble what we've been calling *features* in previous chapters, so you may think that we're dealing with the same kind of task and can use the same tools we've already described. But the devil is in the details: because we don't know in advance the groups we want to define, we don't know which labels to apply. So far in the book, we've used a subset of ML called *supervised learning*. The typical recipe for a supervised learning task is the following:

1 We have data on a group of customers characterized by certain features.
2 These customers also have a label: a target value we're interested in predicting (for example, whether they churned or not).
3 The supervised learning algorithm goes through the customers' data, and learns a general mapping between features and labels.

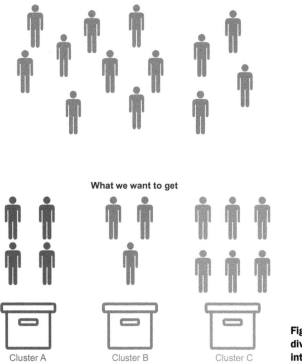

What we start with

What we want to get

Cluster A   Cluster B   Cluster C

Figure 3.5   A clustering algorithm divides a group of uniform customers into three clusters.

In our new scenario, point 2 is missing: we don't have a label attached to each user. This is what we want our new algorithm to find. Therefore, this is what our new task looks like:

1 As before, we have data on a bunch of customers characterized by certain features.
2 We want to divide customers into a certain number of segments (clusters)—let's say three of them.
3 We run some kind of ML algorithm that, looking at the data, determines the best clusters we can come up with and splits the users into them.

This new kind of ML algorithm is called *clustering*, or *unsupervised learning*. Unsupervised learning is another form of ML in which an algorithm is fed with a set of unlabeled examples (just a set of parameters) and is asked to divide the examples into groups that share some similarity. In this sense, unsupervised learning algorithms use the concept of similarity to overcome the lack of a previously defined label, dividing the examples they're fed into groups in an autonomous manner. This is the core difference between supervised and unsupervised learning: supervised learning algorithms learn a mapping between a set of features and labels, whereas unsupervised algorithms just look at labels and group data points based in clusters that share a certain similarity, as shown in figure 3.6.

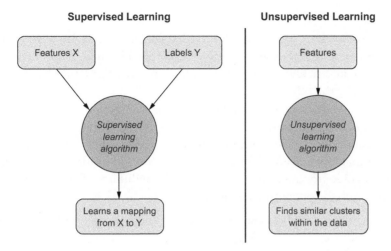

Figure 3.6   The differences in input and output of supervised and unsupervised algorithms

The task of finding similar groups within sets of data is pretty simple when the dimensions that we need to take into account are limited. Take a look at figure 3.7, and you can see that the points naturally condense into two well-separated groups. But what happens when we want to consider a large number of user characteristics? If we want to consider, let's say, 10 attributes, our minds can't possibly identify groups that are similar to each other. This is when unsupervised learning algorithms shine: they can scale the concept of similarity even to hundreds of dimensions without any problem, and we can use the results to gain useful insights.

Right now, you should have a hunch about why the kind of ML we have been using so far is called *supervised*: our algorithms were asked to map a given set of features to a given set of labels. Because we have no labels to begin with, the algorithm has to find them by itself, in an *unsupervised* way.

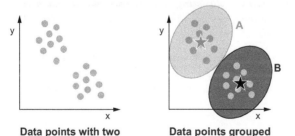

Data points with two features (*x, y*) in space

Data points grouped into similiar clusters

Figure 3.7   The effects of clustering on a simple set of points with two features

You can think about it in this way:

- In *supervised learning*, you already know what you're looking for. If you can classify customers into different classes (for example, churned/not churned as we did before), an ML algorithm can learn how to recognize customers belonging to one class or the other.

- In *unsupervised learning*, you don't know exactly what you're looking for: you can't assign a label to customers. An unsupervised learning algorithm will recognize groups of customers who are similar and assign them a label. It won't tell you what that label means, though: the algorithm will just tell you that customers with label A are similar to each other and are different from customers with label B; it's up to you to understand why.

Let's see how a conversation between an ML expert and a marketer who has read this book would unfold:

Marketer: I'm looking at ways that ML can help our team improve customer segmentation.

ML expert: How did you do customer segmentation before?

Marketer: You know, the "good old way": using a mix of surveys, experience, and gut feeling. I know that there are some ML techniques that can help with that.

ML expert: Yes, I can use unsupervised learning to automatically generate clusters. Let's start with something simple: what are the top three elements that are relevant to segment our customers?

Marketeer: For sure, demographics like age and gender, and I'd add monthly average spending into the mix. This is a good indicator of their likelihood of purchasing new services from us.

ML expert: Nice. I'll get an export from our CRM of these dimensions for 1,000 clients and get back to you. I'll need your help to interpret the results.

[After a while]

ML expert: I've done some preliminary clustering, and it looks like we have three well-defined clusters: young low-spender males, high-spender women in their 30s, and one that is between.

Marketeer: Interesting—we didn't know that women in their 30s were such a profitable segment for us. I'd like to dig deeper; can we add another dimension to the clustering? I'm interested in knowing their purchase frequency: we know that women like to buy more often than men, and I wonder whether unsupervised learning can pick up something deeper in it.

ML expert: Sure, let's define a label that is "average time between orders." I'll look into the results.

As a business person, it's important that you start these conversations with some knowledge of unsupervised learning so you can have a constructive discussion with technical people, and with an open mindset that can accept the inputs that are given to you by them.

A good way to visualize clustering is to picture how stars are scattered over the night sky. Our brain intuitively groups neighboring stars and assigns them zodiac signs. Most real-world applications are a bit more complex, for three main reasons:

- Sometimes, data points are distributed homogeneously, making it difficult to decide how many clusters to consider, let alone how to divide customers.
- As humans, we easily perform segmentation on limited dimensions, but we struggle when the number of dimensions increases. Think back to the zodiac sign examples: we see the sky as a two-dimensional canvas; performing the same task in a three-dimensional space would be much harder. In four dimensions, it would be impossible. What about with 20 dimensions of customer information?
- From a business standpoint, segmentation is not an idle exercise, but is most useful only when the various segments can be linked to a business outcome, often in terms of customer lifetime value, price sensitivity, or channel preference.

In the next section, we'll address these issues through an example. For now, let's dig a bit deeper into the nuts and bolts of clustering. One of the first important decisions to make when tackling a clustering problem is to decide which features (or dimensions) to use for clustering. In our trivial example of a night sky, the choice of dimensions is obvious: the horizontal and vertical position of each star. Real-world applications may be way more complex, though.

3.4.2 Unsupervised learning for customer segmentation

This section will give you more details on unsupervised learning and shed some light on the inner workings of these algorithms. The core concepts you've learned so far are enough to envision new applications for unsupervised learning within your organization. If that's enough for your goals, feel free to skip this section. If you want to know more about how to use these techniques in practice, keep reading.

Let's use the example of an e-commerce website that sells shoes and has access to the purchase history of its customers. Each data point represents a purchase or a return, and contains information about the shoe such as price, brand, size, color, the date and time of the transaction, and whether it was bought together with other items. We could decide to use all these features for the segmentation or to limit our analysis to a subset. For example, looking at the colors of all the shoes a customer bought might help us better understand that customer's taste, or looking at the time of the day for those purchases may provide suggestions on the best time of the day to propose discounts.

We could even extrapolate parameters such as the average amount spent per purchase and the number of shoes bought in a month. These two pieces of information together would likely help the clustering algorithm find a natural distinction between high-frequency/low-value customers and low-frequency/high-value ones.

For the sake of simplicity, let's assume we're building a simple clustering algorithm that looks at three features of each customer:

- Age
- Gender
- Average monthly spending on the e-commerce

Keep in mind that the attributes that are not used for clustering are not thrown away but can be used for *profiling*. This means describing the characteristics of each group to inform marketing decisions.

Table 3.1 shows our data for the first five customers.

Table 3.1   Five customer features before being fed to an unsupervised learning algorithm

Customer ID	Age	Gender	Average monthly spending ($)
1	18	M	14.67
2	21	M	15.67
3	28	M	18.02
4	27	F	34.61
5	32	F	30.66

In some of the most commonly used clustering algorithms, the next step would be to decide the number of clusters we're looking for. This is often counterintuitive: After all, wouldn't you want the algorithm to tell *you* how many groups of users there are? If you think about it, though, there are many ways to slice and dice the population, and choosing the number of clusters up front is the only way to direct the algorithm. Let's keep things simple for now and say that we're looking to get three clusters. The clustering algorithm is going to find a way to divide users such that

- Customers within the same cluster are similar to each other.
- Customers in different clusters are different from each other.

In this way, we are mathematically sure that when we're choosing an action to target customers from a certain cluster, we are maximizing the likelihood that they'll respond in the same way. Two outputs of the clustering algorithm are interesting to look at:

- The cluster that will be associated with each user, as indicated in table 3.2.
- The *cluster centers*. Each cluster has a center, which can be considered the "stereotype" of the kind of user who belongs to that cluster. A marketer would call this a *buyer persona*.

Table 3.2 Adding a Cluster column, identified by an unsupervised learning algorithm

Customer ID	Age	Gender	Avg monthly spending ($)	Cluster
1	18	M	14.67	1
2	21	M	15.67	1
3	28	M	18.02	3
4	27	F	34.61	2
5	32	F	30.66	2

Looking at the cluster centers is crucial, as it gives us quantitative information on what the algorithm has found, which we can then interpret to extract insights. Each center is going to be characterized by the same three features that we used before to describe users (though we may rearrange them to be more meaningful). Typically, we would also add a count of the number of users who fall into each cluster. Table 3.3 shows what the cluster centers may look like, assuming we started with data from 1,000 customers.

Table 3.3 A summary of the characteristics of the three clusters spotted by our algorithm

Cluster number	Age	% female	Avg monthly spending ($)	# of customers
1	18.2	20%	15.24	290
2	29.3	90%	28.15	120
3	22	40%	17.89	590

This apparently innocuous table is packed with useful information. Let's spend some time trying to extrapolate insights and getting to know our segments:

- Cluster 1 is mainly made out of young (average age: 18.2), predominantly male people who are not high spenders (average monthly spending of $15.24). This is an average-sized cluster (29% of users are here).
- Cluster 2 skews toward older females (29.3 years on average) who spend much more than any other cluster ($28.15 average spending compared to $15.24 and $17.89 of clusters 1 and 3, respectively). This is a rather small segment, with 12% of users belonging to it.
- Cluster 3 is almost equally split between males and females. They are not as thrifty and young as cluster 1, but definitely spend less than cluster 2 and are much younger (22 years old versus 29.3).

Marketers can make good use of this information and come up with personalized strategies to market products to each group of people. For instance, customers in clusters 1 and 3 can be offered cheaper products compared to the ones in cluster 2. Adding new features like the colors of shoes bought may give us further insights to take more fine-grained decisions.

Notice how the process started with the data and the algorithm's findings about it, but ended with a human looking at the results and interpreting the cluster centers to extract useful information that is actionable. This aspect is key to any ML algorithm, but is especially critical for clustering: true value is achieved by the symbiosis between what AI can do and what expert and curious humans can build on top of it.

3.5   *Measuring performance*

Because ML-based predictions have a direct impact on the business outcome, evaluating their performance is an important skill to have. Researchers and engineers will often develop models for you, and report the algorithms' performance by using different metrics. Although these metrics do a good job of describing the statistical performance of the models, they don't tell the whole story. In fact, the link between these nerdy numbers and business outcomes can be subtle. It's your job to understand ML metrics enough to make informed decisions about how the accuracy of the model can affect your business goals.

3.5.1   *Classification algorithms*

A big part of working with machine learning is getting comfortable with dealing with errors. Even the best-performing algorithm won't be 100% perfect, and it's going to misclassify some examples. Remember that the process to build ML applications is to perform some training on historical data first and then use it "in the real world": it's important to have a sense of how many errors the algorithm will likely make after it's deployed, and what kind of mistakes.

The simplest and most naive way to evaluate an algorithm is with a metric called *accuracy*, representing the percentage of correct guesses over the total predictions:

$$Accuracy = \frac{Correct\ predictions}{Total\ predictions}$$

However, not all errors are the same. In the case of our churn predictor, there are two possible errors:

- A customer is wrongly labeled by the algorithm as churned but is actually still engaged. This case is called a *false positive* (*FP*).
- A customer is wrongly labeled by the algorithm as active but is actually about to cancel their subscription. This case is a *false negative* (*FN*).

This distinction isn't another fixation for nerds: it has a direct impact on the business, and it's important for you to understand how it's going to affect your business decisions. A good data scientist should not represent performances with a simple accuracy number, and neither should you. A better idea is using a more informative table like table 3.4.

Table 3.4 Visualizing the possible combinations of algorithms' predictions and ground truth

		Predicted (What the algorithm has predicted)	
		Churned	**Not churned**
Actual (What the data says)	**Churned**	True positives (Customers identified by the algorithm as churned, and it was right)	False negatives (Customers identified by the algorithm as not churned, but it was wrong)
	Not churned	False positives (Customers identified by the algorithm as churned, but it was wrong)	True negatives (Customers identified by the algorithm as not churned, and it was right)

Presenting results in this type of table is common for *binary classification tasks* (in which the label has only one of two outcomes—in this case, churn/not churn), so let's spend some time explaining how to read it. The goal of this table is to have a measure of the algorithm's performances in a single snapshot, both in terms of correct guesses and errors.

The top-left and bottom-right cells are relative to the correct guesses. The top-left cell represents the number of customers who are churned and are correctly classified as such by our algorithm (*true positives*, or *TPs*). The bottom-right is for active customers (not churned) that the algorithm identified correctly (*true negatives*, or *TNs*).

The bottom-left and top-right cells are relative to the errors we mentioned previously. Customers who are active but the algorithm misclassified as churned are in the bottom left (*false positives*, or *FPs*), and customers who are active but have been wrongly classified as churned are in the top right (*false negatives*, or *FNs*).

Researchers and engineers spend a lot of time looking at tables like table 3.4, because the numbers they contain often give insights as to how an algorithm will perform in the real world. As someone whose business is impacted by these numbers, it's important that you understand the nuances that can hide behind them.

First, the number of false positives and false negatives are linked together, and it's easy to trade one for the other without substantial changes to the model or additional training. For example, consider a *very* naive model that always predicts that customers are churning: whatever inputs it gets, it always outputs "yes, the customer is about to churn." Metrics for true positives and false negatives will be encouraging (100% the former, and 0% the latter—can you see why?), but false positives and true negatives will be terrible.

A tricky situation and how to avoid being fooled

Imagine that you are building your churn predictor on a sample dataset of 1,000 users, divided as follows:

- 900 of them are active.
- 100 of them are churned.

These kinds of datasets are called *unbalanced*, as the number of examples representative of one label is much higher than the number of examples representative of the other. Now, let's say you build an algorithm that has 90% prediction accuracy. This sounds good, but is it? If you build your algorithm to predict "Active" every time, it will be correct 90% of the time (because 90% of users are active). In this case, we would have the following:

- 100% true negatives (All that are not churned are correctly identified.)
- 0% true positives (The algorithm never spotted a single churning customer.)

In reality, your algorithm performs poorly, even though it is correct 90% of the time. As you can see, looking at true positives and false negatives is a much more useful strategy to avoid being fooled by high-accuracy performances.

Now, false positives, false negatives, true positives, and true negatives are absolute metrics. It's always a good idea to report them to an absolute metric that isn't sensitive to the number of samples combined. Two metrics can help us with this, called *precision* and *recall*. Here's what they tell us:

- *Precision*—Out of all the customers whom the algorithm predicted as churned (true positives), how many were really going to churn?
- *Recall*—Out of all the customers who churned, how many did the algorithm predict?

Figure 3.8 shows how precision and recall are calculated based on the algorithm's predictions.

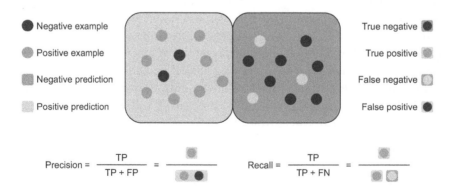

Figure 3.8   A graphical representation of true positives, true negatives, false positives, and false negatives, and how these metrics combined form the precision and the recall

You can imagine an algorithm with a high precision and low recall as a sniper: it wants to be sure before shooting, so it stays conservative and doesn't shoot unless it's 100% sure. This means that it misses some targets, but every time it fires, you're confident that it's going to hit the right target. On the other hand, an algorithm with a high recall and low precision is like a machine gun: it shoots a lot and hits many of the targets it should hit, but also hits some wrong ones along the way. Table 3.5 summarizes the difference between precision, recall, and accuracy, and what these metrics tell you.

Table 3.5   Accuracy, precision, and recall

Metric	Definition	What this metric is telling you
Accuracy	$$\frac{True\ Positives + True\ negatives}{Total\ examples}$$	How many mistakes is the algorithm making? No difference in misclassifying a positive from a negative.
Precision	$$\frac{True\ Positives}{True\ positives + False\ positives}$$	How much should you trust the algorithm when it spots a positive example?
Recall	$$\frac{True\ Positives}{True\ positives + False\ negatives}$$	Out of all the positive examples, how many did the algorithm spot?

3.5.2   Clustering algorithms

When it comes to unsupervised learning, evaluating performance is tricky because there's no objective "greatness" metric: because we don't have labels to compare, we can't define whether the algorithm's output is "right" or "wrong." Remember also that most clustering algorithms require you to define the number of clusters you want it to identify, so another question you'll have to answer is whether your choice for the number of clusters was good. How do we get out of this apparently foggy situation?

First of all, some mathematical tools can tell a data scientist whether a clustering has been done well. Unfortunately, having an algorithm that performs great from a mathematical point of view isn't necessarily a sign of it being useful for business purposes. If you bought this book, we assume that you're not using ML to publish a scientific paper but rather to help your organization. If this is true, mathematical stunts won't be of any interest to you. What you should do instead is look at your results and ask yourself these questions:

1 Are the results *interpretable*? In other words, are the cluster centers interpretable as buyer personas that make logical sense? If the answer is yes, move to question 2.
2 Are the results *actionable*? In other words, are my clusters different enough that I can come up with different strategies to target customers belonging to the different centers?

If the answer to these questions is yes, congrats: you can start testing the results in the real world, collect data, and move forward either by iterating and tweaking your algorithm when you have more data, or by using the new knowledge to redesign your approach. Luckily, underperforming unsupervised algorithms are usually less risky than underperforming supervised learning ones, as the concept of "right" or "wrong" prediction is foggier. For this reason, you don't have to worry much about metrics, but rather about the testing methodology you should have in place to evaluate the business impact of your project. We'll talk about the iteration and design process extensively in part 2 of this book.

3.6   *Tying ML metrics to business outcomes and risks*

Now that you have gained some familiarity with common ML metrics, let's see what they imply in a business scenario. Let's assume you have deployed a great churn predictor that has identified a group of customers likely to leave your service, and you want to reach out with a personalized phone call to each of them.

If your data science team has built a model with high *precision* but low *recall*, you won't waste many phone calls: every time you call, you'll talk with a user who is really considering leaving you. On the other hand, some users are leaving the service, but your algorithm has failed to spot them. A high-recall, low-precision algorithm would instead have you make a lot of phone calls—so you'll reach out to a large chunk (even all) of the customers planning to abandon your service, but you'll waste phone calls to other users who weren't planning to unsubscribe at all.

The trade-off between precision and recall is clearly a function of the business. If each customer has a high value and reaching out is cheap, go with a high recall. If your customers are not making expensive purchases, don't want to be disturbed unnecessarily, and calling them is expensive, go with a high-precision one. An even more sophisticated strategy could be to reserve more-expensive actions like phone calls for customers with higher value or a higher probability of churn, and use cheaper actions like email for others. As you can see in figure 3.9, you can decide whether to focus on recall or on precision based on two parameters: the cost of losing a customer, and the cost of the actions you pursue to try to retain them.

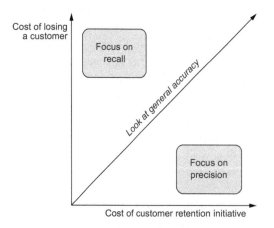

Figure 3.9   A cheat sheet to decide whether to focus on high-precision, high-recall or just general accuracy based on key business metrics

The problem becomes even more serious in safety-critical applications. If we have a classifier used for medical diagnoses, the cost of a false positive and false negative are very different. Suppose our algorithm is detecting lung cancer. In table 3.6, you can see what each error means and its implications.

Table 3.6   Implications of true positives, true negatives, false positives, and false negatives

Metric	What does it mean	Implication
True positive	The algorithm predicts that the patient has cancer, and it's right: the patient really is sick.	The patient gets the treatment needed right away.
True negative	The algorithm predicts the patient is healthy, and indeed the patient is.	The patient goes home relieved.
False positive	The algorithm predicts that the patient has cancer (hence the positive), but the patient actually is healthy (hence the false).	The patient gets scared and maybe starts a trial, but is actually OK.
False negative	The algorithm predicts the patient is healthy (negative), but the patient is sick instead (false).	The patient goes home feeling relieved but actually is sick and doesn't receive the treatment needed.

As you can see, the cost associated with a mistake is very different, depending on whether we're misclassifying healthy or sick patients. A false positive can imply additional exams, or maybe unnecessary treatment, but a false negative will deprive a patient of the therapy desperately needed to survive.

In such a scenario, you clearly see how dangerous it is to optimize for the wrong metric. Having high accuracy here wouldn't be indicative of a good algorithm, as it would weight false negatives and false positives in the same way. What we want in this case is a high recall: we want the highest number of patients who are sick to be identified, even if that means having some false positives. False positives may lead to additional unnecessary exams and frightening some families, but it will ensure that the highest number of sick people are spotted and taken care of.

As you can see, every algorithm has an indicator of its performance, and you need to be able to assess which metric is the most important for you, so that your data science team can work on maximizing it. We've seen that the best choice is not always obvious. From a business point of view, the most powerful idea is to tie each misclassification to a dollar amount. If your assumptions are correct, this will automatically lead to the best business outcome. Our imaginary telecom company could develop a retention plan for disgruntled customers that gives them a $100 bonus if they stay with the company for the next 12 months, thus retaining a customer that would have otherwise defected to a competitor in the near future.

On the other hand, let's assume that each lost customer loses the company $500 in profit. Now that we have all these numbers, we can easily compute just how much money false negatives and false positives cost us. Each false negative (a customer who defected to a competitor before we could entice them with a discount) costs us $500 in lost revenue. Each false positive (a loyal customer who would not have churned but received a gift anyway) costs us $100 in lost revenue. We can now use some basic accounting to tie the performance of the model to a monetary value:

*Total cost = $500 * FN + $0 * TN + $100 * FP + $100 * TP*

Here, *FN* is the number of false negatives, *TN* is true negatives, *FN* is false negatives, and *TP* is true positives.

You can use these same ideas for other situations where you're using a binary classification model. For example, say that you're developing an automated quality control system for a manufacturing line. You can tweak the model to either let more items through (increase the false-negative rate) or reject more items right away (increase the false-positive rate). The former might let more faulty items through, thus leading to more issues downstream in the manufacturing process. The latter might result in unneeded waste of material, as perfectly fine products are rejected. In any case, you can adapt the preceding formula to your specific business situation.

Whatever your strategy, you still need to be comfortable with the fact that no machine learning algorithm will be perfect (if it is, something is wrong). You'll make mistakes: make sure that these mistakes are acceptable and that both you and your algorithm learn from them.

3.7   Case studies

This section presents two case studies from real companies that used AI for their marketing efforts. The first one is Opower, an energy company that used clustering to segment its users based on their energy consumption habits. The second one is a Target initiative: the retail store used the data of its customers to identify signs of a pregnancy early on and start advertising diapers.

3.7.1   AI to refine targeting and positioning: Opower

The relationship that energy companies have with customers is peculiar: although consumer companies normally get paid when the customer makes a purchase, with energy, there's a lag: people first consume energy for a period of time and get billed later. Also, people don't buy energy for the sake of it: it's a necessary expense to enjoy other goods (such as turning on a TV).

These two factors make it hard for every utility to know its customers and interact with them. This isn't a problem just for the marketing department of energy companies, but also for their overall costs and profitability. In fact, producing energy doesn't always cost utilities the same price: it depends on the kind of power plant they use to produce it, a choice that depends on how much energy they need to produce and how well in advance they planned for it.

The best-case scenario is a perfectly flat demand: utilities can start producing X amount of energy using their best power plants and never change. This is, of course, never the case, as daily demand has a duck shape instead, with two peaks usually happening when people wake up and when they come back home from work. To fulfill demand during these peaks, utilities need to use power plants that are easy to turn on and off and modulate, but flexibility comes at a price: these plants are more expensive to run, consume more energy, and burn more-expensive fuels. As represented in figure 3.10, this problem is getting worse: today's habits are making the energy demand curve less flat, with a bigger valley during the day and sharper peaks in the morning and in the evening. The dream of every utility company is to be able to shape their customers' habits by moving their peaks to different times of the day, achieving an overall almost flat demand.

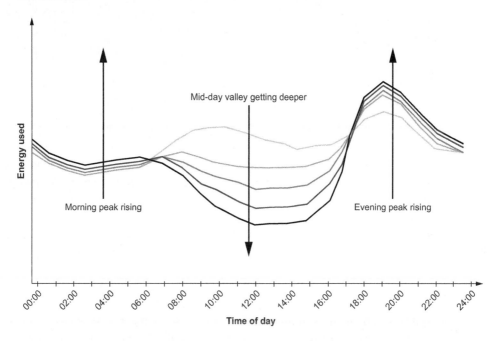

Figure 3.10   Typical load curves for the energy consumption of California homes

OPOWER'S STRATEGY

Opower was founded in 2007 with the mission of providing energy companies the tools to target their users and engage them in changing their consumption habits, both to save energy and to achieve an overall flatter demand. The company was getting smart meter data from utilities' customers, and could send them reports with details on their energy consumption and tips to improve their habits, using mail, email, internet portals, text messages, and sometimes in-home energy displays.

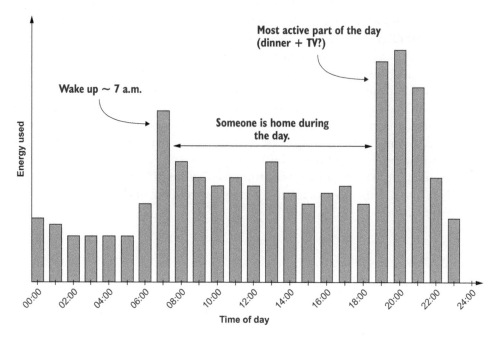

Figure 3.11   **Energy consumption values of a household at different times of the day**

The company's secret sauce is a mixture of behavioral science and data science. Opower turned to one of the core applications of machine learning—unsupervised learning—which it used to identify particular user groups that could be targeted similarly.

The most characteristic element of an energy user is their consumption pattern: how much energy they use during different hours of the day. We can therefore see each user as in figure 3.11: a combination of 24 numbers that represent the amount of energy consumed for each hour of the day. These numbers draw an accurate picture of the habits of the users, just as the number of purchases, average expense, and items bought would be in an e-commerce scenario.

Spotting different groups of users based on their consumption patterns isn't an easy task. If we represent 1,000 users in this way and plot all of them on a graph, we get what data scientists like to call a *hairball*: an intricate mix of lines, one on top of the other, impossible for a human eye to distinguish. On the other hand, identifying patterns is where unsupervised algorithms are the most useful; using these, Opower was able to spot five user clusters. We gathered data from the internet and ran an unsupervised algorithm to mimic the results that Opower achieved; you can see the hairball and the final clusters in figure 3.12.

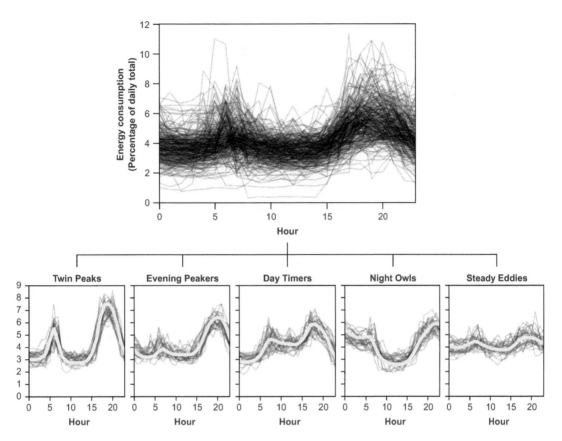

Figure 3.12   Turning a "hairball" of 1,000 users into five clusters

Looking at these clusters, we can try interpreting each of them:

- *Twin Peaks*—They consume a lot of energy in the early morning, way more than users from other clusters. They also have a peak during the evening at about dinner time, but a bit lower than their morning peak.
- *Evening Peakers*—They have a high peak during the evening that they reach smoothly, starting from the early morning. The first morning peak is absent.
- *Day Timers*—They don't have the classic peaks that all other clusters have. Instead, they have a high consumption during the day that ramps up and slows down smoothly.
- *Steady Eddies*—They're the steadiest ones; the two classic peaks are very smooth.
- *Night Owls*—They have classic peaks during the early morning and late evening but tend to consume energy during the night.

Opower used the results of the clustering to target different users in different ways. Its infrastructure allowed splitting each cluster into groups and testing different messages. From the analysis of the results and using behavioral science, Opower was able

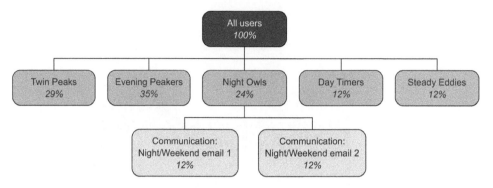

Figure 3.13   Decision tree that Opower used to target its users

to constantly improve its targeting. An example of this segmentation is represented in figure 3.13: Opower could pick a specific cluster (the Night Owls, in this case), and split them into two groups that it targeted with different emails. This approach allowed Opower to optimize its messaging and target people in the best way possible.

Thanks to its approach, Opower was able to help consumers save 10% on their energy bills, while making utilities more profitable, thanks to the better distribution of the total demand. As a result of its performance, Opower was acquired by Oracle in 2016 for $532 million.

CASE QUESTION

How can you persuade a group of people to change their behavior?

CASE DISCUSSION

Think for a second about the complexity of Opower's mission: it has to enable millions of people to change their way of consuming energy by sending them some kind of report. You'd be naïve to think the same message could work for all of them.

Every person responds to different incentives and different messaging, so ideally you'd have to target everyone with a different message. This is, of course, not practical or scalable, but you can still go a long way by splitting your audience into groups that have something in common. For Opower, this first step was done using unsupervised learning. Remember that unsupervised learning is a class of ML algorithms that looks for patterns in data, finding groups of similar data points based on their features. In Opower's case, the most important characteristic was the user's energy consumption habits, so Opower needed a way to account for this. Opower's idea to express energy consumption habits into features (a bunch of numbers) was to consider in each hour of the day the amount of energy a certain user was consuming. The result was a representation of each person made up of 24 numbers, which is easy enough for a human to grasp, but very easy for a computer: once an unsupervised learning algorithm is fed with this data, it can easily compare two users and spot similarities.

Unsupervised learning provided Opower with the first, most important distinction across users: their energy consumption. The second step was measuring the effects of different messages, which Opower did by using behavioral science and A/B testing (sending different messages to different people and measuring the results).

A final implementation note on the number of clusters that the algorithm identified here. Opower had five, but where did this number come from? With some of the widely used algorithms, you need to come up with the number of clusters the algorithm has to look for, and the algorithm will optimize for it.

Mathematical tools provide data scientists clues about what number would yield the best results from a mathematical standpoint, but it wouldn't necessarily be the best solution for your business needs, so there's no "right" or "wrong" solution. Because there's no script for deciding the number of clusters, coming up with this number can sometimes feel like doing grocery shopping: "Do we want five clusters? Let's do six; it's better to have a little more, just in case we run out of them." We can argue that making a decision is actually much simpler.

Think about this: every time you ask the algorithm to find one more cluster, it's going to see new, subtler patterns in the data. Assuming we have 1,000 users, the upper limit would be to find 1,000 clusters, where each user has a cluster of their own. Before you reach that extreme situation, you'll sometimes find that you can't really gain any new knowledge from adding a new cluster. This is a good moment to stop. Adding clusters will make the results of the algorithm more specific, but also less interpretable. Figure 3.14 illustrates this trade-off.

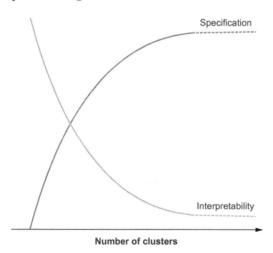

Specification

Interpretability

Number of clusters

Figure 3.14 The relationship between the number of clusters and the interpretability and specification of the results

The ideal process would be to start with a number of clusters that is rather small; ideally, this number can be provided by your data scientists, who will use mathematical tools to find out what makes sense from a technical standpoint. From there, you can move either down, condensing different clusters, or up, increasing the granularity of the clustering. Every time you increase or decrease the number of clusters, try interpreting the results and ask yourself whether a higher number of clusters helps you better understand the phenomenon. If the answer is no, we can argue that you found the optimal number of clusters. This may not be what the data scientists found as the technical optimum, but it will be what's optimal for the business.

3.7.2 *AI to anticipate customer needs: Target*

The birth of a child can be not only a joyful event for a couple, but also the beginning of a new stream of costs. Suddenly, the parents need to include new, expensive products in their usual shopping, such as diapers, baby food, a stroller, and so on.

Such an event is extremely lucrative to retailers, which try to attract new parents to their stores to become their trusted point of reference for purchasing all they need for their newborn. The strategy that retailers usually use is offering discounts and promotions to the newly formed family, and the earlier the retailer can put its coupons in their hands, the more advantage it wins over the competition in acquiring the new customer.

Among all the new expenses that families need to sustain, diapers is an extremely important one. According to a Nielsen report for 2016, American families spend an average of more than $1,000 per year per newborn for diapers. Revenue isn't the only reason diapers are important to retailers, as they also play a strategic role as *traffic builders*: products that a family can't live without and so attract young mothers and fathers into a store where they then end up spending money on other goods as well.

The result of the economic and strategic value of acquiring a customer who has just had a baby results in a "coupon war" between retailers: all of them fight to be the first ones to place offers in the hands of the new mother and father, and attract them to buy diapers and other products at their stores.

The first approach that retailers tried to win these new customers was to get the openly available registry office data for newborns and send targeted offers to the new fathers and mothers, incentivizing them to shop for their first diapers in their shops. However, many retailers quickly started using this strategy and began competing for attention from newborns' families right after the baby was born.

To get ahead of its competitors, Target, the eighth-largest retailer in the United States, decided to investigate a new, bold strategy: provide families offers *before* the baby was born. If the retail chain could know that a couple was waiting for a baby, it could outpace its competitors and reach the family first.

The retail giant used its fidelity card data to identify patterns in the shopping habits of pregnant women, and prepare a specific set of coupons and promotions that would entice that category of shoppers to expand the range of items that they choose to buy at Target. In a 2012 *Forbes* article (http://mng.bz/PO6g), we get some indications of the results that Target's statistician Andrew Pole was able to find:

> *As Pole's computers crawled through the data, he was able to identify about 25 products that, when analyzed together, allowed him to assign each shopper a "pregnancy prediction" score. More important, he could also estimate her due date to within a small window, so Target could send coupons timed to very specific stages of her pregnancy.*

Target was reportedly able to increase sales thanks to its new strategy. However, increased revenue came at a cost: people started sensing they were being spied on and weren't happy with that. The first warning sign that the general public might not like such intensive targeting techniques came when a disgruntled father complained about the coupons for baby products that his high-school daughter had been getting from Target. As reported in the same *Forbes* article, he complained to the store manager, shouting:

> *My daughter got this in the mail! She's still in high school, and you're sending her coupons for baby clothes and cribs? Are you trying to encourage her to get pregnant?*

It turns out, the girl was actually pregnant, and Target had figured it out before her father did. The Target's manager reportedly called the angry father a while later, and got his response as reported by Forbes:

> *I had a talk with my daughter. It turns out there's been some activities in my house I haven't been completely aware of. She's due in August. I owe you an apology.*

As reported in the *Forbes* article, Target ended up mixing personalized recommendations obtained through ML with seemingly random items from the catalog (for instance, adding a coupon for a lawn mower right next to one for diapers), to avoid making customers feel like they were being stalked.

CASE QUESTION

Are special discounts an effective way to win customers over competitors?

CASE DISCUSSION

Special offers and coupons are an extremely common strategy that retailers use to attract customers. However, when everybody knows a person is looking for a specific product that everybody can sell, the effects are usually a promotions war, eating retailers' margins. This may be good for customers but definitely is not for retailers. We argue that offering discounts to customers can be a valid marketing idea if the following are true:

1. The retailer knows who to send the coupons to (it's effective at targeting its users).
2. Other retailers are not targeting that person at the same time, to avoid the price wars mentioned previously.

The initial strategy that retailers adopted was clever: using openly available registry office data for newborns to target families immediately after a baby is born. This strategy is effective at point 1 (targeting the right customer), but fails at point 2: as the name says, open data is open, and every retailer can use it.

Target's case is a perfect example of how you can use data and machine learning to win over competitors, targeting the perfect customer before anyone else. Target started from its *core business sales data*: the shopping habits of customers, collected through fidelity cards. It was also able to build a label "is waiting for a child"/"is not waiting for a child" for past customers, by looking at whether this customer actually started buying diapers in the future. We hope you already figured out that this looks like a classic supervised learning classification problem:

- The features are the shopping habits of the customer (let data scientists figure out how to build them exactly).
- The label is whether that customer is waiting for a baby, according to feature purchases of baby-related goods.
- After the model is built for past data, it can be applied to current customers, identifying the ones waiting for a baby.

Notice that the label wasn't immediately available: Target's customers don't call the retailer, communicating that a baby is born. However, this label can be assigned to past customers by looking at their past purchasing behavior: if a customer started buying diapers or a baby stroller six months ago, she must have been pregnant within the nine months before and can be labeled as a positive example.

Think about how powerful this approach is. Patterns exist in the purchasing habits of pregnant women: they may stop buying certain foods like sausages or sushi, eat healthier food, or quit cigarettes. The problem is that when there's a lack of clear indicators (for example, the purchase of prenatal vitamins or diapers) it's hard for a human to spot patterns by looking at customer purchases. But it's not hard for an ML algorithm, which can figure out which purchasing habits suggest a pregnancy.

Something else you should keep in mind is that what may sound like a nice story, and a great move from Target to boost sales, can also be a ticking PR time bomb due to aggressive targeting in such sensitive domains.

To summarize, you should keep the following in mind from this case:

- ML can help you predict future purchases, anticipating competitors.
- Core business data has a much higher value than openly available data (more about this in chapter 8).
- Be on the lookout for the creepiness factor: ML can be so powerful that people might feel like you're spying on them.

Summary
- The core reasons behind the effectiveness of AI in marketing and sales are the ability to target specific customers at scale and make data-driven decisions.
- A churn prediction model is a typical application of AI in marketing, and can spot which customers are most likely to quit your service.
- Likewise, machine learning can help marketers find upselling opportunities by identifying which customers are more inclined to buy more.
- Unsupervised learning is a subset of machine learning that enables computers to find structure in data, finding clusters of similar data points. Clustering also has uses in marketing.

- There are different ways and metrics to evaluate the performance of classification algorithms (we covered accuracy, recall, and precision). Each one tells us something different about the algorithm, and you can look at your business objectives to choose the most appropriate one.

- Opower used unsupervised learning to divide energy consumers into clusters and then targeted them individually to optimize their energy consumption patterns.

- Target used supervised learning to identify which of their customers was about to have a baby, and then offered them coupons for diapers and baby products.

AI for media 4

This chapter covers

- Using AI to understand the content of images
- Using deep learning to solve challenges in computer vision
- Detecting and labeling human faces
- Creating original artwork with deep learning
- Using AI with audio data
- Case study: automating vegetable sorting with a $1,000 robot

Images and videos are probably the richest source of data that humans use to understand the world. Sadly, they were largely off-limits for computers until the 2010s. While cameras had been getting better and better for decades, computers still couldn't understand the content of images. A pivotal moment was the development of a new field of machine learning called *deep learning (DL)*. This family of algorithms has unsurpassed (for now) learning power that can reach superhuman accuracy in important tasks like detecting objects and faces in images. These abilities allow businesses to supercharge their existing products with abilities that would have been considered magical just 10 years ago, from automatically creating photo albums based on the content of images, to automating industrial processes with robots.

4.1 *Improving products with computer vision*

FutureHouse's home-price-prediction tool that we developed in chapter 2 is a resounding success. Customers are really happy with the pricing suggestions they get from the AI model and are rushing to list their homes on the website. Newly listed homes are sold fast at a price very close to the algorithm's suggestion. Business is going well, but this only fuels your ambitions.

During another brainstorming session, the user experience team brings up behavioral analytics data for the marketplace and breaks some alarming news. A good chunk of users are dropping out of the step-by-step flow for listing their property. The biggest drop happens when they're asked to upload images and manually pick which room of the house they depict (bathroom, living room, and so forth). This process is long and tedious, and your team is motivated to start a new project to streamline the user experience: we can use AI to automatically label images and get rid of all the manual work. The experience for users would be much easier: they simply upload a bunch of pictures, which are then automatically tagged as bathroom/kitchen/living room/etc. The overall flow will become much faster and more pleasant.

What we're designing is an algorithm that has as an input the picture of a room, and as output its type (bathroom, kitchen, and so forth), as shown in figure 4.1. Notice that our AI will have to learn how to map these inputs to a specific target (the room category); therefore, we're dealing with a supervised learning problem. More specifically, it's a *classification* problem, because the target is a category, not a number. For obvious reasons, most engineers use a common name for this task: *image classification.*

Now that you know what type of problem we're dealing with, you also know what type of training data we need to collect: a collection of labeled pictures that have already been grouped according to the room they were taken in. Luckily, we know just the right place to get them: users have gone through the painful process of uploading

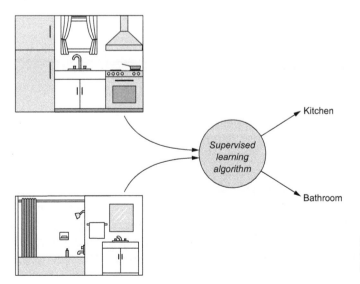

Figure 4.1 An overview of the inputs and outputs of the image classifier

pictures of rooms and tagging them with a category. Now, we can take all this *labeled data* and build a model that tags images automatically, so that future users won't have to do all this boring work. This pattern is pretty common when building AI applications in business: a manual process has already produced a lot of labeled data, which can be used to develop AI-based automation.

If we had to follow the blueprint in the previous chapter, the next step would be to identify relevant features so that the algorithm can learn which elements make a bathroom and which elements make a kitchen. Remember: a *feature* is any aspect of each input item that you believe is going to be useful for the algorithm when it comes to learning how to classify items. Table 4.1 shows examples of features you might want to use.

Table 4.1   Domain knowledge is often the best tool for choosing features.

Objective	Possible features
Predicting the price of a house	Square footage, location, renovation year
Deciding whether a tumor is benign or malignant	Size of the tumor, age, blood-test results
Deciding whether a customer is going to unsubscribe	Use of the product, age, monthly spending, products purchased

The *learning* part of machine learning begins only *after* engineers have defined which features to use for a specific problem. While humans are pretty good at doing this task by using intuition and experience, traditional ML algorithms need to be told exactly which numbers to use. The question you should ask yourself to identify relevant features is "If I had to classify this picture myself, what would I look for?" It would be natural to use features like these:

- Is there a toilet in the picture?
- Is there a refrigerator in the picture?
- Is there a shower in the picture?

The task seems so easy that we don't even need machine learning to solve it: if there's a shower, we know we're looking at a bathroom. (We suggest having a face-to-face chat with your architect should your kitchen have a shower!) Sadly, from the point of view of a computer, things are not that easy.

When programmers write code that processes digital images (this field is called *computer vision*), all they have to work with is a long list of numbers that represent the color for each spot in the image. Figure 4.2 shows an example of the numbers that form an image with a few dozen *pixels* (individual points). Pictures taken by your smartphone will have millions of these colored pixels (this is what *megapixel* means).

Given that the data we have is just a collection of apparently random numbers, how can we define features? For the first time in this book, we're struggling to do so. If we could just recognize some of the shapes contained in a picture, our job would be easy; but, unfortunately, our data is just a bunch of raw numbers. The first approach that

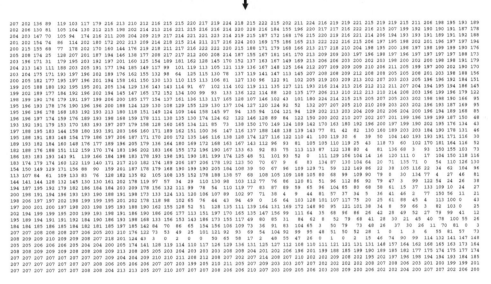

Figure 4.2 An image of a cat, and the same image as read by a computer (scaled to 40 × 40 pixels to fit on a page). Each number represents the brightness of a pixel.

computer vision researchers tried in order to solve this problem was to find clever ways to extract features by hand. They would build complex mathematical tools called *filters* that can spot basic shapes in images, and then try combining these to detect elements.

This approach can work for basic objects. If you think about the shapes that form a shower head, you'll probably picture a circle and a cylinder that represents the handle. That can work for many shower heads, but what about design items like the one on the right in figure 4.3?

You can probably imagine the frustration of a computer vision expert who has to build by hand new filters to catch every possible shower head shape. The approach of hand-building a feature set for every image to tell computers its content clearly has severe shortcomings.

The key to conquering computer vision has been a special class of machine learning algorithms called *deep learning*. To give you an idea of its power, let's talk about the

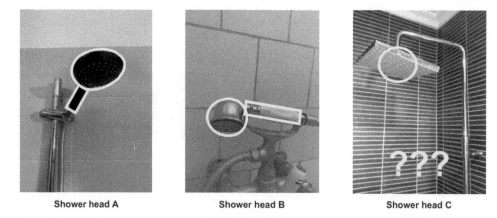

Shower head A   Shower head B   Shower head C

Figure 4.3   Although it's possible to identify A and B as shower heads because of their basic shapes, identifying C is more difficult.

benchmark used to evaluate computer vision models: the ImageNet dataset. This dataset has more than 14 million images, each labeled with one of around 20,000 classes, including a few hundred breeds of dogs and types of food. Traditional computer vision approaches topped out at around 75% accuracy in the early 2010s. Considering that the average human is 95% accurate, that wasn't too great. Deep learning crushed this record, surpassing humans in 2015 before the competition was finally closed in 2017 with 97.3% accuracy (see figure 4.4).

Why is deep learning so powerful, and what price are we paying for this newfound power? The rest of this chapter will make that clear.

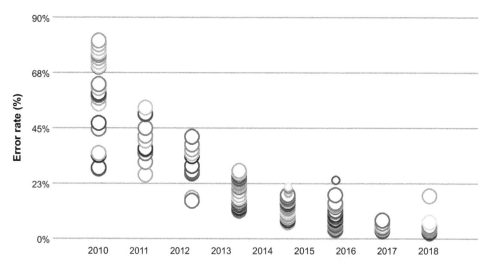

Figure 4.4   Deep learning has been dominating the ImageNet competition since its arrival on the scene in 2013.

4.2 *Using AI for image classification: deep learning?*

First of all, deep learning algorithms aren't entirely different from the machine learning ones we've played with until now. A DL algorithm at its core is still a supervised learning algorithm: it learns a mapping between an input and an output from training data. The main difference is in the kind of input data it works with: while traditional ML algorithms need refined features (top half of figure 4.5), DL algorithms work directly with raw numbers and can understand relevant features automatically (bottom half of figure 4.5).

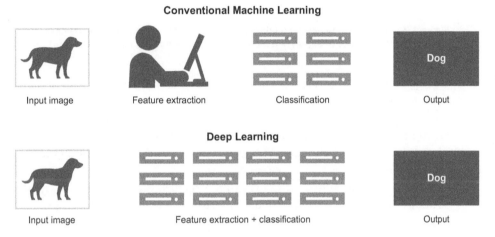

Figure 4.5 **In traditional ML, engineers have to develop algorithms to extract features that can be fed to the model. A DL model doesn't need this complex preliminary step.**

Let's understand why deep learning has such a magical ability. Deep learning is based on a special class of algorithms called *deep neural networks*. You might think that the magic is in the word *neural*, which brings up pictures of an all-powerful artificial brain. Actually, artificial *neurons* are nothing like their biological counterparts. They're extremely simple: they can perform just multiplication and addition. As shown in figure 4.6, each neuron receives the input numbers, does simple mathematical operations on them, and produces an output number.

A neuron alone is simple and, frankly, useless. However, as you connect many neurons together to form a network, they become capable of sophisticated computations. A simple network is shown in figure 4.7: the first column of neurons receives the initial input and passes on the processed information to the middle column of neurons, and so on. Finally, the lonely neuron in the right column produces the final output of the network.

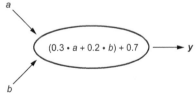

Figure 4.6 **A single artificial neuron receives two numbers (a and b), performs simple mathematical operations, and outputs another number, y.**

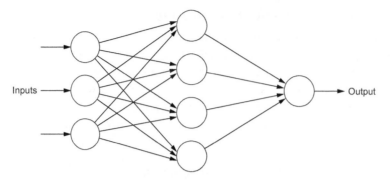

Figure 4.7   Things start to get interesting when you connect multiple neurons together, as they become capable of expressing more-complex mathematical operations.

Going back to image classification, what we want to do is create a network that receives the image pixels, does some internal computations, and outputs the (hopefully) correct class for the input image. Figure 4.8 shows how this all fits together. Of course, real-life networks are going to be much more complex than the one in figure 4.7: a competitive model for ImageNet has around half a million neurons all working together!

In deep neural networks, neurons are organized in columns (or *layers*), and this structure is what makes them capable of extracting features from images without specifying them by hand. Why and how, though?

You can imagine each layer as a step in a production line: the raw numbers composing the image get inside the first layer, where the neurons in it process them by applying their mathematical operations (multiplication and addition). The result is that these raw numbers are modified and transformed into other numbers that are

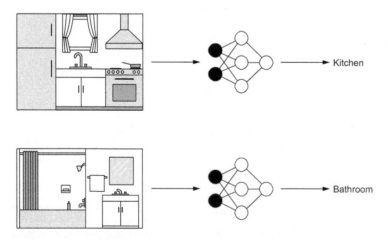

Figure 4.8   Deep neural networks process the input images (on the left) and produce a classification that's consistent with the training labels (on the right).

then passed to the second layer. The second layer applies other transformations and sends its results to the third layer. This process is repeated for each layer until the final one will say, "The image contains a kitchen" or "The image contains a bathroom."

The analogy to a production line makes sense because there's no magic machine that can turn raw materials like steel and leather into a shiny new car in a single step. If you've ever seen a video of a production line, you'll see that the process to build a car is divided into small steps: raw materials are first shaped by machines into small basic components including knobs, gears, and so on. These components are then processed by other machines that form the shift, the steering wheel, the radio, and so forth. Only after these complex parts are built are they finally assembled to form a car; it would be impossible to have a single, gigantic machine that turns raw materials into cars in a single step. Each layer of a deep neural network pretty much does the same thing, except it works on numbers and not steel.

These transformations are the key to the magical power of automatic feature extraction. When a neural network first starts being trained on a large number of images, its initial accuracy is horrible, as the neurons in the various layers haven't yet figured out how to meaningfully process these numbers. As the network sees more images and its training continues, a special mathematical technique called *backpropagation* encourages each neuron to tweak the transformations that it applies so that the overall network improves its classification accuracy. The more images the network sees, the more its neurons will learn meaningful transformations.

But what are these transformations? They sound vague, and in the early days of deep learning, they were also a bit mysterious for the researchers building this technology. After deep neural networks achieved amazing performance, researchers started to dig deeper into their inner workings. What they found was extremely interesting: when neurons in the first layers optimize their transformation, they do so in a way that allows them to recognize simple lines, edges, and corners from the raw pixels, similarly to the hand-built filters that the first computer vision engineers were trying to craft. The next layer will receive this information that is much richer than the initial raw numbers: these new numbers represent the presence of shapes in different parts of the image rather than the color of a single pixel. This second layer will build up on this information, and apply another transformation that allows it to recognize more-complex shapes like circles and squares, starting from simpler lines, edges, and corners. Going forward, a layer eventually will have recognized the shapes we cared about in our bathroom versus kitchen example: showers, ovens, toilets, microwaves, and so on. Figure 4.9 show what these increasingly complex shapes look like. Finally, the last layer will have to make the final decision about which class the image belongs to, based on the elements extracted by the previous layer.

The magic of deep learning is that all these neurons and layers have autonomously learned to decompose the millions of numbers that make an image from basic to complex shapes, and then make a prediction based on them. Basically, the modular structure of a neural network allows it to process information in steps, and thanks to clever

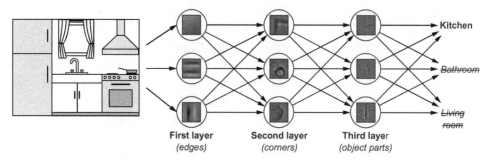

Figure 4.9   Internal representations developed by a deep neural network trained to recognize cars, people, and animals

mathematical formulations, the network learns to adjust these steps to recognize the more characteristic traits of the images it's learning from: in our case sinks, fridges, ovens, and so on.

These shapes look exactly like the features we were looking for at the beginning of the chapter. Thanks to the magic of deep learning, they've been identified *automatically*: no one has told the first layer how to recognize lines and corners, no one has told the following ones how to combine them to form circles and rectangles, and no one has come up with a clever way to teach the last layers how to recognize complex elements like a shower head. All we do is take a neural network with a bunch of layers, feed it images of kitchens and bathrooms, and let the math behind backpropagation do the rest.

Does all this deep learning magic come for free? Unfortunately, no. We're asking our networks to do a lot, and the Gods of Deep Learning demand a sacrifice: a lot of computing power and a lot of data.

Although computing power is getting cheaper and cheaper, acquiring more labeled data isn't that easy. In the case of the house broker, you'd need to wait to reach thousands of pictures of house rooms, and it may be painful to wait. Does this mean that if your business doesn't own large datasets, you have to give up deep learning? Luckily, a technology called *transfer learning* is an invaluable asset that can allow you to build state-of-the-art algorithms starting from small datasets and open source code. Let's see how.

4.3   *Using transfer learning with small datasets*

Transfer learning is kind of a trick that takes advantage of the layered structure of deep neural networks to transfer their "knowledge" from one task to another. As you can see in figure 4.10, deep neural networks work by recognizing basic shapes in images. For instance, to recognize an oven, you'd need to spot circles and rectangles, and combine them to recognize the knobs, the handle, the glass, and so forth.

If you think about it, circles, rectangles, and other basic shapes are not unique to the room-labeling problem. If you had to tell a dog from a cat, you'd still need to recognize circles, triangles, and rectangles before you could recognize eyes, ears, tails, and so on. After all, circles and lines look the same no matter whether they appear in a picture of

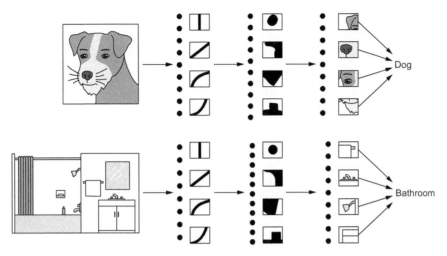

Figure 4.10   Similarities between DL-based classifiers for rooms and animals. The first layers learn to identify the same general geometric patterns.

a dog or of a bathroom. Only the last layers are specialized for a given classification task, as shown in figure 4.10.

Because the internet is full of images of cats and dogs, can we use all this data to train a large neural network and reuse what we can for our room categorization task? We can, and this is the core concept of transfer learning: the basic geometric features learned in the first few layers are largely the same across most image classification tasks, as shown in figure 4.11. This allows you to take advantage of huge datasets (like ImageNet) to *pretrain* your neural networks, and later *specialize* them for room classification by training on the real estate dataset.

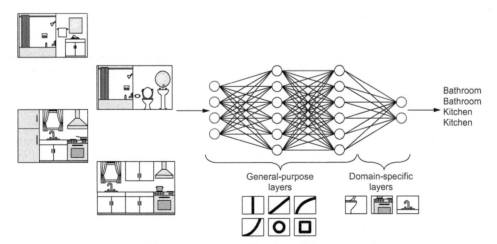

Figure 4.11   In transfer learning, general-purpose layers are reused for multiple tasks, whereas domain-specific ones are trained for a specific problem.

The good news doesn't end here: many open source releases of neural networks have been pretrained on large datasets like ImageNet. Going back to our original task, these are the steps your data scientists will follow to build our room classifier:

1   Download an open source implementation of a neural network that has been pretrained on generic datasets like ImageNet.
2   Keep the first layers, as they're the ones capable of recognizing basic shapes (circles and rectangles), and scrap the last ones, as they're tuned to recognize the specific images contained in ImageNet (from trucks to leopards).
3   Take your relatively small dataset of room pictures (hundreds of pictures instead of thousands), and retrain the last layers of the network. These layers will use information about basic shapes contained in the picture and learn to identify elements such as shower heads, ovens, and so on.

As you can see, the process is relatively streamlined, but the advantages of this technology for any organization are significant:

- You can get state-of-the-art performance without massive datasets, with only a few hundred images from your specific domain.
- You don't need much computing power, as the baseline network you're using has been trained by someone else who released it as open source (generally, large companies like Google or Facebook).
- Training a large neural network on large datasets isn't easy; by using these open source versions, you're building on the experience of seven-figure researchers of tech giants.

4.4   *Face recognition: teaching computers to recognize people*

The landmark movie *RoboCop* came out in 1987. In this dystopian future, crime is surging in Detroit, and the police department is underfunded, leaving space for megacorporation Omni Consumer Products (OCP) to provide experimental high-tech products for law enforcement. Officer Alexander James "Alex" Murphy gets brutally tortured and, declared dead, becomes a testbed for a new OCP cybernetic technology that transforms him into a cyborg called RoboCop. Still haunted by his past life as a human, one day RoboCop spots a group of people he recognizes as being related to his execution and takes a picture of one of them. He uploads it into a police computer, which scans the police records and discovers the identity of the person. This application is called *Face Recognition*, and in 1987 it was the subject of sci-fi movies.

If you recently bought a smartphone, this technology is probably in your pocket now. The only difference is that while in old movies it was used to search for criminals, now its most common use is to . . . unlock phones. Face recognition is another application of deep learning (figure 4.12) that looks like a traditional classification problem but adds some interesting aspects.

Let's say that you're trying to build a smart door lock that uses images from a camera to unlock the front door of your home based on who's standing in front of it. If you, your partner, or your daughter are knocking at the door, a camera will take a picture of the face, and if it recognizes the person as one of these three, it's going to open the door. If it doesn't recognize anyone, it's going to stay locked. How would we build something like this? Let's start by breaking down the problem.

Our input data is an image of a face. The task is to understand whom it belongs to: you, your partner, your daughter, or somebody else. Just like the kitchen/bathroom example at the beginning of the chapter, it's a supervised classification task. As we've seen, deep learning is the best tool to solve most image classification problems. We might even take advantage of transfer learning by retraining the last layers of a network that was trained on ImageNet.

As always, the next step is to find the training data: you open your family album and take a few hundred pictures of your family. It's important that you get as many as you can, so the algorithm will have examples of your faces in different light conditions, different haircuts, and so on. To complete the dataset, you download a few hundred pictures of random people from the internet and label those as "other." This is so the model will learn to spot the most distinctive features in your family's faces, and ignore any attributes that are shared by all human faces.

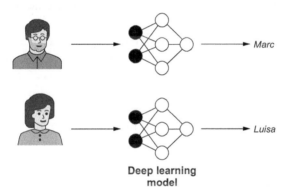

Deep learning model

Figure 4.12   Face recognition is a specific application of image classification in which the input images are human faces.

This approach sounds like it should work, and it does. Here's the challenge, though: your daughter is in high school, and her friend Catherine often visits your home to do homework with your daughter. It would be nice to add Catherine to the list of trusted people so the door will unlock for her too. You now have five classes instead of four:

- You
- Partner
- Daughter
- Catherine the study buddy
- Other

You'd have to ask Catherine for a few hundred pictures of her face and train a whole new model. Neither you, Catherine, or her parents would be happy to do that just to speed up the door-opening process.

This problem is similar to the face-recognition technology that is now present on many smartphones. When Apple released the iPhone X with Face ID, it worked great without needing you to upload hundreds of pictures and wait a few hours to retrain a neural network. You just look at the camera for a few seconds, and you're done. Is this magic, or what?

It turns out that it's not magic; it's a technology called *one-shot learning*: another trick that allows special deep neural networks to learn to classify items by using a single training example instead of the thousands that are usually needed.

It all comes down to the ability of neural networks to recognize shapes and patterns in images. If you train a network to recognize faces, it will follow the same steps we highlighted for the "kitchen versus bathroom" task, recognizing first lines and edges and then gradually more and more complex shapes. What will these complex shapes be in the case of facial recognition? They'll be facial traits: the different shapes that a nose, a forehead, or lips can take.

Inside the software of each iPhone, a neural network is trained on thousands of faces. When you're setting up Face ID and it looks at your face for the first time, it will break down your face's image to recognize basic shapes and then key facial traits, which it will encode into a small list of numbers (from hundreds to thousands). This list of numbers is called an *embedding*.

Every time you unlock your phone, it takes a picture of your face, runs it through its neural network, gets its embedding, and compares it with the one it saved when you first set it up. If the numbers are close, it means that the facial traits of that image are similar too and therefore belong to the phone's owner, and the phone unlocks (top two rows in figure 4.13). If the embedding is very different from the "golden" one, it must be a different person (bottom two rows in figure 4.13). That's it! Simple, fast, efficient, and accurate.

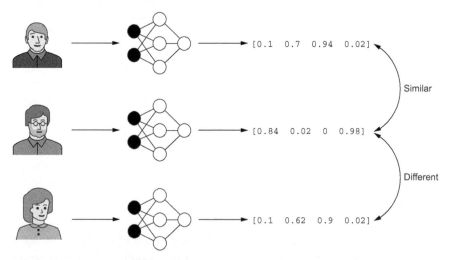

Figure 4.13   In face recognition, selfies are translated into an embedding (a list of numbers) that can be compared to those of a known image.

Embeddings (or *encodings*) have this name because they *embed* the information in the original image into a few numbers, encoding the large amount of information contained in a raw picture into something more compact, convenient, and meaningful (from millions of numbers from the front camera to only a few hundred).

Embeddings open up many opportunities, and you just saw how one-shot learning is a great way to implement features like face recognition with few examples, and without having to keep retraining the models. Many other interesting applications can be built using encodings, and you're about to learn more.

4.5 Using content generation and style transfer

Content generation and style transfer are up-and-coming applications of AI that finally push AI from understanding to *creating*.

The first application we'll talk about is automatic *content generation*. Earlier, we said that a neural network will figure out which relevant elements make up a car, a motorcycle, a ship, a face, and so forth. When trained with different faces, the neural network will focus on the specific task of recognizing faces, and therefore will create a representation of the shapes of different cheeks, foreheads, noses, and so on. What happens if we feed a neural network with thousands of images of people smiling? Well, it will learn what a smile is (which color and shape combinations form the impression of a smiling face). What happens if we train it with thousands of pictures of people with curly black hair? Well, it will now learn what curly black hair looks like, purely from the input data.

Now, if a neural network knows what a smile is, can we find a way to make this network generate a whole new smile? Or even better, can we take a sad face and ask the neural network to modify the pixels so that it puts a smile on that face? It turns out that we can go even further. If a neural network trained with images of smiles understands which elements make a smile, what happens when we train it with thousands of images of a certain celebrity, let's say John Oliver? The network will encode the facial traits that make up his face, of course. What if we feed the network with videos instead? Well, provided we have enough data, it will start learning not only which elements make Oliver's face unique, but also his most distinct movements and facial expressions. Can we also try to take these features and turn them into somebody else? We sure can, and the results are astonishing, as you can see in the before/after image in figure 4.14.

Figure 4.14   In this AI-generated clip, John Oliver's facial traits are applied to an image of Jimmy Fallon. (Generated by Gaurav Oberoi, https://goberoi.com/.)

Unfortunately, some people have used this powerful tech in unethical ways. You'll see more about the risks connected with automated content generation in the last chapter of this book. For now, let's jump back to the more uplifting side of this technology. You've seen how a network can learn relevant characteristics of classes of pictures and transpose them from one image to another, and we focused on people's faces. What other applications can be built on the same technology?

One example is *style transfer*: taking the *style* from a picture and applying it to another. In figure 4.15, the model makes zebras look like horses (top row), and horses look like zebras (bottom row). The top row looks great: even the fur of the colt is picked up. However, it seems that the model has trouble telling human skin apart from horse fur: the woman in the bottom row also ends up "zebrafied."

This is undoubtedly fascinating, but what can you do with it? Well, apart from generating beautiful pictures, we honestly don't know yet! But don't be too quick to disregard the artsy aspect of this technology, as some companies have built successful products that do just that.

A good example is Prisma, an app that allows you to take pictures and apply different styles using the techniques we just mentioned. One week after its debut on the iOS App Store in June 2016, the app was downloaded more than 7.5 million times and received more than 1 million active users. Just a month after, it was installed in more than 12.5 million devices with more than 1.5 million active users worldwide, and was listed in the top 10 apps in the App Store in 77 countries.

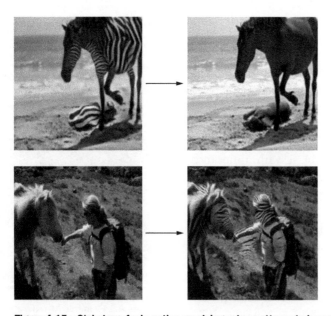

Figure 4.15   Style transfer in action, applying zebra patterns to horses (and humans). Images were generated using code from "Unpaired Image-to-Image Translation Using Cycle-Consistent Adversarial Networks" by Jun-Yan Zhu et al., https://arxiv.org/abs/1703.10593.

4.6   *What to watch out for*

DL models are the most complex flavor of AI we have seen so far, and this means that they also come with subtler gotchas. For one, the power of deep neural networks lies in their ability to automatically extract and compute features from input images. This is great because they perform better than human-engineered algorithms, and you don't need to pay salaries either. However, the flip side is that we don't really know *why* deep neural networks work so well. Just to give you an idea, the behavior of your average image classification model is governed by roughly 50 *million* numbers that are tweaked and optimized during training. Even the smartest researchers and engineers have little hope of wrapping their heads around this complexity.

Within the ML community, DL models are effectively considered a *black box*: they're powerful and accurate, but we struggle to explain *why* they make certain decisions. Understandably, researchers first focused on making this technology work, and only now are they starting to peek inside the black box. We usually say that deep models lack *explainability*, and this is a problem for their application in safety-critical applications.

For example, a self-driving car might deploy a 99% accurate model to detect pedestrians crossing the street. This looks great on paper but might not be enough to create a safe product: what happens in the remaining 1% of the cases? In conventional machine learning, engineers have at least *some* degree of insight into how the model operates and makes decisions. This is often not the case for deep learning, spurring a new field of research called *explainable AI*.

Research into explainable AI follows two main directions: developing families of models whose decisions are intuitive for humans to understand, and creating new tools and techniques to explain the decisions of the models we already have. In both cases, the idea is that we don't want to sacrifice accuracy for the sake of explainability. While research into new models is still in its early stages, there have been many interesting results in visualization and model debugging tools. One example is a 2016 paper by three researchers from the University of Washington: "'Why Should I Trust You?': Explaining the Predictions of Any Classifier" by Marco Ribeiro et al. (https://arxiv.org/abs/1602.04938) gives a lot of food for thought (and even comes with a catchy title).

One of the paper's examples is a computer vision application that uses a deep neural network trained to classify huskies and wolves. This is a hard task, as the two animals look similar. The researchers did something sneaky: they collected pictures of household huskies while they were at home, and of wolves living in the wild in cold places. A classifier trained on this data performs surprisingly well, and a naive ML engineer might be tempted to call it a day and ship the product. However, if you dig a bit deeper and try to understand what the algorithm is looking at—which features it's building in order to understand the type of animal—you discover something funny.

The algorithm didn't care at all about the animal. The only feature it identified is whether there is snow in the picture. Because all the pictures of wolves had a snowy background, it was pretty easy for it to understand "If I see a white background, then it's a wolf." Should you decide to test the algorithm with a husky on snow, it will say "wolf" each time. Actually, even if you put a pug on the snow, it will keep on saying "wolf"! It's funny: we were trying to build a smart algorithm that could discern wolves from huskies, and what we got was an algorithm that counts white pixels.

What's the big takeaway, then? A great philosopher once said, "With great power comes great responsibility" (it actually was Spiderman's uncle Ben). This is especially true with deep neural networks. Their ability to learn features autonomously is extremely powerful but must be handled with care: the model may have learned something you didn't expect.

Checking everything that an algorithm trained on millions of images has learned is impossible, so you need to play smart. The way you play the smart game is by remembering what we said in the beginning of this book: in AI, the single most important thing to pay attention to is the *data*. If the model develops a bias, you should look at the data to find both the cause and the solution.

4.7   AI for audio

Audio data presents many of the same complexities of images, as the data looks similar: a ton of numbers representing waveforms and audio peaks. Therefore, we'll limit ourselves to mentioning the three main applications of AI to audio:

- Speech to text, or *speech recognition*
- Text to speech, or *speech generation*
- Trigger word detection

Let's spend a few words on each. *Speech recognition* is about understanding words from an audio recording of a spoken dialogue. The input is the raw audio, and the output is its transcript (figure 4.16). You've used this technology every time you've asked anything of Siri, the Google assistant, or Alexa.

This is another technology that wasn't very accurate until deep learning matured and we were able to collect and process large datasets. If you think about it, the problem is the same as with images: if you listen to an audio file with a recording of someone saying "Hello," you should be able to recognize the utterings that make up the sounds of the different letters, and then recognize the word. Does it remind you of the layered structure of a deep neural network?

Even if deep neural networks have brought about major progress in speech recognition, today's solutions still have severe shortcomings. The algorithms have pretty good performance, but one of the biggest bottlenecks is data. To train a DL algorithm

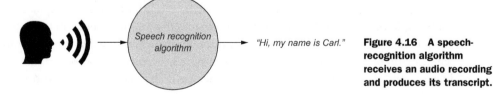

Figure 4.16   A speech-recognition algorithm receives an audio recording and produces its transcript.

to perform speech recognition, you need labeled audio files: recordings of someone's voice alongside the transcript of what was said. A natural fit for this data need comes from movies: you can use the audio as input, and the subtitles as labels. However, not every language has a strong history of cinematography, and some languages have small datasets available. Also, most actors have perfect pronunciation, and therefore it's hard for an algorithm to generalize to broken English.

Text to speech is the task of generating audio from text. Just as speech recognition is the technology used by Alexa to understand your voice, *speech generation* is what it uses to talk back to you (figure 4.17). This technology has also evolved quickly thanks to deep learning, and the voice produced by these algorithms is much more natural than the robotic, metallic voices we were used to hearing in the subway. However, one of the main problems of these new algorithms is that they're still power-hungry, and it's hard to use cutting-edge technology on mobile devices.

Figure 4.17 A text-to-speech algorithm speaks sentences aloud with a natural-sounding voice.

The last task we want you to know about is *trigger word detection*. This technology unlocks your phone when you say, "Hey, Siri" or "OK, Google." Compared to generic speech recognition, it's optimized to watch out for just that one expression, and thus can run in the background on your phone without draining its battery.

Along with trigger word detection, speech recognition and speech generation are both advanced and hard to develop for a small organization; even tech giants like Google and Facebook are still doing research on them. Luckily, you'll see in the second part of the book that most of these companies offer their technology as a service, and that's almost all you need because they're pretty standard applications that don't usually require specific customization.

4.8 Case study: optimizing agriculture with deep learning

Makoto Koike is a software engineer based in Japan. As he started helping out at his family's cucumber farm, he couldn't help but notice that his parents were spending a lot of time sorting the produce according to its quality. Japanese agriculture takes great pride in the quality of production, which means that Koike's mother would spend up to eight hours a day sorting cucumbers according to their shape, color, and number of prickles. Since there's no standardized classification for the quality of cucumbers in Japan, Koike's farm has adopted a nine-class approach, from the best to the lowest-quality examples. You can see these classes in figure 4.18.

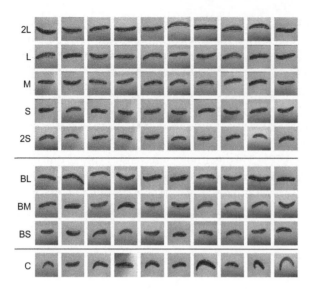

Figure 4.18   Examples of cucumber classes. Cucumbers can vary in shape and size.

Koike decided to try to automate this process so his family could focus on optimizing the cultivation. Thanks to his background in automotive engineering, he was able to design and build the mechanical components for an automated sorting machine based on a conventional conveyor belt design.

Automated arms (controlled by a computer) push each cucumber into one of the bins based on its quality classification. Once the machinery was built and tested, Koike had to implement the control algorithm for the arms. From the point of view of implementation, the hardest tasks to complete are as follows:

1 Identifying distinct items as they move through the conveyor belt
2 Classifying each item based on shape, color, surface appearance
3 Coordinating the movement of the arms to push each item into the correct bin

Koike could leverage his expertise to tackle tasks 1 and 3, which fall into the realm of conventional automation engineering. He then recognized that task 2 is an *object classification* task, for which he could use a vast amount of research and open source code. This reduced the conventional software engineering effort to the few hours needed to set up one of these freely available frameworks, and he was off to the next real challenge, collecting training data. As often happens in domain-specific situations like this, the only avenue for data collection is to fall back on the only humans that have the necessary expertise. Koike collected examples (pictures) and labels as his mother patiently classified around 8,000 cucumbers according to the farm's stringent quality criteria. The dataset is freely available at https://github.com/workpiles/CUCUM-BER-9.

After enough training data for a prototype has been collected, what remains is just routine software engineering: plugging the predictions of the model into the control system for the conveyor belt. Figure 4.19 illustrates the process: a camera takes an

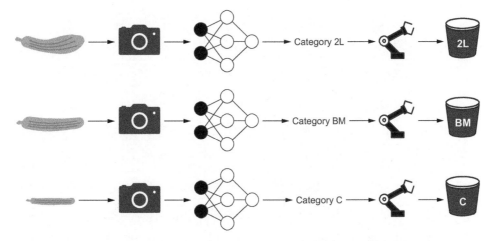

Figure 4.19   The core steps of Koike's system, from taking a picture of the cucumber to its final placement into its right bucket

image of a cucumber that is then processed by a neural network; based on the prediction of the network, a robotic arm places the cucumber in the bucket corresponding to its class. The whole process happens on a small conveyor belt. You can see the final product in figure 4.20.

Koike claims 70% accuracy for the complete system, even if the accuracy measured on the *test set* often topped 95%. This suggests that the test data does not accurately capture the variability of the samples in real-life situations. For example, some shapes or colors of cucumbers might be underrepresented in the training set. Typically, this would happen if all of the training examples and labels were collected at the beginning of the harvesting season, while cucumbers were growing larger with the passing of the seasons.

To improve his system's performance, Koike decided to adopt a multicamera approach: different cameras take images of the cucumbers from different fixed angles, which are then fed into a neural network to classify the cucumber. You can see the upgraded version of Koike's dataset in figure 4.21.

Figure 4.20   Part of the final cucumber-sorting machine, where cameras take pictures of the cucumbers and a computer elaborates the prediction, before moving the cucumber forward, where it's placed in the right bucket.

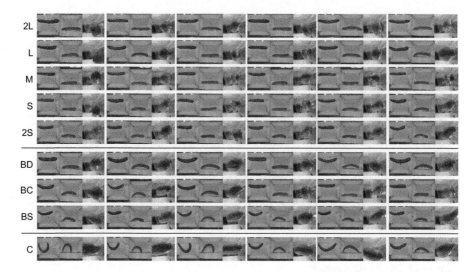

Figure 4.21 The upgraded version of Makoto's dataset, which results from each cucumber being photographed from three different angles

Koike's story has fascinated many news outlets, which reported on this David versus Goliath story indicating that even a single engineer can build AI applications that rival those of big corporations. Many of these reporters failed to mention that Koike took three months to collect the 8,000 samples needed for the prototype. The images he captured were also of such an extremely low resolution that it's physically impossible for the model to recognize prickles and scratches. On the other hand, Google's blog released its own version of the story, which emphasized the role of its open source libraries and the cloud services it offers to speed up training.

4.8.1 *Case questions*

1 Why is this problem a good fit for machine learning?
2 What key choices and trade-offs allowed Koike to quickly develop a prototype with minimal investment?
3 How would you design guidelines for measuring the success of this project?

4.8.2 *Case discussion*

The business case for automating production processes has been clear ever since the time of the Industrial Revolution. This project is an example of AI bringing about a new wave of improvements by focusing on advanced perception for robotics. Many plants are designed so that industrial robots can complete tasks with a minimum need for flexibility: think about a conveyor belt carrying open cans while they're being filled with a product. In a case like that, the algorithms that control the plant have little need for cameras or other advanced sensors, because the process is strict. The situation with the cucumbers is dramatically different, as it's hard to control what kind of shapes cucumbers will come in (Mother Nature doesn't like standardization), and you need to sort them yourself. Coming up with hardcoded rules is hard, and therefore ML is a natural fit for this kind of decision-making progress.

Koike's project is also a relevant example of bridging 20th-century technology (industrial automation) with 21st-century AI and software. After the mechanical machinery had been built, the algorithm was a textbook application of supervised classification, about which researchers have written thousands of papers. This allowed Koike to leverage well-known techniques (like the ones discussed in this chapter) and even reuse open source code.

Even though it's small, this project contains all the steps in the pipeline for building an AI application: recognizing the business value (saving time), collecting training data, and plugging the model into the business process. In technical terms, this is a good example of what happens when you use the right mental model for a problem: everything becomes easier as you can communicate with engineers more effectively, and can use a wealth of prior art. Once Koike figured out that the core of his tool was an object classification model, he could delve right in and start collecting labeled training data, and then use open source code from the internet.

Notice that building the technology was not hard for Koike, as he was able to use cloud providers and open source tech. What took time was the creation of the dataset. This is another example that should highlight that data is the most valuable asset when building AI applications. This is particularly true for this case; the data that Koike collected had some different properties compared to the images he was collecting in the actual application, as the difference between the performances on the test set and in real life suggest. This could be an important aspect to work on in case the project had to be scaled further.

Finally, consider the initial issue that Koike had: he struggled with measuring the performance of his model because it seemed to perform better on never-seen-before examples (test set) than on the ones it had learned from (training set). This is, of course, fishy, and probably due to the fact that the cucumbers in his training set were produced during a different season than the ones in his training set. This challenge highlights the importance of carefully choosing your data: big datasets are not enough; you also need them to be representative of the potential cases you are going to experience in the real-life application.

In terms of minimal accepted accuracy, Koike could have used his mother's decisions as the ground truth and come up with a threshold that made sense for him. However, it's also important to think critically about what a mistake means: what is the cost of placing a cucumber in the wrong box? Because errors in this application won't bring destructive consequences (unlike in medicine, for instance), Koike could have decided to accept not-super-exciting performances in favor of completely offloading this taxing task from his poor mum.

Summary

- Deep learning is the family of machine learning algorithms that powers most AI applications dealing with images and audio.
- The secret sauce of deep learning is its ability to automatically extract relevant features from data, saving engineers from lengthy (or just plain impossible) work.
- Transfer learning is a technique that helps reduce deep learning's otherwise insatiable thirst for training data.
- Face recognition and automated content generation are clever applications that take advantage of the flexibility of deep learning models.
- Deep learning works as well with audio as it does with images, and is today's state-of-the-art method for recognizing and producing speech.

AI for natural language

This chapter covers

- Understanding the main challenges of natural language processing
- Measuring opinions from text with sentiment analysis
- Searching for textual content with natural queries
- Building conversational interfaces (chatbots)
- Case study: ML-assisted language translation

Making computers understand language has been a pipe dream of computer scientists since the 1950s. This is probably because most human knowledge and culture is encoded in written words and the use of language is one of the most powerful abilities that sets us apart from animals. The umbrella term for these techniques, which includes both understanding and producing language, is *natural language processing* (*NLP*).

Unfortunately, giving machines the ability to understand and produce language is as hard as it is desirable: the technology to sustain such a seamless computer-human interaction simply isn't here yet. This didn't stop companies, agencies, and media from overselling the potential of end-to-end solutions. *Chatbots* are a prime example of this phenomenon, hyped as autonomous agents capable of messaging with customers, seamlessly augmenting or replacing human workers for complex matters like sales or after-market service. Results were underwhelming: in 2017, the Silicon Valley blog *The Information* published its research about the performance of Facebook's Messenger personal assistant, M. The blog reported that M was failing to handle 70% of user requests. As you can imagine, broken promises yield nothing but wasted money, wasted time, and frustration.

If this introduction doesn't seem encouraging, there's good news. The first is that technology is evolving rapidly, and the horizons of possibility are expanding accordingly. The second is that you're about to learn how to find and develop the hidden projects that can benefit from simpler, more mature NLP tools. These opportunities too often are undervalued in the midst of the hype bubble around NLP, but can be a powerful success story for your AI efforts.

This chapter has two broad goals:

- Give you the knowledge to judge whether an idea is feasible with today's technology (and your resources)
- Teach you how to plan a natural language effort with an eye to maximizing return on investment. This will enable you to be the one lifting the fog and finding hidden opportunities in your organization.

We'll start by explaining why language is really hard for computers, and how machine learning, once again, came to the rescue over the past few years, allowing us to build amazing products and solutions.

5.1   *The allure of natural language understanding*

Let's face it. The way we consume information on the internet has been stuck in an unnatural compromise for a while: we're still clicking buttons and selecting drop-downs, while in the real world we simply use plain language. *Natural language processing* is the technology that can allow us to remove this barrier and allow people to use the digital world in the same way they experience the physical one.

Let's try to imagine how NLP could change the game in the by-now-familiar world of a real estate brokerage website. We'll put ourselves in the shoes of one of its users: a wealthy startup investor from San Francisco who wants to purchase a home. She wants a big villa with at least four rooms, close to the Highway 101, with a mandatory ocean view.

Right now, when she visits the website, she's faced with the classical internet portal view we all are used to: a menu, some boxes for prices, location, bedrooms, and a bunch of information for each listing (images, description, and so forth).

Playing with all these buttons, selectors, and drop-downs can feel like being in the cockpit of a jet when all you wanted was a simple answer to this question:

What are the villas in San Francisco that are close to the highway, have an amazing view of the ocean, and at least four bedrooms? I want to visit the best ones this weekend.

Every flesh-and-blood broker can answer this question, but we can't have a dedicated human for every person searching for homes on the internet. But what if we could, thanks to AI? This is the promise of machine language understanding: a superior experience for everyone interacting with a computer, increasing their satisfaction and efficiency, at scale.

You're already aware that completely matching human capabilities in using language is out of reach for today's technology. The way out of this challenge is designing solutions that reduce the complexity to fit the technology available. The first step is understanding and measuring complexity. Let's get started.

5.2 *Breaking down NLP: Measuring complexity*

Language is one of the most important abilities that distinguishes humans from animals. While the family dog can use sounds to communicate, it's limited to a small set of moods (for example, pain, sadness, and anger). On the other hand, humans can use words to communicate (almost) anything: from expressing our feelings to the love of our life, to ordering a double cheeseburger.

Obviously, a whole spectrum of complexity ranges from the simple capabilities of a dog to the nuances that a poet can express with language. In technology, complexity is the enemy: the more complex a task, the more chances we have to fail and ship underwhelming products, especially with immature technologies like NLP. How do we measure complexity in the realm of NLP tasks? Based on our experience, there are two qualitative key metrics:

- *Width*—The diversity of topics or language domains required to perform a task. How large is the vocabulary that our algorithm has to master?
- *Depth*—How sophisticated is the result of our algorithm? How many things does it have to understand or do?

Table 5.1 lists examples of NLP tasks and indicates their width and depth.

Table 5.1 NLP tasks and an evaluation of their width and depth

Task	Width	Depth
Understand whether an Amazon product review is positive or negative.	High: The review can be about a wide range of products and attributes.	Low: We have just two possible outputs (positive or negative sentiments).
Help travelers book and manage their plane tickets.	Low: The text we'll be dealing with is relative to a restricted subset of topics (flights, bookings).	High: The agent must understand a vast range of options, from checking prices to changing tickets, addressing complaints, providing airport assistance, and so on.
Help a manager plan their time and appointments (a secretary bot).	High: A secretary needs to understand queries about many domains—scheduling. appointments, invoicing, travel, and so on.	High: In each of these topics, a secretary-bot should have a solid understanding and perform complex actions, such as setting up a meeting at a comfortable time while making arrangements for transportation.

Notice that because both width and depth contribute to the complexity of a task, we can say that the overall complexity of the task is proportional to their product:

Complexity = Width × Depth

If we draw a graph with these two metrics on the axes, we get an effective way of visualizing the complexity of NLP tasks. Tasks that form a rectangle with a large area are more complex than tasks with a smaller area, as shown in figure 5.1.

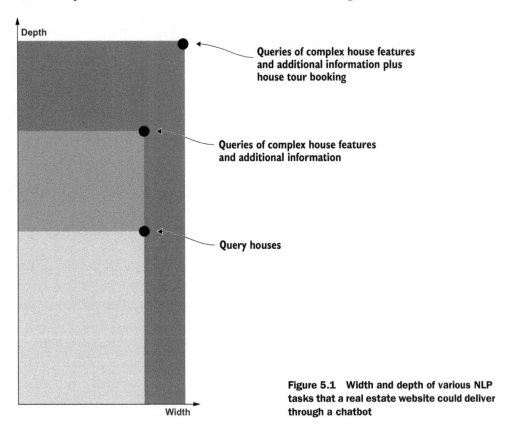

Figure 5.1   **Width and depth of various NLP tasks that a real estate website could deliver through a chatbot**

Let's go back to the example of a chatbot for our real-estate website. A simple action that this chatbot could perform is understanding basic user queries, basically replacing the conventional search interface. This is an example of a query:

> *Show me homes with more than four bedrooms in downtown San Francisco that cost less than $2 million.*

In this case, the chatbot needs to perform a single action—querying a database—related to a single domain: house properties. We could ask more from our chatbot, and extend its functionality to extract meta information out of this database or answer more-complex queries, for instance:

> *What is the average price for a home in the Presidio neighborhood, with an ocean view, four bedrooms, and that's less than 10 minutes away from Highway 101?*

This wouldn't increase the width, because the language domain is still limited to houses, but depth is way higher, as the number of possible actions that the bot must be able to handle has increased. The last step could be to manage the booking of home tours as well. This would increase the depth again as the number of actions increases. Now, width increases too, as the bot needs to understand new language expressions relative to bookings.

Keep in mind that two very different tasks can have similar complexity. Let's switch gears for a second and look at two typical examples of NLP that you're likely already familiar with:

- *Sentiment analysis on tweets*—For this task, the model reads a short text and must decide whether it expresses a positive or negative sentiment. In other words, sentiment analysis is about finding out what the author thinks about the main subject of the text. Examples: "I loved Spielberg's new movie" is positive. "The camera of this new phone is awful" is negative.
- *Classification of customer support tickets*—For this task, the model reads complaints from customers and assigns them to one of several classes of potential causes. Examples: "The password is wrong" is an authentication issue, and "The site doesn't load" is a connectivity problem.

The first task has high width, as it can deal with a lot of subjects (people use Twitter to talk about everything), but low depth as it has only two possible outcomes: a positive or negative review flag.

The second task, on the other hand, has low width because it needs to deal with tickets that will all be somehow related to the same domain (IT stuff not working), but it has higher depth because it needs to put the tickets into several buckets. On our width/depth graph, the two tasks would look something like figure 5.2.

How do we translate these insights into actionable information? Looking at an NLP task in terms of width and depth helps assess its feasibility. In general, you want to keep both as low as possible by starting to design your NLP application from the lowest width/depth combination. You'll be building on top of it according to your

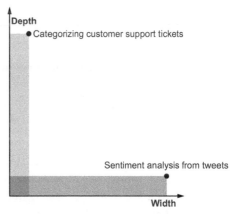

Figure 5.2 Two tasks on the width/depth diagram: categorizing customer support tickets (high depth, low width), and sentiment analysis from tweets (high width, low depth)

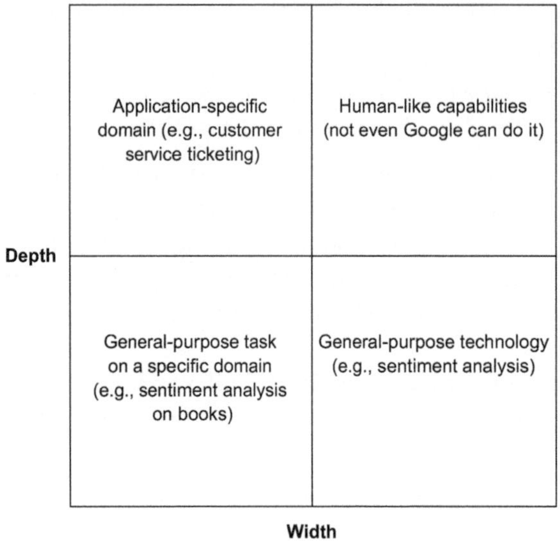

Application-specific domain (e.g., customer service ticketing)	Human-like capabilities (not even Google can do it)
General-purpose task on a specific domain (e.g., sentiment analysis on books)	General-purpose technology (e.g., sentiment analysis)

Figure 5.3   NLP applications based on their width and depth. The closer an application is to the top-right corner, the more unlikely it is to be feasible with today's technology.

needs, and depending on the performance you can achieve. In figure 5.3, you can see a representation of the feasibility of an application depending on its depth and width.

In the next part of this chapter, we'll use this mental model as our guide on the path to add NLP capabilities to our home listings site.

5.3   *Adding NLP capabilities to your organization*

Let's bring back our real estate brokerage site from where we left off in the previous chapter. Our DL-based picture classifier has greatly improved the user experience, and the number of monthly visitors is growing fast. Customers visit our website, can quickly find the details they're interested in through the images of each listing, and move along the process by asking for more information about their favorite home. Right now, someone who's interested in a specific listing has two options to find out more:

1 Spend a long time reading through the description left by the homeowner and all the reviews by other persons who visited it (let's just assume that our real estate platform has reviews on houses).

2 Call customer service, which will connect the customer to the broker who is handling that home.

The first option is not a great user experience, and the second is really expensive for your business. We already pictured a human-like computer program (often referred to as a *bot, chatbot,* or *agent*) that can completely take over the role of a house broker, but we also understood that such an application of NLP is unlikely to work with today's technology. We can call this advanced application the *brokerbot*: it has both high width and high depth.

Let's take a step back and look at our business objectives. The business goal is to allow customers to quickly find the information they need about each listing. If you look at it this way, the brokerbot is a bit of overkill: we can still inch toward a better user experience and faster search while using simpler technology.

We know that users spend a lot of time going through reviews written by other prospective home buyers. These reviews are packed with information that often isn't included in the house description, such as firsthand opinions of the lightning fixtures, the neighborhood, and so on. We would like to use this information to help other users make the best decisions possible, but few would take the time to read all this material.

What we'll do in the next chapters is progressively come up with more-complex NLP features for our website, by taking advantage of the primary natural language content that we have: user reviews. You'll find that even basic NLP functionality can be useful for people, without having to design super-complex human-like features that will probably end up being underwhelming and frustrate users. As you can see in figure 5.4, in a complex and immature field like natural language processing, increasing the complexity of your product exponentially increases the technological risk, while business value plateaus after a while.

The first step toward adding NLP capabilities to our website should be the easiest thing we can build that still delivers value to people. In our case, it can be developing a system that classifies each home review as positive or negative, making it easier for new users to understand how good the listed home actually is.

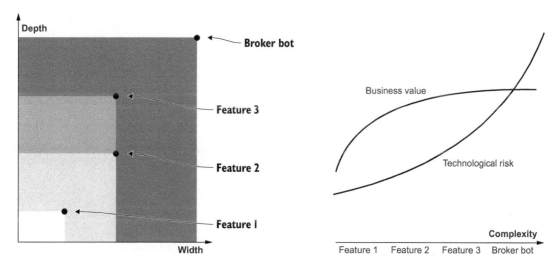

Figure 5.4 Different features with increasing complexity bring exponentially higher technological risk, while the business value plateaus quickly.

Basically, we want to go from an unorganized review section like the one in table 5.2 to a much more digestible and informative layout, as in table 5.3.

Table 5.2   A list of positive and negative reviews all mixed together

Reviews
Great location!
The house is very old and run-down.
The view from the rooftop is breathtaking.
I'd never live on the ground floor in such a dangerous neighborhood.

Table 5.3   An organized table of positive and negative reviews

What people liked	What people didn't like
Great location!	The house is very old and run-down.
The view from the rooftop is breathtaking.	I'd never live on the ground floor in such a dangerous neighborhood.

Let's see how sentiment analysis fares in terms of depth and width. Remember that the *depth* of an application is related to how complex the capabilities of the model need to be. In this case, the only thing we're asking our chatbot to classify is a review into one of two classes (positive or negative), and the depth is therefore low. *Width* measures the size of the vocabulary that the model has to "know" (the number of words it has to understand to classify a review correctly). In this case, the kinds of words required are limited to positive words like "beautiful," "safe," "breathtaking," and negative words like "worn," "awful," "dangerous." These words are the union of general positive and negative words like "beautiful" and "ugly," together with some domain-specific terms like "spacious" and "worn" that are specific to the houses domain. The width is therefore a bit higher than that of a standard sentiment analysis task, but not dramatically so. Figure 5.5 compares sentiment analysis with the brokerbot on the width/depth diagram introduced in figure 5.1.

As you can see, it's a much smaller area compared to the brokerbot, and therefore it's much easier to build while still bringing significant improvements to the user experience.

Sentiment analysis is such a classic and important application of NLP that it's worth going into a bit more detail. We'll also use it as a tool to shed some light on the inner workings of NLP algorithms in the next section.

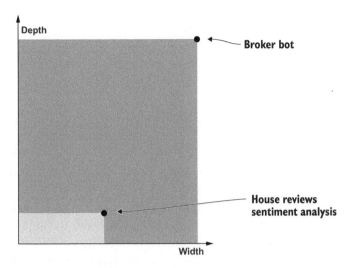

Figure 5.5   The brokerbot versus sentiment analysis on the width/depth diagram. Sentiment analysis has less depth and width because its final outcome is narrow and it deals only with words that express opinions.

5.3.1   *Sentiment analysis*

A surprising amount of textual content produced by users on the internet deals with opinions and feelings. For example, think about user reviews on Amazon, Twitter replies, or even blog articles. *Sentiment analysis algorithms* digest all this free-form text, and figure out whether the author had a positive, negative, or neutral opinion about the subject.

Sentiment analysis is an important task, and it can be used for much more than sorting reviews of houses. You could monitor the results of your marketing campaign in real time by following feeds from social media, or even gauge the reaction to individual presentations during a conference. Wall Street trading firms routinely use sentiment analysis to measure what the public thinks about a company and to inform their trading decisions.

But let's go back to our real estate listings website. These are excerpts from some of the reviews posted by users:

- The kitchen appliances are old and smelly.
- Views from the living room are amazing at sunset.

What we want to do is build an algorithm that can label each sentence as positive or negative, as in figure 5.6.

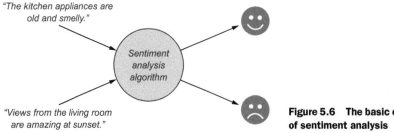

"The kitchen appliances are old and smelly."

"Views from the living room are amazing at sunset."

Sentiment analysis algorithm

Figure 5.6   The basic concept of sentiment analysis

Let's suppose that we don't know machine learning, and we need to explain to a computer how to rate these sentences by developing an algorithm. A good rule of thumb would be to look at certain telltale words, such as "terrible" and "amazing." In fact, this is exactly how the earliest algorithms for sentiment analysis worked: researchers painstakingly built a dictionary of important words, and labeled each as positive, negative, or neutral. For example, such a word-sentiment dictionary might look like this:

- *Delighted*—Positive
- *Killed*—Negative
- *Shout*—Negative
- *Desk*—Neutral

Once you have an *emotional glossary* like that, you can classify each sentence by counting the number of positive and negative words and get a final score for the sentence.

This simplistic approach has a bunch of problems. Language is extremely complex, and we use it in very different ways from person to person; the same word can be used in different ways to communicate completely opposite messages. Let's say you listed "nice" as a positive-sentiment word, and one of the reviewers writes this:

It would be nice if they completely removed that tapestry.

Even if the sentence has an overall negative opinion of the house, our naive system would consider it positive, because of the positive connotation of "nice." Maybe you could try improving this system by adding more-complex rules, something like this:

'It would be [POSITIVE WORD] if ..' => negative

Although this rule would work on the preceding snippet, it's still easy to fool. For example, the following sentence is actually extremely positive, but would be ranked as a negative opinion:

It would be nice if I could move into this place right away!

Should we keep adding hardcoded rules? The game is already becoming complicated (and boring), yet it's still easy to fool our system. Notice also that we're still playing with just a few words; we haven't even started mapping the vast ocean of the English vocabulary. Even if we did get to the bottom of this, we would almost need to start all over again for other languages.

By now, you're probably starting to think that this approach is doomed to failure. If you are familiar with the main theme of this book, you might think that we have something much better coming up for you, and you would be right. Maybe a machine can find out how to perform the task by itself, without us explaining it.

We can try looking at sentiment analysis in the same way we looked at other ML problems in the previous chapters. Given a piece of text, we want to decide if it belongs to the "positive" or "negative" class: a *classification* problem. The classes (labels) will simply be "positive" or "negative," and the features will be the words of the sentence. Instead of manually creating rules to classify each word as positive or negative, we can train an ML model to do that job for us. It turns out that the presence or absence of specific words in the text is enough for the model to figure out whether the opinion is negative or positive.

This approach is simple yet effective. One of the first to sketch out this idea was Paul Graham, the legendary founder of Silicon Valley's most successful startup accelerator, Y Combinator. He thought of this approach while trying to fix what he thought was one of the biggest threats to the early internet: spam email. Back then, your email inbox would fill up with advertisements for all sorts of frauds, from fake lottery prizes to counterfeit Viagra. In 2002, Graham came up with a new method that he described in his essay "A Plan for Spam" (www.paulgraham.com/spam.html).

Graham's plan begins with the realization that most developers will be drawn to programming explicit rules to detect spam email. Back in those early days of the internet, by using explicit rules, it wasn't hard to correctly identify almost 80% of spam. However, catching that last percent of spammers would turn out to be extremely different. On the other hand, a simple ML approach was more effective right off the bat. The concept was pretty simple: let an ML algorithm see a bunch of spammy and not-spammy emails, and let it figure out by itself which are the words that are most likely to be indicative of spam.

With limited effort, Graham's algorithm was capable of beating the most complex hand-coded rules that expert programmers painstakingly encoded. It also found surprising correlations between weird words and spammy email that no one had thought of: it turns out that ff0000, the color code for "red" used on the web, is as good of an indicator of spam as pornographic words.

Graham's experience provides two interesting takeaways. First of all, in 2002, Graham was considering autonomous spam filtering to be AI. Today, we take this feature for granted and think it's less sophisticated than a coffee maker. Also, we won't get into the details of the specific classifier that Graham used (for your information, it's called *naive Bayes*), but it's probably one of the simplest algorithms a mathematician can think of. Yet, it was still able to outsmart him and some of the smartest engineers in the world. Learning by experience beats hand-coded rules, once again.

5.3.2   *From sentiment analysis to text classification*

Sentiment analysis has already improved the experience of our users on the site, but we want to take some more steps toward the brokerbot. We decide to tackle another problem: reviews are wordy and talk about all sorts of aspects about the house, from the lighting in the living room to the neighborhood. A potential buyer who is particularly interested in a specific topic would have to go through all the reviews to find the ones that talk about that topic. Tagging each review by its topic would be an awesome feature that allows potential buyers to quickly find the information they want.

Instead of having just two classes (positive and negative) as in sentiment analysis, we now have many more, as reviews can be about the furniture, the view, the prestige of the neighborhood, and so on. This task is usually called *text* or *document classification.*

Is document classification more or less complex than sentiment analysis? Again, let's use the width/depth diagram to visualize the difference. The *width* of the task is higher, because document classification models need to understand a bigger vocabulary of words. Terms like "shelves," "dishwasher," or "orchard" can be ignored in sentiment analysis, but are clearly important for classification. The *depth* of an NLP application measures how complex the task is. In the sentiment analysis case, we simply wanted to put our review in one of two buckets. For text classification, we could have as many buckets as the categories we want to divide our reviews in; for example, reviews about the living room, the wear and tear of the house, the neighborhood, and so on. The more classes we decide to use, the deeper the model becomes, as shown in figure 5.7.

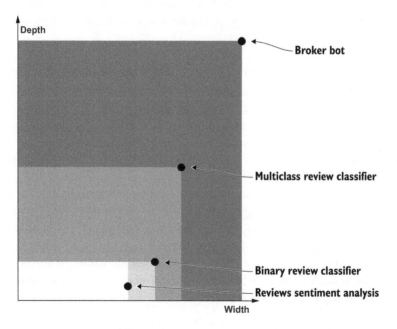

Figure 5.7   Comparing the brokerbot to the other, simpler NLP applications we've developed in this chapter

Basic ML models are usually good enough for sentiment analysis, but start having problems with more-complex tasks like classification, mostly because they ignore the *meaning* of words, and simply count how often they appear in the labeled dataset. This means that the classifier has no insight about the fact that "awesome" and "breathtaking" have similar meanings. Why is this a problem? Suppose you have 20 training examples with the world "awesome" but none with the word "breathtaking." A model that doesn't have any knowledge about the meaning of words will learn to classify as a positive example every review with the word "awesome" but won't know what to do with the word "breathtaking." If a model can grasp the meaning of words, it's enough for it to see a few examples with a few positive words to extend its classification power to all the words that are positive (that is, it will correctly interpret "stunning," "fabulous," and "gorgeous" even if the training example contains just "awesome").

The high variability of words is creating a problem similar to the one we had in chapter 4 with images. When we started talking about computer vision, our main issue was that images are made of millions of pixels, and it's hard for us to find ways to break the complexity of this data into simpler items, like the presence of basic shapes. Our solution to the problem was using deep learning, a special class of algorithms that are capable of autonomously extracting complex features (in the case of images, from basic information like corners and edges, to complex ones like facial traits for face recognition). You also saw how to use these algorithms to build *embeddings*, a computer-friendly summary of the contents of an image.

Luckily for us, deep learning also works on text and can help us build more powerful features than the simple presence of certain words in a sentence. In the same way we used embeddings to transform raw image pixels into meaningful information (for example, pointy nose or big ears), we can use them to transform words into a set of numbers that represent abstract word features, like "positiveness" and "strength." Just as two images with similar objects have similar embeddings, similar words will have similar embeddings as well (that is, similar words like "awesome" and "fabulous" will be transformed into similar sets of numbers).

If we interpret the numbers of a word embedding as coordinates in space, we can visually understand the power of this representation. For instance, in figure 5.8, you can see words represented on a 3-D plane. In the left plane, you can notice that positive words are close to each other, and they're far away from negative words (which, on the other hand, are close to each other). The same applies to the diagram on the right: objects that are related to the furniture in a living room tend to cluster together, and lie far away from adjectives related to the neighborhood. In this setting, *closeness* simply means that the word embeddings of two near words are similar, which allows our text document classifier to greatly simplify its work: it can now ignore the differences between similar words like "amazing," "fabulous," or "beautiful," and consider all of them as similar numbers that represent "positive" feelings.

Just like computer vision, NLP applications can also take advantage of *transfer learning* to reduce the amount of training data needed. As you saw in chapter 4, transfer

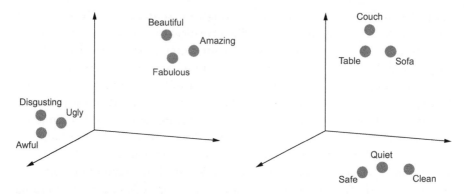

Figure 5.8   In these word embeddings represented on 3-D planes, positive and negative words are on the left, while words related to neighborhoods and living rooms are on the right.

learning is a way of "warming up" a model with large amounts of easily available generic data before training it by using domain-specific training data, which is often harder to get. Just like computer vision applications, in which models can learn simple shapes and patterns, NLP models will pick up basic vocabulary and grammar, which are useful for pretty much everything ("beautiful" has the same meaning whether you're talking about houses or anything else).

The NLP research community has released several DL models that were trained on huge text databases and can thus understand and create embeddings of almost a complete vocabulary. Figure 5.9 sketches out the basic idea behind adopting freely available embeddings for your specific classification task.

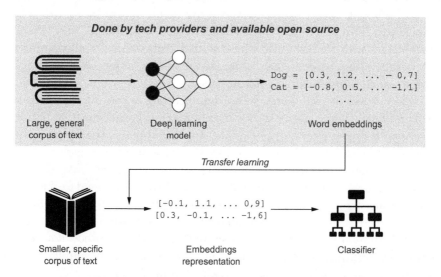

Figure 5.9   A typical NLP pipeline: For the first three steps (in the gray box), you can take advantage of open source models and embeddings. The last three steps involve domain-specific datasets.

The plan is to use the freely available pretrained models to compute embeddings of your own text (for example, the collection of home reviews on the website). These models do all the hard work of understanding grammar and vocabulary because they've been trained on a large corpus of text that allowed them to learn all those complex rules. When you have the embedding vectors for the text *you* care about (for example, the home reviews), it's much easier to build a classifier for sentiment analysis or other tasks, because embeddings express much more meaning than the raw text would.

5.3.3 Scoping a NLP classification project

Text classification is a generic and useful application that can be helpful in different contexts across an organization. Table 5.4 gives you some inspiration.

Table 5.4 Three examples of NLP-based classification for business applications

Application	Input data	Possible classes
Automatic ticket dispatcher	Tweets and email sent to customer service	Root cause of the issue (lack of internet connection, wrong billing, and so on)
Automatic car insurance claims categorizer	Insurance claim report	Kind of damage (broken engine, scratch, and so on)
Medical claims classifier	Doctor's report	Disease

When applying document classification to business problems, it's important to keep in mind that risk and performance depend on the number of classes we want to identify. On the width/depth graph in figure 5.10, you can visualize how complexity increases by imagining that the more classes we're asking our AI algorithm to identify, the more the depth of the application will go up, making the task more challenging.

Something else to keep in mind is that if you have a limited number of examples for a class in your training data, it will be complicated for the algorithm to learn to recognize elements from that class, as it won't have seen enough cases. Going back to our home review classifier, say you have a situation like the one in table 5.5. In this case, we have a lot of training data for the first three classes, but we're short

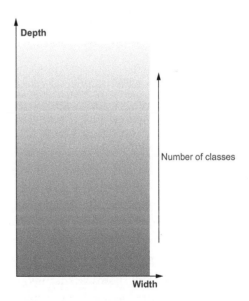

Figure 5.10 The depth of a classification NLP task increases as the number of classes grows, while its width remains the same.

on examples for the last. Class 4 has only three examples, compared to hundreds of reviews in the other classes.

The solution for this kind of situation is either to get more training data, or simply to *merge* the unlucky class with another similar one. For instance, classes 3 and 4 are both related to the neighborhood, so we could just merge them into a broader class of "reviews about the neighborhood," which would have 988 + 3 = 991 reviews in total. The final dataset has one fewer class, but is much more balanced in terms of examples, as represented in table 5.6.

Table 5.5   Initial example dataset of home reviews

Class ID	Class name	Number of examples in class
1	Wear and tear review	1,541
2	Furnitures review	769
3	Public service in neighborhood reviews	988
4	Neighborhood safety reviews	3

Table 5.6   The same dataset after merging classes 3 and 4

Class ID	Class name	Number of examples
1	Wear and tear review	1,541
2	Furniture review	769
3	Neighborhood reviews	991

Reducing the number of classes also helps keep down the depth of the task, increasing overall accuracy and therefore reducing the risk that the system will make mistakes when used in the real world.

5.3.4   *Document search*

In the beginning of this chapter, we pitched the brokerbot: an AI application capable of interpreting text as a human would. It's too complex for modern AI technology, so we started from the simplest application we could build: a sentiment analysis classifier. The next step toward deeper language understanding was text classification. Unfortunately, it still suffers from two important limitations:

- It's a classification task, which means we need to collect labels.
- The classes are defined up front: if a user wants to search for something that is not included in the classes, we can't help them.

It's possible to overcome the first problem either with a clever data collection hack or simply by paying humans to add labels by hand. The second problem is more challenging, and it's exactly what Google is great at: its little search bar allows you to type in anything you're interested in and immediately get a list of results sorted by relevance. This task is a branch of NLP often called *document search and retrieval.*

What we're trying to do is the following: we want to have a search bar at the top of our website, and when a user types something they're interested in (let's say "house insulation"), the algorithm will search through all the available reviews and pick the ones that are the most relevant to their search, as in figure 5.11.

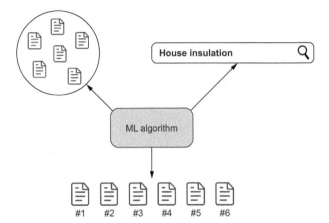

Figure 5.11   In document search, the algorithm is trained on a set of documents (top left). When it receives a query by the user (top right), it produces a list of the most relevant content.

For document search, the concept of word embeddings can help us big time. Recall that a *word embedding* is a set of a few hundred numbers that encode the meaning of a word, with the property that similar words have similar embeddings. Embeddings allow us to transfer the meaning of *similar* from the nebulous world of literature into the cold world of numbers. We can take advantage of this so that when the user asks about "house insulation," we can transform these two words into their embeddings, and if we've done the same with all the reviews, we can then look for the reviews whose numerical representation is closer to the one we got for "house insulation."

We want to help you visualize this concept in your head, so imagine a two-element embedding: each word is represented by only two numbers, as drawn in figure 5.12. Of course, such an embedding won't be very useful in practice, because two numbers are not nearly enough to capture the richness of vocabulary (the embeddings used in real-world applications are made by hundreds or thousands of numbers).

Imagine drawing a point for each of the documents we have in our database, and then drawing a new point corresponding to the embedding of the user query. Thanks to the way the embeddings are built, the documents most similar to the user query will be physically close to the query point. This means that it's easy to answer to the user query: just pick a few of the points that are closest to it, and those will correspond to the most similar documents. This solution also works when embedding vectors have more than two numbers; it's just harder to visualize them.

Document search is a fairly mature application of NLP that often plays the role of a building block in more-complex products. It's obviously not as fancy as other

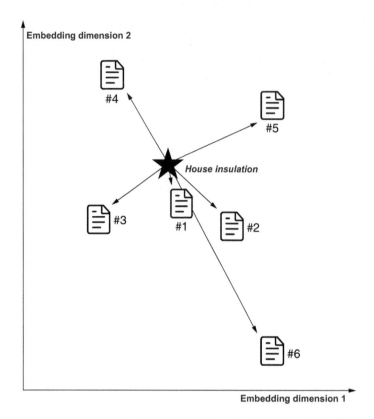

Figure 5.12   Document search algorithms answer user queries by looking up documents that have similar embeddings to the query sentence (shown with a star in the plot).

techniques, but it's often one of the first steps you can take in getting value out of your text-based data assets. In particular, the flavor of document search that we have explained here can't really answer any query that depends on logic or interpretation; the only thing it can do is return documents that sound similar to your query, hoping that you'll find them somehow useful.

5.3.5   *Natural conversation*

In all our efforts to get closer to the brokerbot, we always relied on human-generated text, and were happy to create algorithms that made it easier for people to access that information. A natural improvement would be a model that can generate language on its own, instead of cobbling together premade sentences.

We want to break the bad news right away: this field is still very much at the cutting edge of research, and today's technology is not ready for prime time (yet). Our goal with this section is to show you where the limits are, and how to work around them given what we have today.

The most advanced piece of technology on the market is a model called GPT-2, developed by the nonprofit research organization OpenAI. This model is capable of a variety of tasks, and one of the most impressive ones is generating text based on a human prompt. We downloaded an open source implementation of this model and tried it ourselves:

- *Our prompt*—Achieving human-like performance in language generation would be an amazing milestone for AI. Can the new OpenAI's GPT-2 model be a turning point?
- *GPT-2 completion*—And what impact can this model have on other artificial intelligence projects like AIQ and HCI?
- OpenAI was born to tackle this kind of problem. We were working in the field of speech recognition for the last five years. While working in this space we developed our speech recognition in the open source code. After the GPT-2 announcement some weeks ago, it is time to take the next step in speech recognition and we are proud to present the version 2.
- The biggest challenges facing AI, the most important problems for it are
  - Information in general
  - Knowledge is often not accessible
  - Information can be obtained from many sources that can conflict

As you can see, the results are fairly convincing. The content itself doesn't necessarily make sense, but stays on topic with almost flawless grammar. This was made possible because of the gigantic amount of data that the model has been trained on: more than 8 million web pages. Going back to real estate, here's a last try of GPT-2 with another sentence related to a house:

- *Our prompt*—This house is an amazing deal: the view from the living room is outstanding, and the neighborhood is very up-and-coming.
- *GPT-2 completion*—I'm hoping to upgrade to a two bed as I really love this house and this neighborhood. If you live in central Florida you should probably go check it out.

  My husband loves my house on the north side of town and we are close to Miami and many beach places. Our neighborhood is just a block away. We are both super happy and our home is super cozy. We did get moved but never planned to leave. We have also had other places to take a break and have never had such a convenient place for vacationing. I highly recommend it! We love it!!!

The model "noticed" that the text it was fed resembled a review of something like an Airbnb house listing, and it kept adding text as if it were a home review.

You can also use GPT-2 to answer questions about a body of text, which would probably be a more interesting application than generating random sentences. In fact, this would be extremely close to the brokerbot, as we could use GPT-2 to answer users who have inquiries about houses in plain language. Here are a few examples of the Q&A capabilities of GPT-2:

- *Our prompt*—The GPT-2 model was developed by OpenAI, training an advanced deep learning model on over 40GB of internet text from 8 million web pages. The model has amazing performance, but it's far from perfect.

  Q: Who developed GPT-2?

- *GPT-2 answer*—GPT-2 by OpenAI was developed to develop and train a deep learning model, which can then be used in machine learning applications. The team has made the goal to build a "machine learning engine for the internet" for the next generation of applications.

- *Our prompt*—*From Zero to AI* is a book about artificial intelligence written for nontechnical people. The book will help you understand the core principles of AI and how to apply them to your business. It's written by Nicolò Valigi and Gianluca Mauro, and published by Manning Publications.

  Q: Who wrote *From Zero to AI*?

- *GPT-2 answer*—*From Zero to AI* has always been written by Nicolò Valigi. I always have been an ardent fan of Valigi, and his previous books are quite influential in my writing today. I know him from his work for Apple in their Mac, iPod, and iPhone. He also worked on the screenplay for "The Lego Movie", "Hobbit" the movie, and "Serendity". I had the opportunity to write the book for my daughter's first year of college this past summer, and it was quite interesting to read how he uses his years of experience and successes at the highest level of the industry to help write a book that will appeal to a wider audience. That being said I want to thank Nicolò Valigi, and hope that he will continue to write a great book to help all of us become more intelligent.

Even if these performances seem amazing, severe limitations still affect this technology, and researchers are working hard to fix them. Examples are as follows:

- It's hard to control the output of the model. For instance, we had to try three to four times before getting the results presented here. Even with highly popular topics that are widely present in the training data, OpenAI researchers reported that the model can produce credible results only about 50% of the time.

- When the model doesn't know a topic, it invents stuff based on what may be plausible, even if it's completely false. A good example is the last one: the model invented that one of us authors had experience at Apple and wrote screenplays, just because the prompt was about technology and books.

- The model doesn't really understand the meaning of what it's saying: it sometimes mentions impossible scenarios like fires burning under water.

- It can get stuck and start repeating words on a loop.

- It may switch topics unnaturally.

Arguably, the biggest limitation of these models is that they may seem to understand the concepts in the prompt, but are actually tricking us: all they do is guess which word is more likely to follow in a sentence, based on the billions of sentences they've seen. In other words, they're parroting their huge training datasets, not understanding.

You can visualize the difference between understanding and probabilistic reasoning by comparing a doctor and an ML algorithm. A doctor can diagnose a patient by reading a textbook, understanding its content, and perhaps practicing on X-rays. On the other hand, no ML algorithm today can do the same. To make a diagnosis on a scan, an ML algorithm needs a large number of examples, and having "read" just a single book before won't help it improve its diagnosis in any way.

How do we get closer to the brokerbot, then? Do we just have to sit around waiting for text generation to mature? Thankfully, no. You can adopt other strategies to create value today, so bear with us.

5.3.6 *Designing products that overcome technology limitations*

Let's imagine we really want to build the brokerbot with whatever technology offers us today. We could go back to our sentiment analysis algorithm and our topic classifier, having a nice list of ready-made sentences for each topic. Say the user writes something like this:

> *What are the apartments with the best view?*

Our topic classifier may understand that the topic of the question is the panorama that you can enjoy from the apartment, and our sentiment analysis knows that we're interested in something positive (we also know that this is a question because of the question mark in the end, no fancy tech needed). Now, you may have a series of questions that match the requirements "topic = view" and "sentiment = good," like so:

> *Would you rather be by the ocean or close to a park?*

Notice that this question isn't generated by any clever AI algorithm; a human came up with it and stored it in a database with a bunch of other questions. The user may answer something like this:

> *I love trees! Golden Gate Park is my favorite*

Again, our sentiment analysis will understand that the sentence has a positive feeling, our topic classifier will understand that we're talking about trees (which have an embedding similar to the parks mentioned previously—you see how powerful embeddings are?), and therefore the answer to the question is "parks." If you built the classifier to do so, you may also catch the reference to Golden Gate Park and look for houses close to it. From there, you may have scripted something that understands it's the right time to show properties, and suggest best homes for that specific user.

It looks amazing and smooth, right? But what if the answer that the user gives to the previous question is something like this?

> *I'd say that I love the ocean, but when it's winter, there are many storms here, so I'd go with something else.*

This is probably the unluckiest we can get. Clearly, the user prefers a view to a nice park, but the sentence offers several challenges:

- It talks about the ocean view.
- It never really mentions anything related to parks.
- It says "love," which conveys a positive meaning.
- No words hint to a negative sentiment about the ocean view.

An algorithm will most likely be confused by a sentence like this, and move along the predetermined script with the wrong follow-up questions. Even worse, the user may answer as follows:

You know what? I really like looking at tall buildings with nice architecture.

What if you haven't thought of this answer? The user followed a script path with a dead end, and you don't have an answer. You probably will answer with something generic like this: "I don't get what you mean, can you repeat?" The user will never be able to answer the question in a way you can manage (you simply didn't precode anything that matches those interests!) and will become frustrated and abandon the product.

Does it sound familiar? It certainly does to us, and this is the frustrating experience that consumers get from companies that decided to use chatbots without making sure that their functionality matches what today's technology can deliver.

The solution lies in the way you scope your application. If you're aware of the limitations of today's technology, do your best to stay within these limitations, building your application around them and keeping complexity low, both in terms of width and depth. In the case of the brokerbot, we might explicitly limit the functionality of the brokerbot to a small subset of actions, like just querying houses based on basic parameters (location, size, price). Also, try avoiding natural language as much as possible, using either close-ended questions (yes/no), or buttons that allow the user to choose from different options. For instance, the bot might be the one starting the conversation with a user so that it can lead toward specific topics, thereby limiting the width of the answer. The bot might kick off the conversation by asking this:

Hello! I'm the brokerbot, I'm here to help you find your new house. First of all, what's your budget?

Here, you may decide to let the user give an answer in natural language or provide a slider for choosing the price. The latter is the safest, but because we know that the user's answer will be about pricing, we are also confident that we'll be able to understand an answer in natural language. From there, the bot could move forward with questions about location, size, and so on, until it can finally show the user a selection of homes, and eventually even ask for feedback.

Conversation scripting and design is still the only way to build technology that brings value to people. We encourage you to use the knowledge you gained in this chapter to think critically about what you want your chatbot to do and how you want it to relate to users.

5.4   *Case study: Translated*

In 1999, Marco Trombetti and Isabelle Andrieu decided to start a business together. Trombetti was studying physics, and Andrieu was a linguist. To use their skills, the young couple came up with the idea of building an internet-based translation company. They called it *Translated*, and launched it with an initial investment of $100 for the internet domain Translated.net. In the following 20 years, Translated would become the largest online professional translation company in the world, growing organically without any external investment.

Translated focuses on professional translations, like medical journals and engineering user manuals. Such translations are traditionally performed by professional translators contracted by companies that act as brokers. Matching a body of text with a translator is not trivial: many documents need both deep language skills and subject matter expertise. For instance, translating a paper about transcatheter aortic valve implantations from English to German would need a cardiologist skilled in both languages. Translation brokers that own a database of translators can take advantage of this and charge large premiums to provide clients with the right translators. The larger the translation company, the larger the challenges and inefficiencies in matching translators with jobs. This was an opportunity that Trombetti and Andrieu set out to exploit.

The first challenge that Trombetti and Andrieu had to face was building a large database of translators. From the outset, the duo invested in search engine optimization (SEO) so they could land at the top of Google searches for professional translation services. These being the early days of the internet, their investment quickly paid off, and Translated started receiving hundreds of resumes per month. The early success led to a new challenge: many of the translators sending their resumes didn't meet the quality standards of the company, and sorting professional translators from nonprofessional ones required a great deal of human effort. Translated risked falling into the same inefficiencies as other translation brokers.

The inspiration for how to address this challenge came to Trombetti in 2002, when he read the very same Paul Graham essay "A Plan for Spam," that we talked about earlier in the chapter. Trombetti thought that the same method used to discriminate between spam and not-spam email could be used to make a first assessment on whether a resume they received was from a professional or nonprofessional translator, as depicted in figure 5.13.

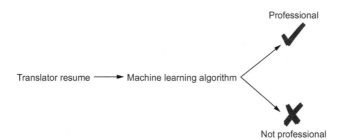

Figure 5.13   Translated's ML algorithm helped the company automatically identify professional and nonprofessional translators.

The algorithm was first introduced in 2002, when the company started receiving hundreds of translation requests per day, and it has been improved ever since. The next evolution of the algorithm was to turn it into an automatic translator-document matching AI, training it using the matchings made by Translated's project managers (PMs) over the years. Once deployed, at any new translation request, the algorithm would look at the document and at the company's pool of translators and calculate a *match probability* for each translator. Translated's PMs would then validate the matches and assign the task. This process allowed the young startup to handle many clients and translators without compromising delivery speed (a factor often crucial for clients) and to keep their overhead low by having a smaller team of PMs.

Today, Translated acts as a double-sided platform: from one side, translators apply to offer their services; and from the other, customers submit the documents they need to have translated. In the backend, Translated matches the right translator for each job and delivers the final result to the client, without them needing to interact with each other. The current version of their algorithm is branded as T-Rank.

The algorithm takes into account up to 30 factors from the source document, including the translator's resume (area of expertise) and previous projects (quality and timeliness of previous jobs). Using this data, T-Rank can rank the translators in the company's portfolio according to their fit with the work and provide the best professional for each task, as in figure 5.14. As in the first versions of the algorithm, the final recommendations are vetted by expert PMs. In case the PM rejects the recommendation, the feedback is recorded and used to fine-tune the algorithm to continuously improve its performance.

Success in the market brought Translated both cash and data. A consistent cash flow enabled Trombetti and Andrieu to run the company without seeking external investments and to keep complete ownership. On the other hand, Translated started collecting the translations made by professionals through its computer-aided translation system called Matecat, improving its matching algorithms and pushing the company toward a new mission: becoming the leader in machine-aided translation.

To evaluate the performance of its ML-generated translation, Translated has always been tracking the percentage of suggested words that are changed by the professional translator. In the early days, translators had to change 45% of suggested words.

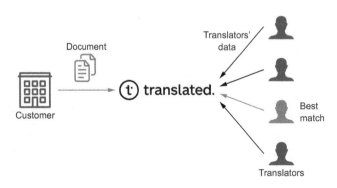

Figure 5.14   Translated is a double-sided platform: customers send documents, translators send their data, and the company finds the best translator in its portfolio for each document to translate.

Together with AI-assisted matching of translators, this was enough to deliver translations quicker than the competition. In 2018, the company could count on more than 1.2 million professional translations, and percentage of words changed by the professional translator dropped to 24% on the eight most-spoken languages, 30% lower than other translation engines.

To further improve the experience and productivity of translators, the company has invested in a technology branded as ModernMT, the first adaptive neural machine translation. Traditionally, ML algorithms are trained on a large amount of data (training phase) and are static while they're used (inference phase). If a translator is presented with a poor suggestion and fixes it, this fix won't be taken into account by the machine translation (MT) algorithm until training is repeated with the new data. This means that while a translator is working on a document, the same fixes might have to be applied multiple times. The result is a frustrating and inefficient experience for the translator.

As illustrated in figure 5.15, ModernMT learns and adjusts in real time while the translator is working through the translation. If the same phrase occurs more than once in a document and the translator fixes it once, ModernMT will learn the correction the first time and avoid repeating the mistake.

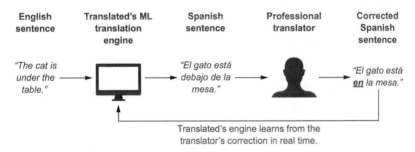

Figure 5.15   Translated's ModernMT translation engine proposes a translation that can eventually be corrected by the translator. The translator's correction is then learned by ModernMT.

As of 2019, Translated receives 2,000 resumes a month from translators. The company has brokered 1.2 million professional translations for more than 130,000 customers, and the translations are performed in 151 languages by more than 180,000 professional translators. The algorithms built on this dataset allow state-of-the-art machine translation performances on the 27 most common languages. Translated's algorithms facilitate, but don't replace, the work of professionals. They provide a first automatic translation of the sentences that just need to be refined and fine-tuned: today, translators need to change just 24% of the words suggested by the company's platform. This is 30% better than any other solution currently on the market. Translated reported revenues of €21 million in 2018, with 51 employees: 12 developers, 35 in operations, with an expected growth of 40% for 2019.

Translated is still investing in improving its translation engine. The goal is not to get AI to produce perfect translations. In fact, if a translation performed by a professional translator is reviewed by another professional, that person would still change about 11% of the words. This is because of the extreme expressiveness of language: the same concept can be expressed with different words to express slightly different meanings and nuances. According to Trombetti, this is the most important and fulfilling task required for a translator: making sure that the richness of the document is expressed in the translation. His goal is therefore improving the company's AI algorithm to allow translators to focus on the 11% of the words they need to change to convey the original message of the document in the most expressive way possible.

Trombetti and Andrieu want to allow translators to perform a more fulfilling and higher-quality job, and democratize translation along the way. Here's what they said during our interview with them:

> *Our technology is creating a lot of opportunities not just for us but also for the translators, who are finally not working on correcting again and again the same tedious stuff but are spending their time in being more human, communicating what the text actually means and being more persuasive and creative.*

5.4.1 Case questions

1 How can you develop a strategy for AI in NLP tasks?
2 Is AI a tool to replace humans?

5.4.2 Case discussion

Translated is a great example of a successful incremental strategy for AI. In its beginnings, the company used AI technology to address a simple use case: classifying translators' resumes into professionals or nonprofessionals. Notice that this first use case was one of the simplest applications the company could have built, but its technology risk was very low because Trombetti and Andrieu knew that the same approach had been tried in other domains (email spam classification). Even if simple, this use case had several characteristics that made it a good fit for AI at the time, such as the following:

- It played a highly strategic role in outperforming competition.
- It had a short time to ROI (its results could be seen immediately).
- It carried low implementation risk.

The success of this first application brought more customers and more data. The enriched data asset of Translated allowed a positive loop, making the translator-matching technology more powerful as data volume increased, and allowing new applications that weren't possible in its early days, such as AI-assisted translations.

Even if AI-assisted translations would have been a killer feature 20 years ago, the company didn't start investing in it immediately. Lack of data was the first reason not to do so, but the biggest reason why Trombetti waited was that the technology wasn't ripe enough. It's a prime example of *riding the technology wave*: letting research take the first hard steps toward the maturity of a technology, and using the findings together with strategic data assets to build on them, reaching state-of-the-art performance. Great timing can be the key success factor for a company like Translated working at the edge of technology.

Notice also that Translated knows that machine translation is an extremely complex task, which would fit well up and to the right on the width/depth diagram, but framed the technology in a way that allows it to be extremely useful anyway. The company does it by giving the professional translators the last word: the technology doesn't produce the final document, but a first approximation that an expert human can work on.

This focus on user experience was a key element in the company's strategy. Translated focused its ML research efforts on solving problems that their translators were experiencing the most, and this led to the development of ModernMT: the first neural network that adapts to the typical translation workflow. This innovation allows translators to avoid fixing their translations multiple times along the same document, saving them time and frustration. Achieving the same performance using standard static neural networks would have required massive effort in terms of research and data.

Let's talk now about the relationship between AI and replacing humans. As you now know well, modern AI is based on machine learning: a technology capable of learning how to perform tasks from data. This means that AI applications today can handle single well-defined tasks, with a specific output and a clearly defined evaluation metric.

Most human jobs are more complex than this. A job may require performing a series of tasks that, taken singularly, may be a fit for ML algorithms—but as a whole require additional skills to be performed properly. Examples of skills required are as follows:

- Exceptions handling
- Empathy
- Creativity
- Making decisions based on incomplete data

On the other hand, AI algorithms are usually better than humans at these tasks:

- Making decisions based on large amounts of data
- Speed
- Objectiveness (provided that they're trained on unbiased data)

If we look at the tasks that humans do to fulfill their jobs, we find a subset that doesn't require human-specific skills and are a good fit for AI agents. For Translated, this was scanning through resumes. If the company employed people to scan thousands of resumes and find the best match for a translation, it would have needed a large team of people to make straightforward decisions (for example, discarding resumes of doctors to translate an airplane manual). This high-level selection requires mostly speed and the ability to process large amounts of information, two characteristics that ML algorithms excel at.

When identifying high-potential ML projects, Trombetti has a simple rule:

> *Look at the tasks that a company could perform using 1,000 untrained interns. These are tasks that can be automated by AI.*

The company knows that selecting a translator for a delicate job requires sensibility and experience. For this reason, the final call is not left to the algorithms: its output is still vetted by a project manager using soft skills to validate or reject the algorithmic pick.

What about Translated's AI-aided translation services? Performing a high-quality translation of a document requires empathy and creativity. These two characteristics are the domain of human beings, and ML algorithms are notoriously not a viable solution for such problems. Yet, Translated has successfully used AI for this application as well.

The main reason behind Translated's success in offering AI-aided translations is that it has never marketed the AI as a replacement for humans. This would have meant overstepping on AI capabilities and delivering a poor product. What the company has done is use AI while clearly stating that its results aren't perfect, but just good enough to make translators' jobs easier. In this way, their attention can be directed at the parts of the document that require more empathy and creativity, while leaving to Translated's AI the task of translating the easiest sentences.

Summary

- Natural language processing models can understand and classify the meaning of text, and even write something of their own.
- Today's NLP technology doesn't always live up to the hype. Framing complexity in terms of width and depth helps your team understand what's possible and what's not.
- By breaking down and scoping an NLP project, you can work around limitations in state-of-the-art algorithms. Sentiment analysis, text classification, and document search are all examples of these more mature building blocks.
- A staggered rollout of AI features is a great way to build confidence in NLP models and build an AI-based powerhouse, as you saw in the Translated case study.

AI for content curation and community building

This chapter covers

- Using recommender systems to suggest engaging content and products
- Understanding the two approaches to recommender systems: content and community-based
- Understanding the drawbacks of algorithmic recommendations
- Case study: using recommender systems to save $1 billion in churn

Recommender systems are the workhorse behind today's "personalized" experiences, and a fundamental tool to help consumers navigate huge catalogs of media, products, and clothes. Anytime you click a related offer from Amazon or check out a suggested movie from Netflix, these companies are taking advantage of recommender systems to drive user engagement and top-line growth. Without them, navigating the vastness of products and digital content available on the internet would be simply impossible.

In the case study at the end of the chapter, you'll see how Netflix believes that its recommender system has been saving the company more than $1 billion each year since 2015.

6.1   *The curse of choice*

Have you ever entered a large mall to shop for clothes and felt disoriented? It's hard to find the T-shirt of your dreams when there are hundreds to choose from, with different colors, fabrics, brands, and prices. The internet has no real estate limitations, and therefore you potentially have to choose from not hundreds, but tens of thousands of T-shirts. Or movies. Or songs. Or news articles. Or dishwasher tablets. Frustration is around the corner, and frustrated customers are not good for business.

The internet is so brimming with choices that we *need* to find a way to help make them. In chapter 3, we tried to find a way to group users according to their tastes and target them with offers that match those tastes, using a set of techniques called unsupervised learning. However, that is still not enough to reach the *marketing singularity*: the holy grail of one-to-one communication, whereby each customer gets fully personalized offers and recommendations for maximum satisfaction. This is the topic of this chapter.

How can you help people make choices? If we look at great shop assistants, they do either or both of these two things:

- They know their catalog. If you like a pair of jeans, they'll be able to suggest others that are similar and quickly direct you toward the perfect choice.
- They know you. If you are a returning customer, they learned about your tastes and can suggest items you're likely to like: "You must try these jeans; they're so trendy right now and they really match your style."

Throughout this chapter, you'll see how to build algorithms that can do both of these things, even better than humans. These algorithms, called *recommender systems*, produce tailored recommendations to customers at scale.

6.2   *Driving engagement with recommender systems*

Thanks to the AI-based features we built in the previous chapters, FutureHouse has been drawing more and more users. The free estimate of the sale price and automated listings have attracted many new sellers too. All this success has brought a new challenge: so many properties are listed for sale now that it's hard for buyers to find the perfect home. We need to find a way to highlight the properties that match their tastes, and make it easier for them to find the home of their dreams. The solution is clear: we need to build a Recommended Houses for You feature that learns the taste of each user and preselects houses for them.

Let's try to think about how FutureHouse could decide which homes to show to each user. How would an experienced human approach this problem? A real estate agent may look at one or more houses that the customer has liked and propose others that are somehow similar (for example, in the same neighborhood or with the same number of rooms).

How do we translate this approach to the world of the internet? An obvious idea would be to keep track of the homes that each customer visits on the site, and suggest that they check out similar properties to the ones they have already found. For example, if a prospective buyer has already looked at several three-bedroom homes close to train stations, it's likely that they would be interested in others that share the same attributes.

How do we define the meaning of *similar*, though? If we had a clear idea in mind of how to measure similarity, we could just explain that to a computer. However, our idea of *similar* is intuitive and natural, and therefore we struggle to do so. By now, you're familiar with the fact that this is a perfect starting point for machine learning.

In chapter 2, we introduced the concept of *features*, measurable aspects of each individual home that can be used as inputs for ML algorithms. More specifically, the groundwork we did to build the price-prediction model suggested that the number of rooms, the square footage, and the distance to public transportation were some of the most important factors to take into account. Similarly to what we did for price prediction, we can lay down the feature values for each home in an Excel spreadsheet, as we did in figure 6.1.

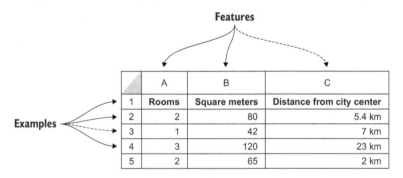

Figure 6.1 An Excel spreadsheet is great for visualizing the features of homes. Each row is a different property, and each column is a feature.

Let's start simple and consider a single feature of the homes: square footage. It's obvious that a 1,000 sq. ft. home and a 1,100 sq. ft. home are more similar to each other than to a 12,000 sq. ft. home. Therefore, our algorithm should recommend the 1,000 sq. ft. home to a user who has visited a 1,100 sq. ft. home, and avoid surfacing the 12,000 sq. ft. villa. In ML terms, this is formalized by the concept of *distance* between the feature values: 1,100–1,000 is much smaller than 12,000–1,000, so the algorithm can figure out they're more similar to each other.

As you've seen in chapter 2, most real-world ML applications don't use a single feature, but tens or even hundreds. Let's now step up our game a notch and consider a second feature: the number of rooms. If we drew a circle for each home in a (very small) dataset of homes, the diagram would look like figure 6.2.

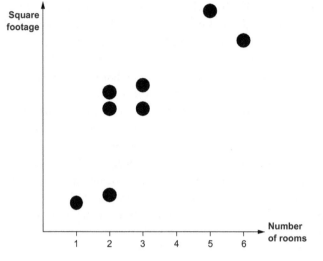

Figure 6.2   A representation of houses based on two features: number of rooms and square footage

Let's imagine the experience of a new user we'll call Lucie. Lucie signs up on Future-House and starts browsing around. She immediately clicks one of the houses and spends a lot of time on its page, looking through the pictures, reading the descriptions, considering the reviews, and so on. We can assume that this is a clear indication that Lucie likes that house. If we take the plot in figure 6.2 and turn the dot corresponding to Lucie's favorite house into a star, we get figure 6.3.

Our task is to help her find other houses that match her tastes: houses that are similar to the one she just spent a lot of time looking at. Even just by staring at figure 6.4, it seems intuitive that three other homes are quite similar to Lucie's favorite. The other four houses seem to be much more different: the two on the bottom left are too small, and the ones on the top right are probably too big.

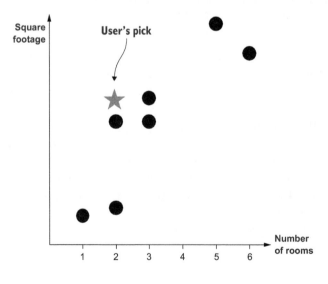

Figure 6.3   Lucie really likes one of the homes, highlighted with a star.

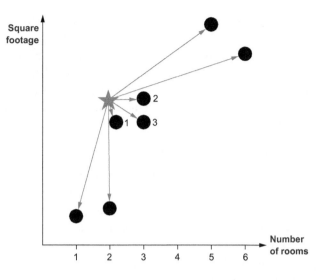

Figure 6.4 A computer takes each pair of homes and measures the straight-line distance between them.

Now we need to translate this reasoning into computing terms so that we can automate it and help thousands of people like Lucie at the same time. We'll again use the notion of *distance* that we introduced earlier. Imagine using a ruler to measure the distance between the points (that is, homes) printed in figure 6.3: this is exactly what a computer does, as shown in figure 6.4.

After we've measured the distance from the starred home to all of the other ones in the dataset, we can ask the computer to sort them from shortest to longest, and pick the top two or three to show Lucie.

Of course, we're still considering only the square footage and number of rooms, so our notion of similarity is rough and incomplete: we're ignoring many other important house features including the location, year of construction, and more. Luckily, it turns out that the algorithm doesn't really change when we add all of the other features back; it just becomes harder to draw it on paper and conceptualize it for us poor, limited humans. Engineers can easily build distance algorithms that work with all the features that we used in chapter 2 for price prediction, and a computer can effortlessly compute them.

What we have just described is the simplest recommender system ever, but it's still effective, and this basic concept is easy to deploy in a variety of business situations. Take the page that shows details and pictures of each home. It's easy for engineers to add a sidebar with links to the three or four homes that are most similar to the one the user is browsing, and enjoy the additional traffic.

More-sophisticated models also keep track of how the tastes of the users evolve over time, by considering all the homes that they have ever interacted with. Even better, we could group choices based on the category of the items and on the time of the year, instead of treating all preferences the same. For example, an e-commerce site would choose to recommend your kids' favorite brand of pencils during the back-to-school season, but recognize that the very same recommendations are not useful during the summer.

Notice that Lucie's recommender system was looking only at the features of Lucie's favorite home and completely ignored who she is and what other users in the community have done. This is also true for the more sophisticated examples we made: we're still focusing on only the content for now. This is why this family of recommender systems is called *content-based*.

6.2.1 *Content-based systems beyond simple features*

While our fictional FutureHouse examples have served us well so far, you're likely wondering how recommender systems can be adapted to other types of items, such as the clothes in your favorite e-shop. When talking about homes, we were lucky to have a set of descriptive features that are also reasonably easy to collect. Again, those are the same features that we used in chapter 2 to predict the sale price of the home.

However, many organizations deploy recommender systems on catalogs of items for which it's much harder to select features. Imagine the example at the start of this chapter: finding the best T-shirt for you. What kind of features could we use?

- Predominant color (black, white, and so forth)
- Fabric (cotton, synthetic)
- V-shaped or c-shaped neck
- Fit (slim, regular)
- Sleeves (long, short, three-quarter).

If buying a T-shirt was so easy, many fashion designers would be out of a job. The reality is that it's hard to come up with criteria that capture the style of a T-shirt, as with any piece of clothing, or in general with any visual media.

Luckily, we already solved the same challenge in chapter 4, when we realized the shortcomings of conventional machine learning and introduced advanced models based on deep learning, a family of algorithms that automatically extracts features from complex data sources. These models were capable of transforming an image into a small set of numbers called *embeddings*, which represent high-level characteristics of the image in a compact form.

Let's recall what we said about deep neural networks when they're trained to recognize faces. When you train a face-recognition algorithm, it learns to recognize high-level characteristics of faces and transform each image it's fed into that series of numbers called embeddings. These embeddings represent the presence (or absence) of certain important facial characteristics in the image; for instance, whether the person in the image has a pointy nose, large ears, and so on.

What happens if you do the same with T-shirts? Well, you'll magically have a way to transform the picture of that T-shirt from millions of pixels to a few hundred numbers that express some of its high-level style characteristics. These may be the presence of vertical stripes, horizontal stripes, prints of different objects, sentences, logos, and more. While we intuitively know that all these features are relevant to characterize a T-shirt, we have no way of doing so by hand. A deep learning algorithm can do that automatically, saving the day for us all.

Once we have transformed an image into its embeddings using a deep neural network, we suddenly find ourselves in the same situation that we described in the previous section: we can transform all the images into a set of points in space, and use the similarity criterion to spot T-shirts that are similar to the user's favorites. Obviously, embeddings will be made by hundreds or thousands of dimensions, in order to capture the nuances of a T-shirt's style. To visualize the concept, we drew a 2-D representation of the embeddings of three T-shirts, as in figure 6.5.

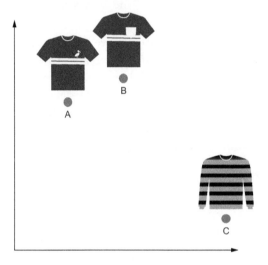

Figure 6.5   Embeddings of three T-shirts represented on a 2-D plane. T-shirts A and B are similar, so their embeddings are close. T-shirt C is different from A and B, so it's far from both.

Imagine now that a user clicks on the product page for T-shirt A and spends time looking at it, checking the available sizes, colors, and materials. We can interpret this as a manifestation of interest in that T-shirt's style, and recommend another one that has an embedding close to it; for instance, T-shirt B. We'll avoid suggesting T-shirt C, as we know that its embedding is far from that of the T-shirt that the user liked, and therefore it probably won't match their taste.

This is again the magic of deep learning and of embeddings: neural networks found a way to "understand" images and transform them into a small set of numbers that actually make sense (for a computer, at least). If you think about it, images are not the only applications where you've seen the power of embeddings. In chapter 5, you saw how powerful embeddings can be when dealing with another complicated kind of data: text.

The same approach we described works with text as well. Suppose we are trying to suggest news articles to a user on a website, and we want to find a piece of news that is similar to the ones where our user spends most of his time. We can transform the words in each article in its embeddings and place our new *vectorized* articles in space, as shown in figure 6.6.

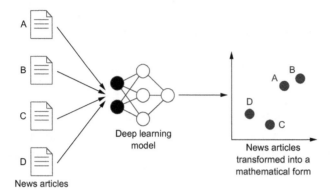

Figure 6.6   Deep learning can translate each news article into its embedding, which is a compact mathematical description that can be used to compare them.

Once we have a spatial representation of the news articles, we can let the concept of similarity guide us in recommending news to a user. If a user reads article A, we know that they're probably going to be interested in article B, because their embeddings are close and therefore their content is too. This is the magic of deep learning and embeddings: they allow us to transform even complex data sources like articles and images into numerical representations that carry meaning, applying the same techniques we used for houses at the beginning of the chapter.

6.2.2   *The limitations of features and similarity*

From what we have said so far, you might think that the concept of *similarity* (together with some deep learning magic) can solve every recommendation problem, from news articles to household products. This section will help you build your intuition about why, in some cases, similarity isn't the best strategy. Let's start with another classic example that we're all familiar with: recommending movies to watch.

Let's tackle this new problem by following the same approach that we used to recommend homes to potential buyers. The first step is to find the *features* that the algorithm can use to describe movies. Most people come up with a list that looks like this:

- Director
- Year of release
- Genre (Comedy, Drama, Animation, Romance)
- Top three lead actors

If we go ahead with this list of features, we'll soon learn that the recommendations produced by the algorithm are uninteresting at best, and downright ridiculous at worst. Throughout their careers, both actors and directors worked on all sorts of movies: even if you liked *Titanic*, it doesn't mean that you would enjoy *The Wolf of Wall Street* just because it stars Leonardo DiCaprio.

We can try to improve our model by turning to the power of deep learning. We could feed all the movie dialogue to a natural language model that can produce additional features capturing the topic and mood of the movie. This would likely work well: the love-themed dialogue and worried discussion of the captain would add more nuance to the recommendations, potentially producing other forbidden-love stories and disasters. However, your future recommendations would likely linger in the love-and-disaster category for a while, which you might find less than alluring.

Sadly, no matter how sophisticated we get with feature building, we're left with a fundamental limitation: our recommendation engine is still based on *similarity*. This means that the model can suggest only items that match the past choices of the customer. This is bound to bore them to death: how many fantasy Angelina Jolie flicks or cheesy dialogues can you withstand before canceling your Netflix subscription? Thus, the Achilles' heel of content-based recommendations is that their outputs can get bland and predictable. While this is not great for entertainment or fashion shopping, it's a great fit for some other industries; say, drug recommendations to doctors.

Unsurprisingly, the best way to add a human touch to recommendations is to bring humans into the mix. By using a community of users who consume and rate the catalog, we can build more nuanced recommender systems. This is what we're going to explore in the next section.

6.3 The wisdom of crowds: collaborative filtering

Just to recap, the type of recommender systems we have explored so far are commonly called *content-based*, as they use descriptive attributes of items the user has liked in the past to find and recommend similar ones in a catalog. However, this approach breaks down in two ways: it might be hard to express meaningful features, and the resulting recommendations can be predictable and boring.

Let's stop for a second and think about how we tackle this problem in real life. People ask their friends for recommendations all the time: books, restaurants, movies, and so on. Over time, most of us have learned that some friends share our same tastes in music or food, and thus we eagerly listen to their recommendations because we anticipate that the similar preferences we had in the past will also extend to the future.

AI can scale this human tradition to much larger groups by taking advantage of a *community* of users who are all expressing preferences about items in a shared catalog. The kind of AI algorithms that build on this concept are called *collaborative filtering algorithms*: a social approach to recommender systems that does pretty much the same thing we do in real life with our friends.

If we can simply rely on the taste and preference histories of similar users, the role of a collaborative model is to match users who share the same tastes, so they can be mutually offered recommendations. In real life, we would start mutually sharing our preference histories and notice that they match up pretty nicely: "Oh, you also like *Toy Story* and *Titanic*! Have you watched . . . ?" Collaborative models can do the same thing, and match users with similar tastes, albeit at a much larger scale.

Just as in content-based models, you'll have to collect the preferences of the users. Let's jump back to our example of a real estate platform and look at example data to understand the intuition behind collaborative models. Table 6.1 shows the preferences of three imaginary users of the platform: Alice, Bob, and Jane.

Table 6.1   Home preferences of Alice, Bob, and Jane

Home	Alice	Bob	Jane
Home A: One-bedroom in the Dogpatch neighborhood	?	Like	Not like
Home B: Three-bedroom in the Financial District	Like	Not like	Like
Home C: Studio in the Mission district	Not like	?	Not like
Home D: One-bedroom in the Mission district	Not like	Like	Not like
Home E: Three-bedroom in the Marina neighborhood	Like	?	Like

Each row of the table shows what Alice, Bob and Jane think of each of the five homes in our (admittedly small) catalog. Just as in content-based models, there are many ways to collect this preference data. The most obvious way is just to *ask* them; for example, with a five-star widget in the home description page. Many savvy organizations go beyond that and keep track of more detailed information, such as how much time users spend reading the description or scrolling through the images. If Bob has seen the listing of a house 10 times over the last two days and has spent five minutes on each session, it's a pretty good indicator that he's really interested.

The example dataset includes homes that Alice and Bob didn't manage to look at (represented with a question mark in table 6.1). Alice never found Home A, and Bob didn't see Homes C and E. As you've learned, the goal of the recommender system is to select which of these "missing" homes they're more likely to be interested in, so that we can place them at the top of their search results and help them find new houses that they'll potentially buy.

By looking at the table, we can already tell that Alice and Jane have similar interests: both liked Home E and didn't like Homes C and D. On the other hand, Bob seems to have completely different taste compared to both Jane and Alice, as he didn't agree on any of the houses that they've rated.

When producing recommendations, a collaborative filtering system would pair up Alice and Jane as two people with similar tastes, and won't show Home A to Alice, as it didn't fit Jane's preferences. Regarding Bob, we know that he's looking for something completely different from Alice and Jane, and therefore we'll suggest that he check out Home C that wasn't liked by either Alice and Jane, and won't propose Home E that was liked by both.

In other words, the idea behind collaborative filtering is to ignore the similarity between *items*, and focus on the similarity between *users*, based on their interactions with items and their preferences. Notice that these models ignore users' features, and rely solely on the ratings given to the homes browsed. This means that in our toy example, Alice and Jane aren't paired based on common social features like gender or age, but are matched because of their taste in homes.

The real magic of collaborative systems is that they don't need to know anything at all about the items or the users in the catalog: as long as there are users who rate things, we can figure out which users have similar tastes and recommend things to each other. The same model works with homes just as well as with movies, as long as the community casts enough ratings. This also makes collaborative filtering systems easier to integrate into existing platforms, because you don't have to fish around for additional data about each item (say, the movie's director), and can instead relax while users are busy letting you know what they think. Even better, since these recommendations are based on the real-world preferences of other humans, they can be novel and surprising, just like those you would get from a friend.

Collaborative filtering systems work well only when there are many more users than items in the catalog. Otherwise, it's hard to select groups of users with common tastes: large catalogs with many items that have never been rated (or just once) don't play well. For instance, let's assume the hyperbolic case in which your real estate website has just Bob, Jane, and Alice as users, but 500 houses are listed for sale. It's going to be highly unlikely that our lonely three users have seen the same houses, which means that we can't use the clever trick of taste-matching that we've described.

An example of a company that is perfectly poised to exploit collaborative filtering is Netflix, which has tens of millions of users interacting with just hundreds of movies. At the other end of the spectrum, put yourself in Pinterest's shoes: while it also has hundreds of millions of users, the content available for those users to interact with is basically the whole web: hundreds of billions of images. In Pinterest's case, the best approach is using content-based recommendations. This is indeed what the company has done: in January 2017, the company announced that its new deep learning system providing content-based recommendations of pins increased users' engagement by 30% overnight.

Another important point is that collaborative filtering works when you have enough user-item interactions to build your model. If you are a young company with a small history of interactions, you may have to ditch this approach altogether. In this case, all you can do is start off with a content-based system so you can start providing recommendations without a large database of existing ratings. As the user base grows, and the ratings start coming in, you can introduce a collaborative component to provide more unique recommendations. As you'll see in the examples, best-in-class organizations actually mix the two approaches, providing a broad range of recommendations that can appeal to most of their user base.

6.4 Recommendations gone wrong

Many of the AI-based tasks that we have discussed so far have straightforward definitions of performance that we usually translate in terms of *accuracy* to compare models in different situations. For example, we have talked about the accuracy in predicting the sale price of a home, or in classifying dogs and cats in pictures. One could easily adopt the same approach for recommender systems—for example, by setting aside a test set of ratings and measuring the accuracy in predicting them. However, this simplistic approach ignores the complex reality of human tastes and preferences, and the effect they have on business performance.

The first problem involves user experience. Automated recommendations work well most of the time, but sometimes we're left wondering how a ridiculous suggestion came about. Screen real estate is limited, and so is the attention of your users; you don't want to waste it by showing useless products.

As you've seen, most state-of-the-art recommender systems operate on a variety of signals, based both on item features and community ratings. Because human tastes are fairly unpredictable, just one off-base suggestion might have a strong effect on customer trust, making it drastically less effective at driving business value. Depending on the specifics of the community, recommender systems might mistake a trivial feature (like the release year of a movie) for an important one, leading to surprising (and disappointing) recommendations. Also, a strategy can work well for a product category but be completely useless for others: it may be nice to see T-shirts similar to ones I bought, but don't fill my screen with air conditioners similar to my recent purchase (figure 6.7 shows a report from the trenches).

Justin Shanes
@justinshanes

(Follow) ∨

Amazon thinks my recent humidifier purchase was merely the inaugural move in a newfound hobby of humidifier collecting.

8:18 PM · 28 Nov 2016

Figure 6.7   An Amazon user isn't particularly impressed with the recommendations he received.

While user experience is an important consideration, it would be foolish to ignore the enormous impact that recommender systems have in shaping public opinion and discourse. Much, if not all, of the media that we consume (whether news, videos, or social media posts) has at some point been filtered by a recommender system. This means that this technology is uniquely positioned to influence our collective world view. We'll keep the conversation strictly about the business implications of this technology for now, and explore the broader impacts on society in chapter 10.

6.4.1   *The recommender system dream*

Let's end this section with some food for thought. Let's assume that as of now, 20% of Amazon recommendations convert to a purchase. Suppose that one of Amazon's data scientists finds a clever way to improve its recommender algorithm so much that now 100% of the recommendations turn into purchases. Why should Amazon wait for you to go online and shop when it already knows exactly what you want to buy? The easiest solution would be to directly ship stuff to your home, with a nice postcard saying "You're welcome."

Of course, a 100% conversion rate seems a bit too much. Yet, the concept is still valid: theoretically, a threshold exists at which product recommendations become so effective that it will take less effort for users to return what they don't like or don't need rather than proactively shop. In such a scenario, Amazon could simply ship us 10 products, and we would ship back what the model got wrong.

This may sound futuristic, but fashion companies are already experimenting with this model. Think about it: improving a single piece of technology can lead to total disruption of business models and customer purchase habits. This is the power of recommender systems and many other AI technologies.

6.5   *Case study: Netflix saves $1 billion a year*

When Netflix was founded in 1997, it started operating a subscription model for shipping physical DVDs to households, who then returned the media through the mail after watching the movie. Over the following decade, large-scale availability of fast internet access and personal devices allowed the company to transition to digital distribution of content. With a single monthly subscription fee, customers can watch as many movies and TV series as they like, using smartphones, tablets, laptops, or smart TVs.

Convenience and lower prices compared to physical media or cable TV made Netflix one of the fastest-growing companies in recent years. From 2005 to 2018, revenues grew from $682 million to almost $16 billion, and the share price climbed by almost 150 times, going from $2 per share at the beginning of 2005 to almost $300 at the end of 2018. In 2018, the company had 150 million subscribers from more than 190 countries.

The main driver of such explosive growth has certainly been its novel concept of internet-based TV with seemingly unlimited choices. However, new opportunities brought with them new, unprecedented problems. Humans are generally bad at making decisions when confronted with too many choices, and picking a TV show to watch is no exception. Consumer research reports that the typical Netflix user will tune out after only 60 seconds spent choosing a new title to watch.

To face this new challenge, the company heavily invested in recommender systems to help users find compelling content within the extensive Netflix catalog.

6.5.1   *Netflix's recommender system*

While the concept of internet TV popularized by Netflix brought along new challenges, it also brought new opportunities to collect data. Thanks to the on-demand infrastructure, Netflix has access to vast amounts of data about what each user does: what they watch, where and when they log in, and so on.

The most important way in which Netflix's recommendation system interacts with customers is the home page they visit right after logging in (see figure 6.8). While the interface changes depending on the type of device, the starting point is a collection of about 40 rows representing different movie categories, and up to 75 items per row. To decide how to populate this screen real estate, Netflix feeds all the data it collects into a group of algorithms, each specialized in a different recommendation task. Together, these algorithms make up the Netflix recommender system.

At the core of the system is an algorithm called the *Personalized Video Ranker* (*PVR*). The PVR, based on the large amount of data that Netflix collects on users' viewing habits, is used to estimate the likelihood that a user will watch movies in all the different movie categories (for example, Thriller or Drama). The Netflix home page also

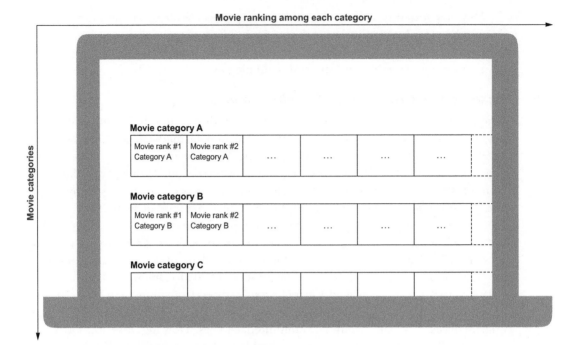

Figure 6.8   The composition of the Netflix home page

has other special rows that have their own specific recommender algorithm. One example is the Top Picks row, which suggests the best content selected across all categories. This algorithm is called the *Top N Video Ranker*. While the PVR is used to find the best movies within a specific subset of the catalog, the Top N ranker looks through the entire catalog.

Another special row is for Trending Now content. Netflix combines personalized recommendations with signals coming from temporal trends. Specifically, the company has found two types of factors that affect users' behavior. The first factor is related to recurring trends, like Christmas or Valentine's Day. The other kind of trend is related to shorter-term events, like elections or natural disasters that generate interest. Even in this case, Netflix doesn't show the same row to every user, but mixes signals from the overall trend with personalized items.

Another distinctive row is Continue Watching. While all other rows focus on content that has never watched by the user, this row is focused on content that the user has begun consuming but never finished. The *Continue Watching Ranker* selects the titles with the highest probability of being finished, using these application-specific features:

- Time elapsed since the last view
- Device
- Point of abandonment (mid-program versus beginning or end)
- Other titles watched since the last view

All the algorithms we have seen so far rely on collaborative filtering techniques to pick their suggestions—inferring the taste of a user by looking at the choices of other users who have similar viewing patterns (and therefore have similar taste). Because You Watched rows are an exception, as they offer content similar to what the user has enjoyed before. This task is performed by the *Video-Video Similarity algorithm*, a content-based recommender system. This algorithm doesn't consider the user's taste: its output is a ranking of similarity between a user's pick and the rest of the Netflix catalog. However, the choice of which movie to use the Video-Video Similarity algorithm on is personalized based on the user's taste.

On top of this series of algorithms, in 2015 Netflix introduced a *Page Generation algorithm* to decide which row to show a specific user in different situations. Table 6.2 summarizes the Netflix algorithms that make up its recommender system.

Table 6.2 Algorithms composing the Netflix recommender system

Algorithm	Use	Criterion
Personalized Video Ranker	Given a movie category, select the movies that a user is most likely to watch among that category.	Collaborative filtering
Top N Video Ranker	Among all the movies in the catalog, choose the best ones for a specific user.	Collaborative filtering
Trending Now	Based on various temporal trends, pick the movies inline with the trend and that the user is most likely to watch.	Collaborative filtering
Continue Watching	Given a collection of movies that a user has started but didn't finish, pick the ones that they are most likely to resume.	Collaborative filtering
Video-Video Similarity	Given a movie, find the movies that are most similar.	Content-based (video similarity)
Page Generation	Select which rows to show for a specific user and in which order.	Collaborative filtering

6.5.2 Recommendations and user experience

The Netflix recommendation system is the primary way customers interact with the service, and as such has shifted to accommodate for the evolution of the platform itself. Throughout the years that Netflix operated by shipping physical DVDs to customers, the watch/rate/watch again feedback cycle that drove customer engagement was much slower than today. Customers would receive new content only once a week, and the weekly shipment had better include something to entertain them on Friday night.

With online streaming, the rules of the game changed: because users can begin and stop consuming any content at any time, recommendations can be more fluid. At the same time, extensive user research has uncovered that the most important driver of retention in the streaming era is the amount of time that customers spend watching content. The goals of Netflix's recommendation system have evolved accordingly. Critics of this (gradual) change suggest that it's overly skewed toward "good-enough" content with the sole purpose of keeping subscribers hooked for multiple hours a day. Riskier suggestions, with a correspondingly higher risk of disappointment, are instead underweighted.

Any algorithm used by hundreds of millions of people worldwide can't be exempt from criticism, and the Netflix recommender system is no exception. While egregiously wrong recommendations often make the rounds on social media, subtler mispredictions also reveal unsolved problems in the domain. Users frequently complain about the model being unable to keep track of multiple independent "moods" and media consumption tendencies. The typical example is a Friday night trash-TV binge affecting recommendation for the following two months.

6.5.3   *The business value of recommendations*

In 2015, Netflix Chief Product Officer Neil Hunt and Vice President of Product Innovation Carlos Gomez-Uribe wrote "The Netflix Recommender System: Algorithms, Business Value, and Innovation" (https://dl.acm.org/citation.cfm?id=2843948). They reported that the Netflix recommender system was responsible for 80% of the hours streamed on the platform, with the remaining 20% coming from the search functionality. However, because users often search for titles that are not in the catalog, a share of that 20% becomes a recommendation problem.

When evaluating the effectiveness of algorithms, Netflix relies on specific metrics. Two of the most important ones are the effective catalog size (ECS) and the take-rate.

The *ECS* is a metric that describes how spread out viewing is across the items in the catalog. The metric has a mathematical formulation, but the main idea behind it is rather simple: if most viewing comes from a single video, it will be close to 1. If all videos generate the same amount of viewing, the ECS is close to the number of videos in the catalog. If the catalog has some movies that are rarely seen and some that are more popular, ECS is somewhere in the middle. The higher this value, the more people are watching all the movies in the catalog, which results in higher customer satisfaction and increased return on the money that Netflix spent to either acquire the rights to distribute the media or to produce it. The goal of Netflix is therefore to maximize this value. To test the efficacy of the recommender system, Netflix tried serving content to users following these two approaches:

- *Using a popularity metric*—Starting with the most popular movie in the catalog and gradually adding other popular movies (black line)
- *Using the personalized system*—Starting with the movie ranking first with the PVR score and adding other movies following the order dictated by the PVR algorithm

Using the personalized system resulted in an increase of the ECS of 400%.

The other key engagement metric used by Netflix is the *take-rate*, defined as the fraction of recommendations offered that results in a play. A value close to 1 means that recommendation will be picked 100% of the time, while a value close to 0 means that the recommendation won't be picked. Netflix tried proposing users a series of recommendations following two approaches:

- Showing the first *N* most popular movies
- Showing the *N* movies that, according to the recommender system, were the best pick for the user

Comparing the two approaches, Netflix noticed that the personalized system delivered substantial improvements over the "most popular" approach, with increases of take-rate of almost four times for the "best fit" movie versus the "most popular" one, and decreasing performance as we move to movies ranked as less fitting.

An improvement of recommendations and of these metrics is tightly related to improved business performance. For a purely subscription-based service like Netflix, the three key metrics to watch are the acquisition rate of new members, the member cancellation rate (churn rate), and the rate at which former customers come back. Hunt and Uribe report that Netflix's efforts on personalization and recommendation have reduced churn rates by several percentage points. Overall, they estimate that the combined effort of all of their recommender algorithms had been saving Netflix more than $1 billion per year, at a time when overall revenues stood below $7 billion.

6.5.4 *Case questions*

- Is a larger product catalog unequivocally better for consumers? And for the business?
- How did the recommendation system evolve with the move from physical media, then online streaming, and finally original productions?
- Besides recommendations, what are other important ways Netflix can use its data advantage when competing with incumbent distribution platforms (for example, TV, theaters, physical media)?

6.5.5 *Case discussion*

Netflix is probably one of the companies that has shaken the entertainment industry the most. Its success was one of the main reasons behind the failure of the DVD rental giant Blockbuster, and its move into original content poses a threat to content producers like TV networks and film studios.

Starting off as an internet-based DVD rental service, the company really started taking off when it pioneered the concept of internet TV. The main alternatives to internet TV at the time were linear broadcast and cable systems. While those two have a predetermined schedule, internet TV puts users in the driving seat, allowing them to pick whatever content they want, whenever they want.

The power of choice seems to be a sure selling point for any business. However, as Hunt and Gomez-Uribe point out, people turn out not to be particularly good at choosing, especially among a vast pool of options. What's the point of having a large collection of movies if users can't find anything they like? This is true not only for the entertainment industry. Think of any e-commerce: what's the value of the catalog of a large brand if users are not buying anything?

The main problem here is that while the offering of a company can potentially be limitless, people have only so much time to browse it. In the case of Netflix, the company reports that most users will give up on their movie search if they don't find anything within 60 to 90 seconds. This means that without helping users in any way, adding elements to a catalog may make it even harder for users to find something they like, and turn out to be counterproductive from a user experience and business standpoint. This is the value of recommender systems: making sure that users are able to find value in your offering with a data-driven approach to suggestions.

One of the key assets of the internet that has been used by Netflix is the opportunity to collect data and monitor user preferences. Think for a second about the difference between the DVD rental version of Netflix and the internet TV one. In the first case, after the DVD was shipped, the company had just one way of knowing whether users liked it: the score that they gave it (if they even bothered to leave one). With the streaming service, Netflix can record much richer information, such as the following:

- When the user watched the movie (time, day)
- On which device
- Did the user watch it all in a single session or pause it several times?

Moreover, Netflix can test different versions of recommendation algorithms and measure their performance according to specific metrics. The abundance of data is a key asset that allowed Netflix not only to drive user engagement, but also to measure its performance and tune its product accordingly.

Summary

- Recommender systems offer personalized recommendations to customers, allowing them to navigate a larger catalog of products or services, and increasing engagement.
- Content-based recommender systems use the past history of users (the pages they visited, the products they bought, and so forth) to recommend similar items from the catalog.
- Collaborative filtering is another approach that finds users within the community that have similar tastes, and shares recommendations between them.
- Recommendation systems are the cornerstone of modern e-commerce and media distribution platforms, as you saw in the Netflix case study.

Part 2

Building AI

Congratulations on finishing the first part of this book. By now, you're quite familiar with the techniques in the AI toolbox. You know about the types of data you can use and which families of algorithms are most appropriate for each. Part 2 will build on your newfound knowledge and guide you as you take your first steps toward bringing AI into your organization.

Chapter 7 teaches you how to select the most promising opportunities for using AI in your organization. The big achievement of chapter 7 is a definition of your very first AI project, formatted into ML-friendly language that's digestible by technical teams. Chapter 8 carries on with this implementation guide by introducing the main ingredients to build any AI project: model, data, and talent. Chapter 9 completes the guide by introducing the processes you can follow to build a successful AI strategy. Chapter 10 is the final chapter, where you broaden your horizons beyond the organization and explore some of the short- and long-term implications of AI for society.

Ready—finding
AI opportunities

7

This chapter covers

- Understanding the difference between an AI vision and an AI project
- Scouting for opportunities for AI in your organization
- Prioritizing and testing your AI project ideas
- Breaking real-world complex AI products into independent ML-powered components
- Translating business requirements into ML tasks using the Framing Canvas

In this chapter, you'll take your first steps into the messy world of AI innovation. Think about machine learning as a toolbox full of various items like hammers, screwdrivers, and saws. After reading part 1 of the book, you know how all these tools can be used to build products. Your next step is to figure out what to build with these tools and how.

This chapter starts by presenting the framework we developed to identify, select, and validate the most promising opportunities for AI in your organization. We'll also show you how to break a complex product into more ML-friendly components that can be built independently. Finally, our Framing Canvas will teach you how to translate the output of all this preliminary work into a description of your project that can be consumed by a technical team.

7.1 Don't fall for the hype: Business-driven AI innovation

The first part of the book followed the story of FutureHouse, a fictional real-estate platform enabling users to buy and sell homes online. We invented fancy AI features and imagined how they could help FutureHouse attract more users. All the while, we tried to explain the technical concepts behind them.

We did *not* focus our attention on the behind-the-scenes story: how did FutureHouse come up with these ideas? How did it choose the best to work on? Unless you work for a tech giant, chances are that your organization is taking its first steps in its AI journey, and you're likely facing these questions too.

This is why we decided to go back to the beginning of FutureHouse's AI journey and imagine the conversations that happened in its meeting rooms. They'll give you a scenario to hold onto while we uncover best practices for introducing AI in an organization. Let's start with a fictional kickoff meeting:

CEO: AI is all over the news these days; it seems like it's going to play a big role in any business. We definitely need to start looking at it before our competition or some tech startup does it first.

CTO: You're right; it's moving so fast, and we need to get ready. I suggest we start investing in infrastructure so we can process all our data. Then we can train our engineers or hire new data scientists and start building AI algorithms.

Marketing manager: Honestly, guys, I think it's a fad. Now it looks cool to say "We use AI," but it will eventually fade out.

AI leader: I agree that some people are jumping on the bandwagon too quickly, but I believe it would be shortsighted to ignore AI altogether. Of course, it's not a silver bullet; we need a strategy to make sure we can get value out of the things AI is great at.

CEO: Mmm, but I'm not sure I'm fully aware of what things AI is great at. There's so much confusion in the media that I struggle to understand what's real and what's hype.

AI leader: This is the first thing we need to fix, in my opinion. How about organizing training for the executive team so we're all more aware of what AI can really do, and then we plan the next steps?

CTO: I think that's a good idea; it would also help the technical team and the business guys learn to work together.

Marketing manager: Okay, let's do this. Maybe it'll help me change my mind about this technology. But I think it's crucial that we start with a strategy. Without some form of AI vision, we'll end up losing time and money.

AI leader: Glad you're all excited about doing AI training, and I definitely agree with you that we do need to have a vision. On the other hand, I think we need more experience to build an AI vision. Training alone won't be enough: we need to start getting our hands dirty before spending time on long-term planning. I suggest that after our training, we go looking for some AI projects to start experimenting with. They'll guide us in defining our AI vision.

CEO: I like where this is going. Do we all agree on getting some AI training and starting to experiment with this technology? I want to have a pilot running four months from now; then we can stop, look at what we learned, and start talking about our overall strategy and vision. How does that sound?

This conversation has many of the elements of organizations that are just starting out with AI. Indeed, parts of this script played out in front of our eyes many times during our consulting experience. Let's look at its most important parts. First, we want you to focus on the *people*. This is a conversation, not a monologue or forced strategy pushed down by someone. To make any fruitful change happen, you need a team, not a lone wolf.

Moving on, this script has four characters with specific characteristics:

- *The initiator*—Someone who starts the discussion. It can be someone who has heard about AI on the news, someone who has experience and sees an opportunity, or just someone who wants to start new projects to advance their career. In our case, we imagined that this person is the CEO of the company. This is an ideal scenario, but the initiator might also be a manager or an employee.
- *The tech guy*—A technologist who has a technology-first approach to AI. In our case, it's the CTO. This kind of person usually tends to look at the technical aspects of AI and forget the business impact. It's important that the perspective of the tech guy is balanced with that of more business-oriented people.
- *The skeptic*—Someone who simply doesn't believe there's any value in AI. Often, these people argue either that AI is just a fad or that it's "just statistics." Sometimes these people will warm up to AI after learning more about it. Sometimes they need to see results with their own eyes. In our case, the skeptic is a marketing manager, but it could be anyone else in the organization.
- *The AI leader*—This is a person who understands AI, hopefully has some experience with it, and makes sure that the technology is used in a way that brings value to the business. They have a deep knowledge of the business and know the core principles of AI to find the intersections between the two. Hopefully, this person can be you after having read this book and gained some experience.

The pivotal element in the conversation is the AI leader. In a couple of moments, this conversation could have taken a wrong turn, leading the organization to a potential dead end in its AI efforts. Luckily for our fictional company, the AI leader intervened and proposed good strategies to prevent this from happening.

The first alarm bell of the conversation is that none of the participants (the initiator, the skeptic, and the tech guy) has enough knowledge of AI to make conscious decisions. In situations like these, the risk is that the organization will follow whomever has the loudest voice, even if they're leading the team blind. To make matters worse, the skeptic might raise objections backed by prejudice and not real knowledge. This is a recipe for disaster.

Luckily, the AI leader proposes to run nontechnical training for all the decision-makers. *Education* is the second focus element of this conversation. Making sure that the "business guys" (CEO, CMO, and so forth) understand AI is important for a successful implementation of AI in an organization. Unless you're in hard-core technology development, the "business guys" are at the helm, and you want them to know how the new ocean they're sailing works.

After the knowledge foundation of the business team is built, the skeptical manager rightfully reminds everyone that AI must be used as a tool that serves the business, and it's important to start from the beginning with a clear *AI vision*: a clear path that defines what it will do in the AI era, how it will help its people work more efficiently, and how it will shape its products to better serve its customers.

Having an AI vision is certainly crucial for any organization, and we definitely encourage everyone to find their own. However, as the AI leader in our conversation points out, your AI vision won't come to you in a dream, or in a PowerPoint presentation put together by a consulting firm. Instead, it's the product of experience and experimentation, successes and setbacks. How can you come up with a comprehensive AI vision if you haven't taken any steps yet in using AI? In our experience, we noticed that companies that neglect experimentation to focus on long-term strategy tend to end in a "brainstorming valley of death": they keep making hypotheses about what they should do, but since they lack action, they miss the information they need to prove they're on the right track. The result is a continuous flow of thinking with not enough action to validate their strategy.

A good way to start building your long-term AI vision is to start focusing on *AI projects*: well-scoped initiatives that use AI to build new products or features, or to optimize existing processes. By running AI projects, you'll gain the experience you need and learn what you don't know yet to form a fruitful AI vision.

AI projects can be more or less complicated (ideally, you start with something small—more on that later), but must always have a solid and measurable business impact. You can see it as a two- to six-month effort: a team from your organization forms an AI task force and builds a single ML-powered product or service, with a well-defined output, a KPI, and an expected business impact. All the industry case studies we've had in this book are AI projects. A perfect example of how an AI project can lead to an AI vision is the first case study in chapter 2, which described how Google revolutionized the way its data center's energy consumption is optimized.

Let's dig deeper into Google's case study to see how it built up to its ML-optimized data centers. The first spark that ignited the revolution was a simple project conceived and led by Jim Gao, one of Google's data center engineers. Gao took advantage of

Google's 20% policy to spend one day of his work week to build a simple ML model to predict one of the key performance metrics of a data center's cooling system, given other operating parameters. This project seemed promising, and the next step was to test Gao's model by simulating the cooling system in different conditions and manually picking the best one.

The next step was to let DeepMind, Google's AI subsidiary, take over. DeepMind refined Gao's model and allowed Google to cut its energy bill by 40%. This wasn't the last step of the initiative: Google was still relying on engineers to vet the algorithm's choices and implement them. The complete vision became closer to reality with the last DeepMind project, which allowed ML to take over the recommendations, with engineers merely checking that nothing went wrong.

The main takeaway from Google's data center experience is that nurturing small projects is the best way to begin forming a broader AI vision. By starting and completing AI projects, you'll learn what you need to know to eventually define a complete AI vision that covers the whole organization, as shown in figure 7.1.

If you look at Google's case, it seems like the final goal of an AI vision should be clear from the outset, and each AI project is simply a part of this bigger plan. This is a convenient lie. Actually, the flow of insight flows the other way. Individual AI projects can (and should) tell you and your organization where there is potential, and where there's a dead end, informing investment and helping you evolve your vision based on what you discovered from each AI project.

In the next section, we'll look into how to design new AI projects, test them, prioritize them, and choose where to focus your energies. Before moving on, we want to warn you of other elements of our fictional conversation that could have been trickier in real life.

First of all, the initiator in our case is the CEO of the company. This is the luckiest case; imagine if the CEO was the skeptic instead. In this case, you'd have to fight to have their buy-in. Another lucky element of our fictional characters is that in our case, the AI leader promptly introduced the two pivotal elements of investing in education

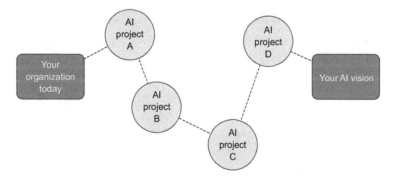

Figure 7.1 Your AI vision will be the product of several AI projects. That vision will rarely follow a straight path: you may have to build several AI projects that go in different directions.

and moving the focus from long-term strategy to shorter-term AI projects. What if you have no AI leader? And what if the skeptic, initiator, and tech guy aren't as easy to convince as our open-minded fictional characters? As we said in the beginning of this section, AI innovation must be done by a team and not by a lone wolf. This means that if you're the AI leader, you'll have to work to bring people on board and enlighten them to help them appreciate the value of education and experimentation.

7.2   *Invention: Scouting for AI opportunities*

Fast-forward two weeks from the previous conversation. Our fictional team has undergone some training on AI and they're now ready to form an AI task force to launch the first projects. This is their conversation after the training:

> *CEO: I really liked this training. I feel like I understand much more about what AI really is and how it can help us. What do you guys think?*

> *CTO: I'll be honest: even if I'm a technical guy, I realized that I had quite a few misconceptions about AI.*

> *Marketing manager: Same. Still, I'd like to see real results before becoming a fan.*

> *AI leader: Awesome, guys; let's start brainstorming a few projects we can start working on to gain momentum, shall we? Do you have any ideas?*

> *CEO: I saw that Google has this new feature on my phone that sorts pictures by their content. What if we help people automatically sort the images of their houses based on the room? This way, it'd be so much easier for sellers to upload images, and for buyers to find what they're interested in (bathroom, kitchen, and so on).*

> *CTO: That's a cool idea. I've also always wondered what we could do with all the data we collect. My team has hundreds of thousands of records of houses sold, and I wonder whether we can use this data to become a financial advisor for real estate investors; I would definitely use that. Maybe the first step can be an algorithm that predicts the price at which a home will be sold.*

> *Marketing manager: On my side, I'm wondering how we can use AI to automate our processes. Maybe we can try cutting costs by automating some tasks that our brokers do, or maybe even think of a super powerful AI-broker?*

> *AI leader: These are all great ideas! I suggest we try to sketch out some projects and prioritize them. What do you think?*

Planning the first step to bringing AI within an organization can be daunting. Where do you start? What if you have no ideas for projects? What if you have too many? Are your ideas good or bad? While creativity and your business instincts are invaluable, it's always useful to have a mental framework to guide your efforts.

There are three phases to go from zero to the definition of a solid AI project:

1 *Invention*—What kind of projects can we build?
2 *Prioritization*—Which project/projects should we start focusing on?
3 *Validation*—Are these projects worth pursuing?

In the preceding conversation, you saw an example of the first step: invention. Our fictional characters are creative and immediately came up with a few interesting and different ideas, but relying on individuals' creativity isn't always a good strategy. This is why we designed a mental model that can help inspire your creativity and business acumen.

The following mental model helps you scout for AI projects that you can then prioritize and validate. It starts by dividing your exploratory space into two parts: within and outside your organization, as shown in figure 7.2.

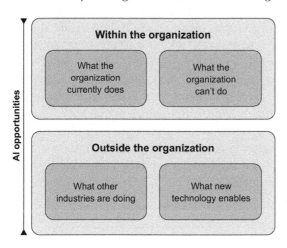

Figure 7.2   Places where you can scout for AI opportunities, both within and outside your organization

As you look inside your organization, you can follow two approaches:

1   Look at things your business does now and ask, "What if I could do it better/cheaper/faster?"
2   Look at things your business does not do right now and ask, "Can AI help me offer this product/service?"

If you look back at the fictional conversation from our real estate team, the marketing manager is doing #1: he suggests analyzing the company's current processes and thinking about how AI can help the organization do better. This approach will typically bring you to incremental innovation projects that will move your organization one step forward, becoming more productive, effective, and efficient.

The second kind of project springs from activities, products, or services that your organization has never built or offered but that could potentially be built using AI. This is what the CTO is doing: he says he would love to have a personal AI-powered financial advisor, and starts wondering how that can be built. These projects are more disruptive and have the potential to define game-changing categories of products. An example is Square Capital's loan eligibility algorithm described in chapter 2. Small business loans have never been a particularly attractive business for banks, as the profit potential is small, the risk is high, and the evaluation process is expensive. Square realized that AI was the key to accessing this almost untouched market.

When it comes to looking for ideas outside your organization, we've found two effective options in our experience: looking at what other industries are doing and at what new technologies are enabling. Our fictional CEO in our conversation is doing both at the same time: he looks at what Google is doing, enabled by new computer vision technology. Most often, looking at other industries means looking at tech companies. If you focus on digital companies in Silicon Valley, most of them are 10 years ahead of the majority of large established organizations in "traditional" industries. This allows us to peek into the future, looking at what AI is capable of doing when applied to large-scale problems and trying to see what can be learned and transposed to your industry of interest. An example is Google's work in its data centers. Google is a leader in deploying AI for its products, and this experience inspired Gao to apply that approach to the new, unexplored field of optimizing energy consumption.

Another interesting example of innovation inspired by new technologies is FaceApp, an app that uses AI to generate highly realistic transformations of faces in photographs. The app can transform a face to make it smile, look younger, look older, or change gender. The app has been on the market for a while, but went viral a few months after NVIDIA released an open source AI model with similar capabilities. Likely, the engineers behind FaceApp took advantage of the new tech available to build a more powerful version of the app, getting the traction needed to go viral.

If you're holding a brainstorming session with your team, the four approaches we just discussed and that you can find represented in figure 7.3 are a good place to start. Likely, at the end of the brainstorming session, you'll end up with some ideas that you'll have to prioritize. In the next section, we'll introduce two high-level concepts that will help you perform a first general assessment of your new ideas' potential.

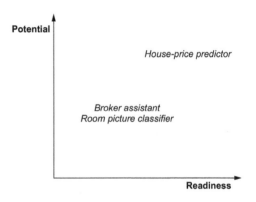

Figure 7.3   Comparison of the project ideas arising from the fictional brainstorming session

7.3   *Prioritization: Evaluating AI projects*

We've all been there: you run a brainstorming meeting with a few people, and everyone has an idea and thinks it's the best one. This may be the case with our fictional gang. Ideally, you'd like to test every idea, but the truth is that most of the time, you'll have to decide what to prioritize. In this section, we'll help you do just that.

The simplest thing that most people usually take into consideration in this phase is the return on investment (ROI) expected from a project: out of all the projects, it seems like a good idea to prioritize the ones with the highest potential. From our experience, focusing solely on a project's ROI is a shortsighted strategy. There's another, maybe even more important variable to consider when selecting a project:

your *readiness*. Without considering how ready you are to tackle an AI project, you risk getting stuck.

For each project, you can estimate how ready you are to face it by considering the following:

- *Complexity*—How difficult is our AI project to build? Can we have a proof of concept in one month, or do we need two years of R&D? (You'll get better at understanding this after reading the next two chapters.)
- *Skills*—Do you already have experience in AI projects and AI talents to implement your new ideas?
- *Data*—Do you have all the data you need?
- *Testing*—What else do we need to test the project? (For example, do we need a mobile app or a website?)

Based on the answers to these questions, you can compare your readiness to solve each of the projects you came up with and make decisions. To make this concept more concrete, we'll tell you the story of a large organization that we helped kick-start its AI efforts.

We'll call it ACME, and let's say it produces a fast-moving consumer good like toilet paper. When we started brainstorming, the company's head of production was extremely pumped about building an algorithm that could improve production planning. The return would have been huge: after all, ACME was producing hundreds of truckloads of toilet paper every day, and being able to have a more efficient scheduling of its production would have improved efficiency, for millions of dollars of potential returns. Yet, there were a few challenges:

- The problem was so complex and had so many variables at play that it required a long, expensive, and risky research effort.
- ACME didn't have any tech talent or AI experience yet.
- ACME's IT department had upgraded its data collection infrastructure only a year earlier, so it only had data on a single year.
- Testing the project was extremely hard: you'd have to change production schedules, which is easier said than done in a company that literally makes tons of goods every day.

Even if the ROI could have been huge, we advised putting this project at the bottom of ACME's list, and picking it up again after they had more data, more experience, and more confidence with AI. Instead, we focused on smaller projects that may have had a smaller return, but that we knew we could deliver in a matter of weeks rather than years. This trade-off between ROI and speed is especially important for a company at the beginning of its AI journey.

If complexity, skills, data, and ease of testing are the four variables to look at to evaluate your readiness to face a project, how do you evaluate the ROI? Sometimes you can be led by your business acumen, but guidelines help.

The potential of an AI project is directly correlated with how much it takes advantage of the two main strengths of AI: scale and accuracy.

Scale refers to the simple fact that there are obvious advantages in letting a computer take over a task. The most common advantages are speed and cost efficiency, but you may have different gains based on your needs. For instance, scale can help you reduce employees' boredom by automating annoying tasks, or improve their safety for dangerous tasks on a production line that you can automate. Obviously, scale is an advantage of every software application, but AI greatly extends what software can touch (for instance, we've seen how traditional software typically can't solve computer vision problems).

Projects that take advantage of scale are typically automation tasks providing a main benefit of cutting costs or reducing time. An example is the cucumber sorting project we introduced in chapter 5 that saved tons of hours for a Japanese farmer.

Accuracy refers to the ability of ML to learn from data and create models with smaller errors than can be achieved with conventional software engineering. Some problems have a direct relationship between accuracy and outcomes, so much so that you can link a dollar amount to each increase in prediction accuracy. An obvious, classic example is in finance: the better you are at predicting the future price of Apple stock, the more money you'll make. The more profit and accuracy are related, the more AI's capability of modeling the world from data will bring positive results for your project.

In this book, you've seen a few projects that were successful mostly because AI allowed making decisions with higher accuracy. One of them was Target's project in chapter 3; the American retailer used data from fidelity cards to target families who were about to have a baby. Probably, the traditional alternative would have been to broadly target all families within a specific age range. It's clear that better targeting accuracy can yield returns that are orders of magnitude higher than the status quo.

The best AI projects take advantage of both AI's scalability and accuracy. These are projects with high disruption potential that can completely change an industry, like the case of Square Capital in chapter 2. Square used small businesses' financial data to decide whether to give them a loan. Square's success is directly tied to how well it can understand how a business' financials impact their ability to repay their loan: the higher their accuracy, the more they'll be successful in managing risk and will give loans to credit-worthy businesses. In Square's case, the scale was actually the main reason for the company's success, as it allowed it to serve the long tail of small business loans that wouldn't be possible to serve otherwise.

Google's data center project took advantage of both AI's scalability and accuracy. Before the AI system was implemented, the data center consumption was optimized by engineers using their thermodynamic knowledge. Even engineers have to sleep, so a scalable system that monitors the plant and makes decisions in real time is immensely valuable. Moreover, Google's algorithms were more accurate than human engineers, contributing to the outstanding results that the company achieved: 40% savings is a lot of money!

If high scalability and accuracy are two key drivers for your project, chances are that you're looking at some very high ROI potential. Once you know this, you can factor in your readiness for each specific project to decide where to focus your energies in the next few months of your AI experimentation.

To clarify what this process looks like, let's take another look at the projects that came out from the brainstorming session of our fictional real estate AI task force:

- *Room pictures classifier*—A feature that automatically sorts pictures based on the room
- *House-price predictor*—A feature that predicts the price at which a house will be sold
- *Broker assistant*—A kind of chatbot that can streamline a broker's job or completely replace them

Let's look at their *potential* first. The room pictures classifier has a high scale factor, as it allows people to upload and sort images in a split second instead of manually sorting them. Yet, the accuracy factor is low: we don't care if our algorithm is better than humans at identifying bathrooms from kitchens, as long as it's good enough.

The home-price predictor has a high scale factor, as right now guessing the sale price is a task reserved for experienced house brokers who are busy and can take days to make a prediction. This project can help clients get a quote in a second rather than days. The accuracy factor is also very high, as the better you are at predicting a house's value, the more you can help clients with their financial planning.

The broker assistant has a high scale value as well, as it speeds up the response times for clients and spares brokers from answering simple questions, helping them focus on the activities they can do best. The accuracy factor isn't very high, though, as brokers are already pretty good at answering clients' questions.

Let's now evaluate your *readiness*. You already have room pictures to build a room picture classifier. Also, the technology isn't particularly hard to build, and it can even be bought from third-party providers. Testing it, on the other hand, requires some plumbing between the model and your current platform.

For the house-price predictor, you already have all the data you need. It's also a *core business data* project with well-structured data, which doesn't bring many technical challenges and doesn't require crazy tech talents (you'll get better at evaluating the complexity of a project in the next chapter). To test it, you also need to plug your website with your model (or some other clever hack—hold on for the next section).

The broker assistant is the most complicated one to build, because as you learned from chapter 5, text data is the trickiest of all the data types. You may have some data for it, and testing it can be done using the Facebook Messenger platform.

If in the Invention phase we came up with a list of projects, in the Prioritization phase we built a first educated guess of their potential based on their scale and accuracy factors, and then sorted them based on both their potential and your readiness to implement it. Now we know that the house-price predictor is the best project to focus on right now, because it has high potential and we're also readier to build it than all the others. Now, let's see how we can validate it and start building it.

7.4   Validation: Analyzing risks

Two major types of threats can undermine the success of your AI project: business and technological threats (figure 7.4). Let's see what each means.

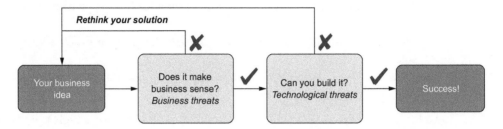

Figure 7.4   On its way to success, your AI project will have to face both business and technological threats.

Business threats are related to the value and usefulness of your new AI-powered product or service as perceived by your customers. Even if your product has amazing tech, it doesn't necessarily mean that people need it or want to use it. In the context of our house-price predictor, there are many potential threats to its business success. For instance, it's possible that customers either don't want it or don't trust it. In both cases, they won't use it no matter how great your technology is. Keep in mind that we use a pretty broad definition of *customer*. Assume that you're building an internal tool for your organization; for instance, an algorithm that helps the quality assessment department of a factory. In this case, the employees of that department can be considered customers, and as "external" customers, they may or may not find your new product useful.

Technological threats are related to the performance of your AI models and what they can deliver for your customers. You're familiar by now with the concept of accuracy of an ML model, and with the fact that no application of ML is perfect. The magnitude and nature of the mistakes that an ML algorithm makes can be acceptable or not, depending on the specific application. For example, safety-critical applications like industrial automation have more stringent accuracy requirements than do most mobile apps.

A good approach to reduce implementation risk is to look at potential threats as if they were a series of assumptions that have to hold for the project to be successful. As you develop your AI project, keep listing any business and technical assumptions you have to make. For our home-price predictor, this is how these assumptions would look:

Business assumptions:

- Customers care about having a quick estimate of the value of their home.
- Customers trust automated price estimates and are willing to stake their finances on their output, no matter how technically accurate they are.

Technological assumptions:

- We have the right data to build the model, and we can keep it up-to-date over time.
- The accuracy of the model is high enough that its estimates can be useful.

Because there's often a way to work around technological roadblocks, we suggest that you test your business assumptions first. There's no fix for a product that nobody wants.

There are ways to test business hypotheses before writing any line of code or collecting any byte of data. For instance, you could add a button labeled Get a Quote for your Home in 5 Minutes and route the requests to human brokers. We can call this validation strategy *concierge AI:* you are using people to test the attractiveness of a new feature that you're intending to implement with AI. This is meant to be a temporary solution that won't scale to millions of users, but you can use it to measure customer interest on a small sample of potential users.

An even simpler test you could run is to insert a fake button labeled Get an Instant Quote for your House that redirects users to a simple web page reading, "We're sorry, this function is coming soon" or "Under maintenance." You can try this trick with a few users, and count how many of them click your bait-button. Faking a function isn't ideal, but it allows you to validate the potential of your AI projects in days (and with basically no budget) rather than months.

The output of such a test can be either positive or negative. If tons of users are clicking your Get a Quote in 5 Minutes button, it's time to move forward to the content of the next chapter and start building that feature! In this case, the AI vision that our marketing manager laid down seems to be fruitful: there's space to transform your real-estate platform into a full-blown financial consultant for real-estate investments.

It's also possible that the results are negative. If not enough people show interest in the new functionality, maybe no one feels like they need lightning-quick home value estimates. In this case, don't despair: your pre-product experiments allowed you to save tons of money and time building something no one wanted. This means that the AI vision of your marketing manager needs to be pivoted to something else, and you can start working on the next AI project in line; in our case, the room picture classifier.

Let's assume that you test the room picture classifier, and it's a resounding success. Its launch has taught you that customers do indeed place a lot of value on a pleasant listing experience. Armed with this additional knowledge, you can decide to focus on creating a real estate platform with the smoothest user experience. By the time you implement and release that feature, you'll be free to jump into future projects with the confidence that all those AI projects have a place in the overall AI vision. Figure 7.5 shows how this flow of experiments and lessons can help you zero in on your AI vision.

Of course, this is just a simplified example. The real world is a messier place, with copious failed attempts and head scratching at every turn. However, the main point still stands: most successful AI-native companies didn't start out with a complete strategy, but rather connected the dots until their AI mission emerged.

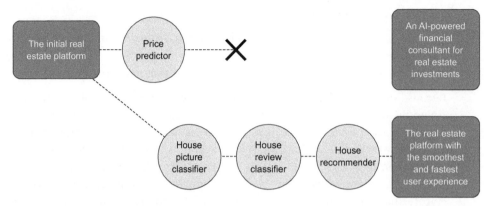

Figure 7.5 The evolution of the AI vision of our real estate platform example, and the different AI projects we discussed in reaching it.

If you want to use AI as a transformative technology, you'll need to transform your mindset too. We encourage every organization, small or large, to adopt a mindset of data-driven experimentation and to invest in AI incrementally, learning from each project and crafting their vision along the way. The best way to do so is to focus on AI projects initially, and try to learn from each. If you're careful to listen, the projects themselves will tell you where your AI vision should head, and they'll be the building blocks of your vision.

Digging deeper into the methodologies of product experimentation is beyond the scope of this book, but you can find many resources online or in other books regarding the topic. Good places to start are *The Lean Startup* by Eric Ries (Crown Business, 2011) or anything by Steve Blank. What we want to leave you with is the idea that there's no free lunch when it comes to developing new products, not even if you use a powerful technology like AI. If you haven't tested your business assumptions and your idea is flawed, even the most powerful AI won't save you.

Once your business assumptions have been tested, it's time to transform your idea into an ML project. This is what we'll do in the next sections and chapters.

7.5   *Deconstructing an AI product*

Let's suppose our real estate company has validated the idea of building a bot to streamline the interaction between users and the platform. The idea is to make the platform feel like a flesh-and-blood broker, so you can ask questions like "What are the houses with three bedrooms in Manhattan's Financial District?" and can receive a curated list of results, as a human broker would do. This is pretty much Apple's Siri for real estate. Since you validated the idea, it's time to go talk to some AI experts to build the product. Here's how a hypothetical conversation would go in this case:

> *Manager: Hey, John, we want to build a Siri for real estate. Is that feasible?*

> *Data scientist (John): Sounds cool, but I need some more information. What's the input data?*

Manager: Our users will directly speak to our app or website and get results nicely presented.

John: Hmm, so this means that the input data is speech, and the output can be . . . anything?

Manager: Yes, the input is speech, and the output is the answer to the user's question. We know that NLP is hard, so we thought we could reduce the complexity by reducing this application's depth: this feature will help users query houses and nothing more. For now.

John: OK, this helps, but I think we're talking about two different AI projects here.

Manager: What do you mean?

John: Well, we can't directly process audio and come up with answers; there's an intermediary step. We first need to transcribe the audio into text; this is a general application called speech to text. Then, after we have the user's question in plain text, we must understand the intention. You can call this application text classification or intent detection. It's doable, but must be broken into in two parts.

Getting your AI project ready to be digested by a technical team might not be as straightforward as you expect. As in some of our examples, many AI-amenable problems are relatively straightforward and can be described as a single idea. For example, the home-price-prediction model is a single product. In other cases, the end goal is more complex and needs to be broken down further before we can talk about translating it into ML-friendly terms. In this case, our manager finds out that his AI project is actually the sum of two well-separated ML algorithms. Now we'll teach you how to understand whether your AI project is a combination of several ML algorithms.

Let's take as an example something that you may be using on a daily basis: a voice assistant like Apple's Siri. Say that we want our personal assistant to do just two things: call people and send messages. Thanks to what you've learned in this book, you know that the first thing to do to tackle any ML problem is to think about the data involved. In our case, the input data is the voice of the person using the assistant, as recorded through the microphone. The output is an action taken by the phone: either sending a message or calling a certain person. Traditional software will take care of performing the action: the only thing we need to achieve is to use speech to decide which action to take, as shown in figure 7.6.

Basically, what we're describing is a supervised classification problem: the input is audio data, and the output is a class. What would the classes be? Theoretically, you should have classes like "text Marc," "call Marc," "send a message to Marc," "answer Marc," and "call back Marc" for each person on your contacts list. It sounds a bit crazy, right? The problem is not only that we have many classes, but also that mapping

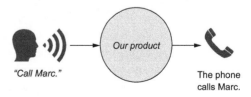

"Call Marc."

The phone calls Marc.

Figure 7.6   Basic scheme of a voice assistant product

audio files to classes directly is extremely hard. In fact, if you tried to remember all the applications we've covered in this book, there's nothing like this.

Let's see what happens if we break the problem into smaller steps, using the technologies covered in this book and starting from the input data. We covered audio data in chapter 3, where we said that it's possible to use deep learning to build speech recognition systems, transforming the audio data in text. This technology is pretty solid and mature, especially for the most popular languages like English and Spanish and for native speakers (we, the authors, still struggle sometimes to be understood by Siri with our Italian inflections). This means that we can be pretty confident that if our user says "text Marc," it's possible to build a system that takes that voice and transcribes it into written words.

After this step, the input data we're dealing with is fundamentally changed: we're now working with text data, and no longer with audio. We still need to understand whether the user wants to call or text, and who they want to communicate with. Let's stay with our approach of breaking a problem into its core components, and focus on the first part. We want to build something that maps a written sentence to one of two actions: calling or texting.

When we covered text data in chapter 5, we extensively described how you can use ML to classify a bit of text into classes. In this case, we can train an ML model with tens of sentences and labels like this:

- "Call Marc" -> call
- "Can you send a message to Marc?" -> text
- "Answer Marc" -> text
- "Call back Marc" -> call
- "Text Marc" -> text

As you may recall from chapter 5, even if there are tens or hundreds of ways to express the same intention, word embeddings greatly simplify our job and allow us to solve this task. Here's where we are now: we know what action the user wants to take, and we're left with understanding which person to pick from the contacts list. This is rather easy, and not an ML task. Because we have the transcription of what the user has said, we can simply check all the words they pronounced and look through their contacts. When we find a name that matches what the user said, we know who to text or call.

As you can see, a problem that seemed impossible can become easy after it's broken into small tasks, each solved with a combination of ML and traditional software engineering. Figure 7.7 is an architectural diagram of the complete product.

You can follow the same process to break down even more-complex projects. For our next example, we'll take an overwhelming case: building a self-driving car. Let's imagine the steps that you would take as a human being to drive your car from your backyard in San Francisco to Los Angeles, and understand what a computer driver has to deal with. As you get into the driver's seat, you'll start breaking down the steps to get to your overall destination: get out of your garage, merge into the freeway, pick a

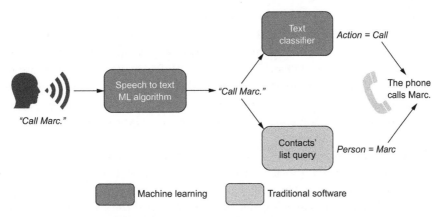

Figure 7.7 A voice assistant can be broken into several components, which convert the user voice to software commands.

radio station, try not to get bored for a few hours, and, finally, pull over at your friend's driveway in LA. Before you can reach your destination, all these high-level goals must be broken down further: which streets to turn into, which lane to choose, and so forth. On top of this, you'll have to observe traffic laws and pay attention to what other drivers are doing so as to not cause an accident.

This intuition will be helpful in starting to break down an AI system to achieve autonomous driving. Road routing doesn't really need AI components, as we can just reuse the same navigation algorithms used in Google Maps. On the other hand, there'll be plenty of machine learning in the *perception* component, which is tasked with figuring out where pedestrians, cyclists, and other cars are in relation to the vehicle itself. Because some of the most commonly used sensors in self-driving cars are cameras, the natural choice is to use deep learning for image classification and object localization models (as we explained in chapter 4). For this component, the input data is images captured from front- and side-facing cameras mounted to the car, and the outputs are the locations of nearby objects.

Understanding that cars and pedestrians are on the street is not enough; you also need to *predict* what other road participants are about to do, so the self-driving car can make the best and safest decisions. For example, other than knowing that pedestrians are on the sidewalk, you also want AI to help you predict whether they're about to cross the street and slow down for safety. This ML task is a bit more exotic than the previous one (classifying objects around the vehicle), so let's see how we would frame it in ML terms. We're not even sure about what we want out of the model: is it enough to have a simple classification such as "likely to move" and "not likely to move," or will the model have to predict the direction of movement too? Both choices are valid (and a real project would probably run both), but the latter is more useful—at the cost of more complexity and training data. From the point of view of the input data, the most relevant bits are probably the location (city or highway), surroundings (street crossing, sidewalk, entrance to an office), and type of entity (pedestrian, cyclist, or vehicle).

All this information feeds into a *decision-making* component that decides how to safely move in the traffic toward the destination. For example, even if the car needs to merge to the left to get onto the highway, it should give up if the lane is occupied and an abrupt maneuver would cause a crash. It probably makes the most sense to implement the decision-making module as a mix of conventional software engineering and machine learning. This is because some of the rules are hard and fast (a red traffic light means "stop"), while many other behaviors are more nuanced (hard brakes are dangerous if a car is tailgating).

Finally, decisions about road behaviors, such as turning right or stopping at a traffic light, must be turned into actions for the steering wheel and gas that actually make the car move (and stop!). This task is not a great fit for machine learning, because we have precise mathematical rules that express how hard the braking action should be based on the stopping distance, the weight of the passengers, and so on. This means that this component is a prime candidate for conventional software engineering.

Figure 7.8 is an overview of all the components that we have talked about, and how they rely on each other to provide such complex behavior. The description is obviously not exhaustive, but breaking down a complex project like this helps you understand how conventional engineering and machine learning can best complement each other. Even the most hopelessly complicated problems can be tackled if you spend the time reviewing data that you could potentially use as inputs and frame the outputs as a measurable value.

Now, self-driving cars are kind of a moon-shot project that is extremely tech-intensive and has some requirements that we can't really argue with: an autonomous car has to drive at least as safely as a human driver, full stop. When you are translating a business opportunity into one or more ML projects, you usually have much more freedom in defining the boundaries of your ML project. For instance, in the case of our initial "Siri for real estate," you could have easily decided to transform the user

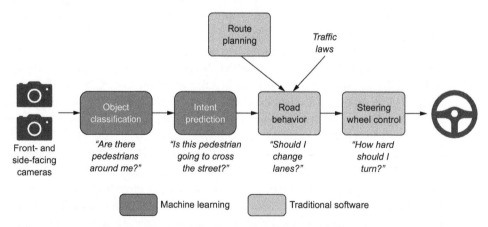

Figure 7.8   A self-driving car is a complex product with many subcomponents, some using AI and others best implemented using conventional software engineering.

experience from speech to text; instead of having people talk to your platform, they could write queries in natural language. This may give users most of the value you expect, completely cancelling half of your AI project (you don't need to build any speech-to-text technology anymore!).

Starting with the idea for an AI project, this section has taught you how to break it into smaller subcomponents that can be tackled individually. The next section completes this preparation work by showing you how to develop an engineer-friendly description of each of these components.

7.6 Translating an AI project into ML-friendly terms

In the previous section, our data scientist John helped us discover that the "Siri for real estate" AI project was more complex than we thought. We then learned that it's important to break AI projects into minimal technological components so they can be a single tech effort. Let's imagine another conversation with John, this time pitching the simpler home-price predictor:

> *AI leader: Hey John, we recently tested a new feature on our website: a house-price predictor. Basically, users input information about their property, and we give them an estimate of the price immediately. We ran a limited test with human brokers that came back after 10 minutes, and people loved it. Now, we would like to build an AI to do it in seconds.*

> *John: Sounds exciting! So the variable we need to predict is the price the home will be sold for, right?*

> *AI leader: Exactly.*

> *John: Based on what? Do you have a rough idea of which features we should use for our ML model?*

> *AI leader: Yes, we interviewed our most expert brokers and listed everything they consider when doing this task. Some features are simple, like square meters and number of bedrooms. Some are more complex, like proximity of public transportation, the reputation of the neighborhood, and so on. I can share with you a report of everything they said.*

> *John: Sounds like we're off to a good start. The best thing to do to build this model is to use past transactions. This way, the ML model will learn the real prices houses are sold for. Do we have such a dataset?*

> *AI leader: Yes, I already checked with IT. We've been collecting information about transactions for the past six years. We have hundreds of thousands of transactions recorded.*

> *John: I think we can build something great out of this. Do we already know what kind of performance we should reach to consider the project successful?*

> *AI leader: We estimate that users will accept a prediction that is ±3% off from the actual price.*

Notice how nicely this conversation unfolds. What makes it so productive is that our AI leader has done their homework: they already knew what the data science team would need from them to build this AI project, and had conducted some preliminary analysis. These are the best ingredients for a smooth cooperation between the business and tech people.

When you're not the person coding AI algorithms, it's easy to forget how they work and to end up in fruitless conversations with engineers, wasting time and getting frustrated. To give you an idea, these are bad starting points for AI projects that would make any technical team cringe:

> *"We'll use internet data to predict what people will buy."*

> *"We'll use our customer data to find the best ones."*

Actually, let us rephrase. These ideas are not *wrong*; they are just too vague. They may be a good fit for marketing material but would make every data scientist sigh, because they don't bring any useful information about the technology. In general, we can say that these are the characteristics that every AI application should have:

- An objective and well-defined output
- One or more datasets that link the input and the output
- A measurable, well-defined success metric

Technical people who are familiar with ML are used to thinking in these terms, and usually can effortlessly frame an ML problem correctly considering these key points. However, from our experience, we noticed that nontechnical people can sometimes get lost in the process, and benefit from a little help in structuring their thinking. For this reason, we designed the *Framing Canvas* pictured in figure 7.9: a five-step tool that you fill out with information about the project you're working on. It will guide you through all the elements needed to kick off a properly scoped AI project.

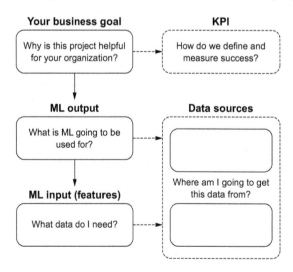

Figure 7.9 The Framing Canvas guides you through the steps necessary to convert a business project into an ML project.

To guide you through the concepts of the Framing Canvas, we'll once again pick up two case studies and an example from part 1, and review them through the lens of the Canvas. The first section is your *business goal*. The business goals of the three projects we'll use throughout this section are as follows:

- *Reduce customer churn*—We covered an example in chapter 3, where we considered a model that identifies which customers are about to cancel a subscription service (for instance, a phone plan).
- *Improve the efficiency of our data center cooling systems*—In the case study at the end of chapter 2, Google used supervised learning to cut its energy bill by 40%.
- *Tackle the small business loan market by offering next-day loans to small businesses*—This is like Square Capital's case described in chapter 2.

For each business goal, it's important to keep in mind its *key performance indicator*, a quantitative metric used to evaluate its success. The first step is finding which parameter will be used to track the ROI of the project. For these three projects, three KPIs can be as follows:

- Customer churn rate (monthly or yearly)
- PUE (power usage effectiveness, a parameter that evaluates the energy efficiency of a data center)
- Percentage of eligible small businesses identified

Now, we need to establish an acceptance threshold for each of these variables. In other words, we need to identify a value for each KPI that represents the minimum accepted performance, below which the product is not ready to ship.

A starting point could be the *status-quo solution*: look at your current solution to the problem, measure its performance on the KPI you identified, and consider that a threshold. If you're introducing a new product or service, you might run financial benefit calculations that tell you the kind of performance you need before the model starts to make financial sense.

Another important point is that you have to choose how to measure your KPI. We've talked about various key metrics and how false positives or false negatives can have deeply different implications for your customers. Let's assume you're developing an AI system that processes brain scans and diagnoses whether a tumor is present. Obviously, a false positive and a false negative don't have the same weight in this situation: a false positive will have a patient go through additional tests that weren't required, while a false negative means that a sick patient is mistakenly sent home to face much graver consequences.

False positives and false negatives also have a different weight in less tragic situations. For instance, if we go back to our three examples, both our churn predictor and our loan eligibility estimator require us to think deeply about which metric we want to optimize for. In the case of the churn predictor, we already talked about the difference between a false negative (a user flagged by the ML algorithms as "OK" but who will actually leave your service) and a false positive (a user flagged by the ML algorithm as "at risk" but who is actually OK). In the first case, you'll miss the chance to try retaining your customer, while in the second case you'll pursue a retaining action that you could have avoided. A cost is associated with both errors, and finding a balance between these is the way to go to decide which is your best KPI.

The same is true for the loan eligibility algorithm. In this case, if we have a false positive, we're giving money to a business that won't repay the loan, and this is a cost for us. A false negative means that we're denying a loan to a small business that would actually repay us, representing a cost opportunity for us (and a missed chance for our customer). Also here, you can do your math and find a sweet spot between both errors that will represent your KPI.

For the sake of argument, let's suppose these are the metrics we find acceptable for our three toy examples:

- Recall higher than 90%
- Prediction within ±3% of the real PUE 95% of the time
- Precision higher than 95%

The *ML Output* block in the left column of figure 7.9 is where ML comes into the equation. Here, you need to be specific about what you want ML to do to help you reach your goals. Going back to our three examples, here are potential choices for the three projects we're working through:

- We'll predict the churn probability for each customer.
- We'll predict the future performance of the cooling systems.
- We'll evaluate the loan eligibility of each customer.

Once you know what your ML algorithm will deliver in order to build your application, you can start thinking about its *ML inputs*. We referred to these as *features* in the first part of the book. Remember that a good starting point for coming up with relevant features is to ask yourself "What information would I need if I had to take over the algorithm's job?" This list may not be exhaustive, and you can always add (or remove) items, especially with the help of a data scientist or after you've gained experience with the model. However, filling in a first draft of these features gives you a starting point to make sure that you're designing something that can be built and can be understood by developers. Here are some examples of how to fill in these boxes with the preceding examples:

- Usage of the product, demographics, kind of subscription
- Outside temperature, humidity, water pressure, data center load
- Cash flow, business size, location, industry

The next and last step is to think about *data sources*. In the previous two steps, you identified the type of information that the model needs to learn from; now it's time to think about where to get this data. You can have as many data sources as needed, and you can draw all the boxes you want in the Canvas to account for all the sources of information you intend to use. For the three examples, here are potential answers:

- For the output, previous unsubscribed customers. For the input, CRM data.
- Logs of the data center appliances and weather data.
- CRM data, transaction data, financial markets data.

The Framing Canvas guides you through a process that produces clearly defined ML specifications that you can pass along to technical people for implementation. In the next section, we'll walk through practical implementations of the Framing Canvas based on the case studies we presented in part 1.

7.7 Exercises

The best way for you to really understand how to frame your AI projects is to fill out the Framing Canvas by practicing on case studies that we have presented throughout the book. We suggest that you apply the Framing Canvas to these three case studies:

- Improve targeting by analyzing customer behavior (Opower case study in chapter 3)
- Automate industrial processes with computer vision (cucumber-sorting case study in chapter 4)
- Help customers choose content (Netflix case study in chapter 6)

For each of these, follow along with what we did in section 7.3, and try to think about what you would do if you were to lead that project. Start by writing down a concise description of the business goal of the project, and define its KPI and the corresponding acceptance criteria. Find an ML-friendly definition of the project in terms of ML inputs and outputs, and brainstorm about the sources of data you could potentially use. By reading the case studies themselves, you should have all the information you need for these exercises. Don't be afraid to walk off the beaten path. At this stage of the process, few choices are wrong, and experimentation is the only way to test them. When you're done, compare your thoughts with our comments and the completed canvas for each exercise.

7.7.1 Improving customer targeting

Let's start with the first practice case study: Opower and its effort to understand the energy use patterns of its customers to refine targeting activities. At first glance, the business goal is obvious: "understand how our customers use energy." This is a worthy goal, which might even make for an exciting startup pitch. However, if you stopped for a second, you'd realize that this is still a fairly abstract statement that needs to be clarified before you can move on. For example, if your business goal is "understand how our customers use energy," how would you even track the outcome and benefit of your model?

In fact, we hope you realized this as soon as you tried defining KPIs for this goal. Instead, try to focus on more-concrete terms for your project. "Understand our customers' energy needs" is focused enough for broad executive-level decisions, but not nearly concrete enough to get an AI project off the ground. What about this instead?

Group customers based on their energy consumption patterns.

Investing the effort to define a more concrete goal will pay off immediately, as you'll find it natural to define an appropriate KPI to track the success of the project. In the case of Opower, an obvious metric would be as follows:

> *Behaviors extracted from energy consumption patterns are accurate.*

Notice that writing down the KPI works as a sanity check on the business goal we found in the previous step. As a rule of thumb, if the goal is not easy to measure, there's still some work to do. Alongside the KPI, you'll also want to define acceptance criteria that will tell you when the project is good enough to ship to customers. Depending on the project, you might take several factors into account when setting these numbers: how critical the project is for the organization, safety and financial risk, and so on. Here's what we think is a good starting point for this project:

> *Fewer than 10% of customers are misclassified when compared to behavioral interviews.*

This is a classic KPI expressed in terms of accuracy of the model. We'll see more composite ways of defining KPIs and acceptance criteria in the following two examples.

At this point in the Framing Canvas process, you should have enough details in your head to start with the ML-specific questions. Based on the business goal we just outlined, the ML output we expect from the model is a *clustering* of energy consumers. In other words, we want the model to group customers with similar consumption patterns together.

When it comes to ML inputs, the obvious candidate for this project is the energy meter data that Opower has been collecting at second granularity. However, we could also imagine adding demographics, weather, and location data into the mix, as they're likely to improve the accuracy of the resulting model. This means that data would be collected through the existing network of energy meters, and supplemented with external data sources bought from third parties.

Figure 7.10 shows the completed Framing Canvas for this exercise.

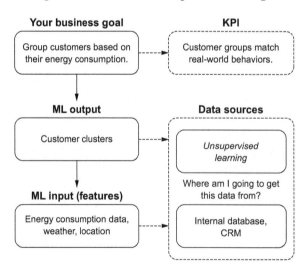

Figure 7.10   The complete Framing Canvas for the Opower exercise

7.7.2 *Automating industrial processes*

Let's move on to the second case study. As you will recall, the project is about automating cucumber sorting in a small-scale agricultural facility. A correct, albeit fairly broad, business goal would be to "increase the efficiency of the farm." However, from our discussion of the previous example, you've learned to be more specific, and thus we propose the following business goal for this project:

Automate cucumber sorting according to quality grade.

A good KPI to go along with this would be the following:

Cucumbers are sorted with no human involvement.

This is a rather ambitious goal, at least as you're spinning up the project. However, it gives us a good base for establishing the acceptance criteria:

Fewer than 5% of the cucumbers are misclassified into a higher-grade class (which is bad for reputation), and fewer than 10% are misclassified into a lower-grade class (which hurts revenue).

Alternatively, we could have framed the KPI and acceptance criteria in terms of human resources saved, or even the increase in the production rate. The ML output for this project is simply going to be the following:

Classification of the cucumber into the quality grades used for sale

This is a fairly standard image classification problem of the sort described throughout chapter 4. For this project, the most obvious candidate for the ML input is also the correct one:

High-resolution color pictures of the cucumbers from a top-down perspective and from both sides

The cucumber weight is also likely to be useful to improve the classification accuracy. The straightforward solution for the data sources is the following:

Pictures collected from cameras mounted in the cucumber selection conveyor belt. Lighting, timing, and orientation can be adjusted for best results.

In conclusion, this exercise is a textbook application of an image classification problem, in which part of the work of setting up the data collection strategy will involve actually setting up the cameras alongside the conveyor belt.

Figure 7.11 shows the completed Framing Canvas for this exercise.

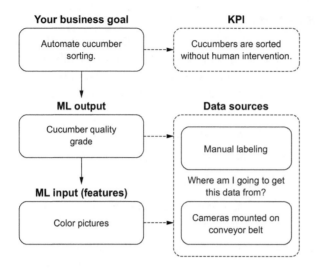

Figure 7.11   The complete Framing Canvas for the cucumber classification exercise

7.7.3   Helping customers choose content

The final exercise is about Netflix's personalized home page of video content. In general, the vision is about "helping consumers find content to watch on the Netflix platform." Here's the business goal:

> *Reduce the amount of time viewers spend choosing what to watch.*

A natural way to find a KPI for this goal is to compare the performance of the personalized home page with a random choice of content on the Netflix platform. This is a great way to immediately track the impact of the project, and one that is going to make it hard for the rest of the organization to ignore your project. This is how this choice looks:

> *Users who browse a personalized home page are quicker to choose which content to watch.*

And here are the corresponding acceptance criteria:

> *Users who browse a personalized home page are 20% faster at choosing what to watch compared to a randomized list.*

In general, you should always try to tie the success of your project to user behavior metrics, as that's the most direct way to measure the impact of your efforts. This concept is widely known as *A/B testing*, because you're comparing a new variant of a feature or product (based on your new AI model) with the status quo. The best candidates for A/B testing are projects for which you have a constant flow of users or items, and thus you can afford to split them into two groups: one that you send to the old system, and one that you send to the new system. By comparing performance across the two user groups, you'll have the best idea possible of how your project is going.

Moving on to the ML Outputs section of the Canvas, we'll need to be specific about how the output of the ML model is going to be used to personalize the home page. Here's the most straightforward option:

A list of the five movies that the user is most likely to enjoy

But keep in mind that, as you saw at the end of chapter 6, a real-world implementation will have several distinct lists to increase its chance of grabbing the attention of the user. We're sure you recognized that this example is a typical application of a recommendation system, which means that the ML inputs are going to look like this:

The viewing history of the target user and all of the others on the platform. Information about the movies (director, year, genre, and so on).

Where are you going to be collecting this data from? We don't have a lot of options here:

Viewing history collected from video servers. Movie information collected from internal databases.

In fact, this example is typical: you won't have to look very far for the data assets, because they're already crucial to the operation of the organization, and thus likely to be collected and managed carefully. Trivially, any video-streaming platform already stores information about movie genres, actors, and directors so that it can use that data when presenting movies to users. It's no big stretch to take this information and use it for machine learning. Likewise, viewing history is also readily available because it must be tracked for accounting purposes (for example, to pay out royalties). Figure 7.12 shows the completed Framing Canvas for this exercise.

We covered a lot of material in this chapter. You learned the difference between a long-term AI vision and individual AI projects, and how the latter helps your organization shape the former. We also explored the attributes that make AI projects valuable

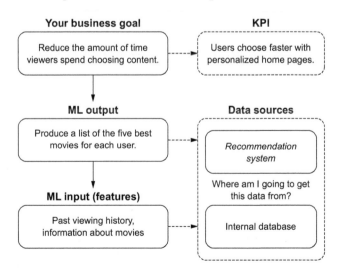

Figure 7.12   The completed Framing Canvas for the Netflix exercise

for organizations, and warned you about the potential risks and pitfalls encountered when rolling out a new project. Finally, we introduced the Framing Canvas as an important tool that helps you distill "business speak" into "machine learning speak."

The next chapter will show you how to take this ML-friendly definition and put together a team and plan that your organization can use to implement your project.

Summary

- Your organization's AI vision is a clear path that defines how it will look in the AI era, how it will help its people work more efficiently, and how it will shape your products to serve your customers.
- An AI project is a well-defined initiative that uses AI to build new products or features, or to optimize existing processes.
- Some complex AI projects need to be divided into independent ML tasks, defining the KPIs, the inputs and outputs, and the data sources you intend to use. The Framing Canvas helps you do that.
- The Framing Canvas helps you phrase the goals and vision for an AI project in ML terms.

Set—preparing data, technology, and people

8

This chapter covers

- Identifying potential sources of data, both inside and outside the organization
- Assessing the quality and quantity of data
- Assembling an effective AI team

This chapter picks up where chapter 7 left off. Now that you know how to use the Framing Canvas to create an ML-friendly vision for your project, it's time to put together the other ingredients that you need. Bringing a project to life requires three main ingredients: the ML model, data, and people. While choosing a good ML model is a task for the technical team, it's your job to recruit them and craft a data strategy so they can get to work. This chapter focuses on how to find and manage data, and how to recruit a team of talented people with the right skills for your project.

8.1   *Data strategy*

One of our goals when writing this book was to make you think critically about data and understand how engineers use it to build ML models. Because data is so crucial, developing a coherent data strategy is critical for the success of any project. In part 1, we talked about data in a way that took for granted that you had it readily available to build your models. You can probably guess that this is rarely the case; this chapter will fill in the gaps and help you understand how much data you need, where you can get it, and how to manage it.

One distinction we have to make is between the data strategy *of your organization* and the data strategy *of your AI project*. When business media or executives talk about a *data strategy*, they're generally talking about the overall company-wide strategy for acquiring, storing, and using data. This strategy is driven by the company's long-term goals and vision for the future.

This book focuses on the data strategy of *your project*, which is specific to a single AI initiative. Having a project-specific focus is better than a broad one for two reasons.

First, developing a data strategy even for a single project forces you to be concrete about the specific data you'll need to collect to build your project, how much you'll need, and where you're going to get it. To develop an AI strategy, you may say, "We'll build infrastructure to collect data from users' interactions with the platform." But to build an AI project, you need to say, "We'll use user clicks, the time they spend on each page, and social shares, and merge that with the CRM data to recommend content." This level of specification helps you think about what you *really* need to collect to build your projects. Someone has to make the decision of what exactly to collect, and if the directions you give the IT team are too broad, they'll make that call for you, often without knowing the business context.

The second (and more important) reason to think about an AI project data strategy is that the organization-wide strategy should be informed by the needs of each AI project that you're planning to pursue. Starting to think about a company-wide data strategy without any experience is like starting to think about your family house when you're single. You simply don't know what you'll need. (Will you have zero, one, or five kids? Which location is more convenient for you and your partner? What's your partner's taste? What can you afford?) Just as individual AI projects help you form a more informed AI vision, likewise building up your data strategy as the minimal set of data needed for the projects helps you make sure you are collecting the data you need.

If you start from AI projects instead, building the organizational data strategy will be a simple exercise of combining the experience that you gained through the implementation of each project (as shown in figure 8.1).

To build the data strategy for an AI project, you need to know where to get data and how much you need. The next two subsections dive into each topic.

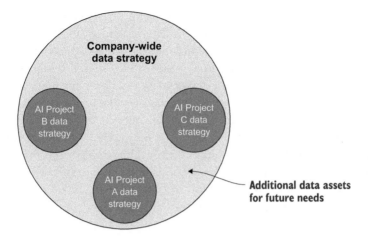

Figure 8.1 The organizational data strategy combines the needs of each individual project (plus some incidentals thrown in for the future).

8.1.1 Where do I get data?

Data has been a fundamental concept throughout this book. We've covered various kinds of data: structured core data, images, and sound and natural language. If you want to build an AI project, an even more important distinction will affect you: data you have, and data you don't.

Let's start by assuming your organization has the data you need to build your AI project. Because this data is produced and owned by your organization, we'll call this *internal data*. Chapter 2 already covered the value of a specific kind of internal data that we called *core business data*: data with a direct impact on the top or bottom line of the organization. For our real estate platform, this can be house-price data; for Square Capital, it's the transactions of their customers; or for Google, the consumption data of its data centers (basically, its only variable cost).

Your organization likely also produces data from business processes that may not be directly linked to your main sources of income or of costs. We'll call this kind of data *ancillary data*. In our real estate example, house pictures and house reviews can be considered ancillary data: still interesting and useful, but not as much as the characteristics of the houses on sale and their selling prices.

As another more concrete example, let's consider an e-commerce platform like Amazon, Zappos in the United States, or Zalando in Europe. In their cases, core business data would be the purchases of each customer, as they're directly correlated to company revenues. Ancillary data may be the pages that a customer visits, the emails opened, product reviews, and so on. You can build amazing projects with ancillary data, but it's most likely not as impactful as what you can build with core business data.

Before moving on, we want to warn you that owning a dataset doesn't mean you can use it pain-free. You may be planning to use customer data but don't have the permission to do so—whether customers denied their permission or, as often happens, your privacy policy wasn't written to account for the use you're planning for now. Even if you do have permission to use data, in our experience, most people underestimate the time and challenges of going from "we have the data" to actually bringing it into the data scientist's laptop, ready to be processed. Even if you're 100% sure that your organization has the data you need for a project, our heartfelt suggestion is that you try to account for everything that can potentially slow you down in actually using it.

In one project we worked on, the legal department of a company made it so difficult to export the data we needed that we literally had to take a plane, get into their building, plug in our laptops, encrypt the data, and bring it home on a hard disk. In another project, we knew the company had the data we needed, but we all struggled to understand what the variables in the dataset meant. The problem was that the person who designed the data collection processes had retired, and we had to spend a whole month running interviews to understand the data we were looking at.

Let's now cover the case in which you don't yet have the data you need for a project. You have three options:

- Start to collect it and wait until you have it.
- Find open data or scrape it from the internet for free.
- Buy it from providers.

The first option is the slowest; sometimes it's also the most expensive, but in some cases you may not have any other choice. Let's suppose you run a brick-and-mortar clothing shop and don't have a loyalty card system or any other way to track who buys what. If a customer walks in, you don't track that his name is John and he just bought some Nike Air Jordan sneakers, size 10, for $129. If you haven't stored this information, do you think any other company has it? Obviously, in this case, your only option is establishing new processes to collect this information and then waiting until you have collected enough data.

On the other hand, sometimes your projects need data that you either can't collect or don't want to make the effort to collect. The second option in this case is to use open data.

It's amazing how much free data you can get from the internet. An example is the open data that governments often open source, which you can freely use for your projects. For instance, you can use income data for your country to focus your marketing on the wealthiest areas. Here are some other great places to look for open datasets:

- *kaggle.com*—A website where companies or individuals can host ML competitions and upload datasets.
- *arxiv.org*—A free repository of scientific papers. As researchers collect new datasets, they write and release scientific papers to present them to the scientific community and often release their datasets as well.
- *github.com*—A repository of open source code.

When using third-party datasets, you should be concerned about the quality of the data and legal issues. Many of these datasets are produced on a "best effort" basis and collected as needed to support new algorithms or fields of application; often data quality is not guaranteed. Also, many publicly available datasets are released with a noncommercial license, meaning that they can't be used for business purposes; always check that you can use an open dataset for the purposes you intend.

The third option is buying data from providers. This strategy can sometimes be extremely expensive, and can also put you in a dangerous position as you may end up depending on these providers forever. Before deciding to go this route, we suggest you first spend enough time evaluating the associated long-term costs and determining whether multiple providers exist to buy it from. If there's just one, you need to find a strategy to protect yourself in case they go out of business or their business strategy changes and they stop selling you their data.

In both cases, we encourage you to think critically about datasets that come from outside your organization. By definition, if some data is openly available—for free or for money—it means that everyone else can get it too. Often, projects based on external data sources will have a harder time on the market because they can easily be replicated by competitors. Some of the strongest AI projects are built on a foundation of proprietary datasets that are hard for others to reproduce.

To sum up, the walls of your organization (or the virtual ones of its data center) make a major difference in the data strategy of your AI project, as shown in figure 8.2. If data sits within the boundaries of your organization, you have a unique and highly valuable dataset you can use. Otherwise, you have to either get it for free or buy it. In both cases, take into account the liabilities that come with those options.

Of course, you can combine internal and external data. Actually, this is often a good idea. An example is our real estate house-price predictor: we could have used free government data on the income of each neighborhood to improve the model. You can even use data from OpenStreetMap or from Google Maps to check the presence of services and public transportation in various neighborhoods, adding another dimension to the house-price predictor.

For a project we built for a large organization, we used all kinds of data. The company had sales data from its stores, but we wanted to see correlations between sales performance and demographics, so we gathered free census data. The census data that was freely available was OK most of the time, but for some cities we needed a more fine-grained picture of the population. We then turned to specialized external providers and integrated their data as well. Notice that whereas sales data is updated

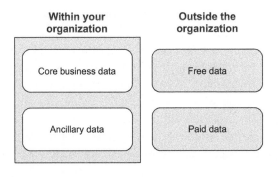

Figure 8.2 The digital or physical walls of your organization define the boundaries between types of data: core and ancillary data within your organization, and free or paid data outside of it.

each day, demographics change much more slowly, so it wasn't a problem to rely on external sources.

Wherever you're getting your data, a piece of information can make or break your project: labels. Remember that if you're training a supervised learning algorithm, the computer needs to learn to produce a number or class (label) based on other numbers (features). Most of the time, you can work around missing features, but you may be in big trouble if you don't have labels. In other words, when it comes to data, labels are way more important than features. Let's use the example of the home-price predictor. Our label is the price a house is sold for, and our features can be the square footage, number of rooms, presence of a garden, and so forth.

Let's assume that when you designed the interface for your real estate website, you didn't think to add a field that lets users specify whether their home has a garden. Therefore, you don't have that information in your database and can't use it to build the model. However, you still have other relevant features included in the house listing form, including the square footage, number of rooms, and location. Even without the "garden" field, you're likely to still be able to build a decently accurate model.

On the other hand, if you forgot to ask users about the sale price, you'd be completely lost. Without labels, there's no way to build a supervised learning model.

Labels can be collected in three ways:

- Naturally
- Hacking
- Paying

Natural labels are generated by your business processes. For instance, if your real estate platform asks clients to input their home sales price as they delete their listing, you'll naturally get the label. Google was naturally saving data on its data centers' energy performance because Google was running them. Amazon stores in a database everything you bought. All this information is stored to make the business run, and can be used as labels if needed.

Sometimes, labels aren't as easy to get, but you can still find clever hacks to get them. An example is what Amazon does with product reviews. When you write a review about your love for your new vacuum cleaner, you also add a star rating (say, from 1 to 5). The score can be used as a label for a sentiment analysis system. Basically, you're giving Amazon both the input (the text review) and the label (the star score) it could use to build sentiment analysis technology, for free. Another example is Facebook, which in the early days asked users to tag friends in pictures by clicking their faces. Facebook could have simply asked you to write who's in the picture, but by clicking a face, you give Facebook an approximate label for image recognition algorithms. Finally, it probably occurred to you that while registering for a new internet service, you've been prompted with a tedious task, like finding cars in images to prove you're human. This service is called Google reCAPTCHA, and by now you probably guessed what it's used for: you're giving the company labels for its ML algorithms, for free.

In some cases, your only option is to pay people to label examples. A common pattern for labeling data is to use a crowdsourcing platform such as Amazon Mechanical Turk, which gives you on-demand, paid-by-the-minute access to a temporary workforce distributed across the globe. With Mechanical Turk, the only thing you can count on is that contractors will have an internet connection: because they're usually untrained, you have to prepare training materials and a labeling interface the worker can use to choose the correct labels for the training examples. Figure 8.3 shows an example of two labeling interfaces for collecting labels for image classification and object localization tasks.

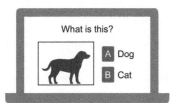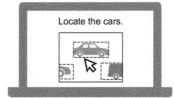

Figure 8.3   Labeling interfaces for image recognition and object localization. Choices can be made using keyboard shortcuts to increase data entry speed.

In general, crowdsourcing platforms are good for labeling tasks that don't need much training. If you're working on a project that requires high-level human reasoning (say, finding cancer cells on microscope scans), you would be better off putting together your own highly skilled workforce.

Table 8.1 summarizes the cost and time required to collect labels for the three labeling strategies.

Table 8.1   Cost and time requirements for the three labeling strategies

Labeling strategy	Cost	Time required
Natural (free) labels	Zero—You are collecting these labels already.	Zero—You already have them.
Hacked labels	Low and fixed—You just need to set up new data collection processes.	Depends on your traffic.
Paid labels	High and variable—You pay based on the number of labels you want.	Depends on the time needed to label an example and the number of labelers you have.

Once you have a clear view of where to get the data you need, the next step is figuring out how much you need.

8.1.2   How much data do I need?

In our experience as consultants, we've often seen people falling into the trap of *big data*. It's reassuring to think that having a lot of data is a silver bullet to unlocking amazing opportunities. But as you'll see in the coming sections, data *quality* is often more important that data *quantity*.

The amount of data that you need to build an AI product strongly depends on the product itself. So many variables are at play that giving precise rules like "you'll need data from 10,523 customers to build a 93% accurate churn prediction model" is just not possible in practice. What we can give you are guidelines that can help develop your intuition about the data requirements for the most common types of problems you'll find in the business world. We think it makes sense to divide our presentation according to the type of data your project will be dealing with, just as we did in the first part of the book.

Let's first talk about projects that require *structured data*, such as predicting home prices (chapter 2) or customer churn (chapter 3). You need to consider three factors:

- Whether the *target* (the thing you want to predict) is a number (*regression*) or a choice (*classification*)
- For classification problems, the number of classes you're interested in
- The number of features that affect the target

Let's start with features. Remember that structured data is the kind of data you're looking at when you open an Excel sheet, and it's organized into rows and columns. A good way to think about data requirements is to picture that, if you could view your dataset in a single screen, you'd want the data to look very thin and tall, as shown in figure 8.4. You want many more rows than columns. This is because rows indicate examples, while columns indicate features that the model has to learn from. Intuitively, the more information a model has to learn from (the more features), the more examples it needs to see in order to grasp how the features influence the target (which means more rows).

If you don't have enough examples and too many features, some of the columns might even be useless or misleading! Take, for example, a home-price dataset like the one in chapter 2. Adding a column with the zodiac sign of the seller is unlikely to improve the accuracy of price predictions. However, ML models can't draw common-sense conclusions a priori: they need to figure them out from the data. As long as you have enough rows (examples), most families of models are indeed able to do so, and will rightfully "ignore" the zodiac sign column. However, if you have too little training data, the model would still try its best to estimate how the zodiac sign affects the price, reaching numerically correct but misleading conclusions.

As an extreme example, imagine that the only $1 million home in the dataset was sold by a Gemini. Surely, this doesn't mean that price predictions for homes sold by Geminis should be higher than those for homes sold by Aries. Most models will be able to avoid this mistake if the dataset contains many million-dollar villas (a dataset with a lot of examples), because buyers will have many different zodiac signs and their effect can be correctly estimated. However, if you don't have many examples, the model could "think" that the zodiac sign is the driver of house value.

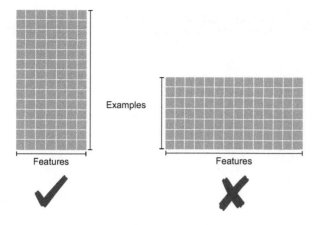

Figure 8.4 The dataset on the left, which has many examples and a few features (tall and thin), is a good dataset for ML. The one on the right, which has a lot of features and a few examples (short and wide), is not a good dataset for ML.

Let's now go into the specifics of classification or regression problems. In classification problems, you're trying to predict whether an example belongs to two or more classes. The first classification examples in this book were as follows:

- The loan eligibility algorithms of Square in chapter 2 that were giving customers one of two classes: either eligible for a loan or not eligible
- The churn prediction of chapter 3 that was labeling a customer as either about to abandon a service or not

Assuming you have a modest number of features (let's say 10), you should budget at least 1,000 examples for each class that you have in your problem. For example, in a customer churn model that has only two classes (loyal versus nonloyal), you might want to plan for at least 2,000 examples. Intuitively, the more classes the model has to deal with, the more examples it will need to see in order to learn how to distinguish all the classes.

It's harder to give similar rules of thumb for regression models because they can model more-complex scenarios and phenomena. Many regression models are based on *time-series data,* a special kind of data that describes how measurements or numbers evolve over time. An example is Google's data center case study from chapter 2 that collected environmental measurements throughout the day. Another example you may be more familiar with is financial data (for example, the price of stocks). You can see what time-series data looks like in figure 8.5.

In time-series data, the number of data points you collect is not as important as the time span along which you collect them. The reason is pretty intuitive: suppose you are Jim Gao, the Google data center engineer from chapter 2, and you're collecting one data point per second from your DC air-conditioning system. If you collect data from January until March, you'd have almost 8 million data points (3 months × 30 days per month × 24 hours per day × 60 minutes per hour × 60 seconds per minute). With so many points, you may think you have a great dataset, and indeed your models may be very accurate . . . for a few days.

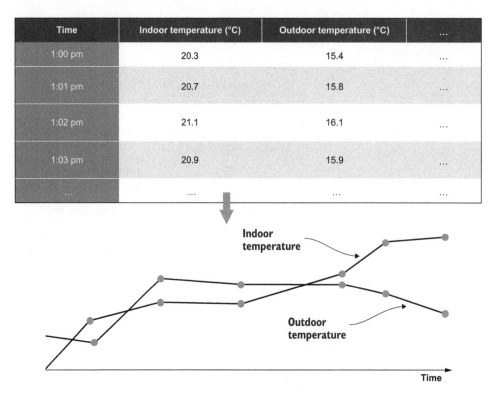

Time	Indoor temperature (°C)	Outdoor temperature (°C)	...
1:00 pm	20.3	15.4	...
1:01 pm	20.7	15.8	...
1:02 pm	21.1	16.1	...
1:03 pm	20.9	15.9	...
...	...	...	...

Figure 8.5   Time-series data looks like a stream of measurements taken over time (for example, of temperatures). Values to the right of the plot are newer than those on the left.

But what happens as summer gets closer and temperatures rise? The model doesn't know how the data center behaves during the hottest months of the year because it's been trained using only winter data.

Talking about *AI for media*, the simplest image classification tasks (think cats versus dogs) need roughly a few hundred examples for each class (the famous ImageNet dataset has roughly 700–800 images per class). If you were to choose classes that are more similar to each other (like breeds of dogs), the number of required samples shoots up into the thousands because the model will need more examples to assimilate the subtler differences. If you're taking advantage of transfer learning, you're starting your training from an existing model trained on huge datasets like ImageNet (as explained in chapter 4), and you can have good performance in the low hundreds of images (or even tens for very simple tasks).

Giving similar guidelines for natural language applications is more difficult, just because the landscape of tasks is more varied. For simpler tasks like sentiment analysis or topic classification, 300–500 examples for each class might be enough, assuming you're using transfer learning and word embeddings.

Now that you have guidelines about *how much* data you should be thinking about collecting, you should understand that not all data points have the same importance when training models. Adding especially bad examples might even backfire and reduce the overall accuracy of the model. This is the subject of the next section.

8.2 Data quality

Much of the discussions about AI in popular media suggest that AI-based decisions are inherently more rational than humans because they're based on math and data. In other words, they insist that AI is data driven and thus immune from human biases and prejudice. The three stories in this section aim to convince you otherwise.

Machine learning is all about finding patterns in data, and training on biased data will cause the model to make biased decisions. What do we mean by *biased data?* You already saw an example in chapter 4, where we told you about researchers collecting a dataset with pictures of huskies and wolves, and setting out to build a model to classify the two. At first glance, the model was doing great, but researchers discovered that it did so only because it was relying on the fact that all pictures of huskies had snow in the background, and those of wolves didn't.

It turns out that even standard datasets are affected by the same problem: neural networks like to hallucinate sheep when presented with pictures of grasslands with no sheep present, as shown in figure 8.6. Likewise, if you show a neural network an image of a kid holding a lamb, it will most likely classify it as a dog. This happens because the training datasets are biased: sheep appear only in green fields, and most animals held in a human's lap are dogs. Because ML models are mostly pattern-matching machines

A herd of sheep grazing on a lush green hillside
Tags: grazing, sheep, mountain, cattle, horse

Figure 8.6 Neural networks tend to associate pictures of green hills with sheep, because that's where most of them appear in the training dataset. (Source: https://aiweirdness.com/post/171451900302.)

on steroids, the model may have learned that a "sheep" is just a tiny speck of white on a mountain landscape, and a "dog" is anything with four legs close to a human.

The underlying problem is that the training set is *incomplete*: it's missing important combinations of factors that would help the model in its (autonomous) quest to find the most important characteristics in the image. For instance, the problem would be solved by adding images of people holding other animals, and other images of sheep in unusual places (on a beach, in a house, on a boat, and so forth). In this way, the models will learn to separate the sheep from its context and correctly "understand" what a sheep really is.

Let's start talking about another subtler and more insidious case of data bias. The goal for this project was to create a model that could automatically screen patients for skin cancer by looking at photographs of their bodies. It turns out that when dermatologists take pictures of sick patients, they often place a ruler alongside the cancer for scale. This means that most photos of sick patients also had a ruler in the frame. Needless to say, the model learned to pick up the presence of the ruler, as that's much easier to recognize than small patches of darker skin. Lacking any ability to recognize that a ruler was a confusing hint, the model was completely useless on future patients.

We like this case because it proves how seemingly insignificant details can affect the quality of the training dataset, and thus of the resulting model. In other words, today's AI models have such a shallow understanding of the world that their mistakes can be devastatingly dumb.

In the case of cancer patients and rulers, at least an experienced engineer would have been able to find and pinpoint the problem. However, some sources of bias are harder to spot. Say that all pictures of sick patients were done in a room with fluorescent lighting, and all those of the healthy subjects in a room with LED lights. The slight color change in the pictures is hard to pick up with the naked eye but is an attractive hint for any neural network. As a result, you're left with a potential disaster: you think your model has learned to spot cancer, but it actually learned to classify LED light.

The common theme of these first two stories is that training data has a direct impact on the behavior of your model. So much for AI-based impartiality and data-driven rationality! In both cases, the problem was a lack of *contrarian* examples in the dataset (say, sheep walking on asphalt, kids cuddling little tigers, and skin cancer under different light conditions). However, data quality can also suffer because of deeper incorrect assumptions. Let's see how in the final example.

During World War II, both the Allies and the Axis powers were constantly looking for ways to improve their fighter and bomber planes. One of the most important goals was to make aircraft lighter so they could fly farther. Because planes need engines and fuel tanks to fly, cutting weight meant removing armor that could protect the vehicle during enemy fire, potentially saving the pilot's life. The engineers were wondering about which areas in the plane were the most vulnerable and thus needed heavier armor.

The military started examining the frame of damaged planes and produced images like figure 8.7. It seems that the fuselage and wings suffered the worst damage. This means that the airplane designers should reinforce the armor in those hard-hit areas, right?

Counterintuitively, this is exactly the wrong thing to do! We're looking only at the planes that made it back home, and not at those shot down by the enemy. All this could teach us is that contrary to what we thought in the beginning, planes can sustain heavy fire on the fuselage without losing the ability to fly. In fact, designers ought to be putting the heaviest armor on the *engines*, even if they found just a few bullet holes there, because that meant that planes shot on the engines were crashing.

Compared to the previous two examples, in which data was simply unbalanced or incomplete, this story teaches us that data col-

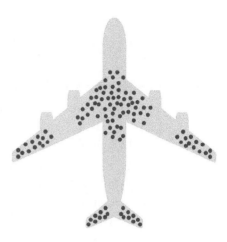

Figure 8.7 During World War II, Allied planes returning home after a mission were often heavily hit on the wings and fuselage.

lection can be plain misleading, and lead us down a completely incorrect path. This phenomenon is commonly referred to as *survivorship bias*, and you'll find it's often applicable outside AI too. In general, anytime you're selecting subgroups of items or people, you should be on the lookout for survivorship bias effects that will thwart your efforts. Say you're constantly surprised by how many 20-year-old cars you see driving around. You might be inclined to think that newer models would never last that long, as cars today are breaking down all the time. Survivorship bias suggests you should also count old cars that are already sitting in a junkyard after breaking down years ago. You won't see any of those driving around, and thus the numbers will be skewed.

These three examples have shown you ways in which your data collection efforts might lead you to miss the forest for the trees and end up with ineffective models. Don't despair, though; these are some of the most active areas of research today. In the meantime, the best antidote is to follow a *deep and wide approach*. *Deep* refers to efficiently collecting the bulk of the data that you need to build an accurate model. *Wide* is about complementing the deep with a (likely smaller) dataset of unusual and tricky examples that you can use to double-check the results.

Remember: the main challenge is that we have limited tools to analyze how AI models make their decisions. Just as scientists didn't know much about bacteria before the invention of the microscope, ML engineers have to guess what the model is doing. Because the only way to learn how the model would react to a specific input is to run it, models must be tested and validated on realistic data. As a practical example, self-driving car companies collect data throughout all four seasons of the year and times of the day to make sure their object detection models can reliably detect pedestrians no matter whether they're dressed in shorts or coats. In other words, make sure that you're mixing up things a bit and snapping those pictures of huskies at the beach.

Now that we have talked about the main aspects of a data strategy, the remainder of the chapter deals with a less technical, albeit equally challenging, type of resource: humans.

8.3   Recruiting an AI team

This section guides you through the process of recruiting a team with the appropriate mix of talents and experience needed for the implementation of an AI project. It's helpful to talk about three main categories of skills:

- *Software engineering*—Extracting data from various sources, integrating third-party components and AI, and managing the infrastructure
- *Machine learning and data science*—Choosing the right algorithm for a specific problem, tuning it, and evaluating accuracy
- *Advanced mathematics*—Developing cutting-edge deep learning algorithms

You may be tempted to find a person who has all of these skills, a figure often referred to as a *unicorn*: it basically doesn't exist. However, you *can* find different people (or teams of people) that excel at one or more of these skills.

In this book, when talking about technical implementation of AI projects, we often refer to the mythological figure of the data scientist. Defined by the *Harvard Business Review* in 2012 as "The Sexiest Job of the 21st Century," every company is looking for one, but no one can describe exactly what it is.

The problem is that in many people's minds, a data scientist is a jack-of-all-trades: someone who can solve any kind of problem that involves data, ranging from simple analysis to the design of complex ML models. On top of that, we often want the ideal data scientist to show business acumen too. The expectations of what a data scientist can do are so high in theory that they're often unmet in practice.

We recommend that you look for a data scientist in the following cases:

- You are not yet sure about the direction that your organization will take. Having someone with a broad skill set can help you be flexible until you have a clearer direction.
- You don't have extremely complex needs on the technical side. If all you need is someone who can analyze medium-sized datasets (up to a few gigabytes) to make business decisions and build some ML models, people who call themselves data scientists are usually a good fit.

In case you are specifically trying to build an AI team that can tackle more-complex AI projects and also deploy them to be used in the real world, you probably want to start recruiting people who are specialized in different skills. We can identify three major categories of talents, each with its own skill set:

- Software engineer
- Machine learning engineer
- Researcher

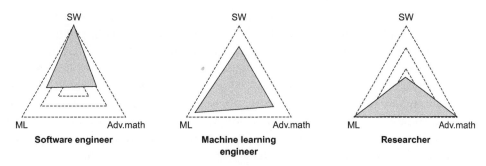

Figure 8.8 The typical software engineer, ML engineer, and researcher have different levels of skills across software engineering (SW), machine learning (ML), and math.

Figure 8.8 helps you visualize how each of these roles has a different composition of the three core AI skills: software engineering (SW), machine learning/data science (ML), and advanced math.

Let's see how each one of these figures fits in the data/model/infrastructure breakdown of AI projects. *Software engineers* work mostly on the infrastructure side of the project, setting up the systems that fetch data (from internal or external sources) and integrating the ML model into your existing products or services.

There's also a special kind of figure referred to as a *data engineer*. This person is usually hired when you're dealing with massive amounts of data (many terabytes), and even computing the simple average of a database column can be a challenge. Because you'd probably use a data engineer for the infrastructure of your project but not for its ML models, we'll consider them a special kind of software engineer dealing with extremely large datasets.

A *machine learning engineer* has specialized knowledge of AI and machine learning. They know the contents of part 1 of the book by heart (and much more), and their job starts with cleaning and analyzing the data and ends with choosing the most appropriate model for your AI project. They will also take care of writing the code to train the model and evaluating its performance. The outcome of the work of the ML team often is a trained model, together with a description of its accuracy and the data that was used for training. ML engineers handle performance improvements to the model, and will guide your efforts in collecting more or better data. Although some ML engineers also know how to deploy models effectively, that's usually not their favorite activity. Out of these three figures, ML engineers are the ones who are most similar to our previous description of data scientists.

Finally, the *researcher* is the most academic role of the three. They can use their in-depth research experience in a specific niche to find solutions to novel problems that are not well explored in industry yet. Of the three components of the project, the researcher sits firmly in the *model* camp, where they can use their knowledge of the state of the art to build AI algorithms that push forward the frontiers of what's possible. Most researchers are great at building models, but lack software engineering skills and are usually not interested in deploying their creations or figuring out all the bugs.

The main difference between a researcher and an ML engineer is that the former is a scientist, while the latter is an engineer. The distinction might seem arbitrary, but they have very different skill sets. If your project is about any problem or algorithm that we have explained in this book, you want an ML engineer. All the research work has already been done for you, and you just need somebody who understands it and can apply it to your specific problem. If you're venturing outside the realm of industry-standard problems and data sources, you want a researcher at hand who has a deeper understanding of the theory and can come up with innovative approaches to novel problems.

That being said, the skill sets of these three kinds of people definitely overlap and might even be interchangeable in some cases. You can look at the three figures as different kinds of chefs. If you want to eat a basic dish, probably any kind of chef can pull it off. As the level grows higher, chefs start to specialize in specific cuisines or disciplines, and in a Michelin three-star restaurant, you may find a pastry chef, a sauce chef, a fish chef, and so on.

Let's see who could have built some of the projects we designed in this book. The price predictor is a pretty standard ML project (there are also many examples online), so you may go with a data scientist or machine learning engineer. The same goes for the churn prediction and upselling classifier projects we talked about in chapter 3. Chapter 4 covered media data, which is a bit trickier. If you have a lot of users using your platform at the same time, you may need a software engineer to make sure your infrastructure is stable and can withstand the load of hundreds of images that need to be processed at the same time. The algorithm is a simple classifier, and probably any skilled ML engineer can pull it off. In chapter 5, we looked at text data, and we saw different project ideas with different levels of difficulty. For the simplest projects like the text classifier or for sentiment analysis, you could go ahead with an ML engineer, but if you want to push forward the boundaries of the state of the art and try building the super powerful brokerbot, you may have to hire a researcher as well. In chapter 6, we talked about recommender systems. Simple models can be built by a single ML engineer, whereas if you want to build particularly complex models, you may look for a researcher to join the team. It's possible that you need your recommender system to be extremely fast and stable. This is the case if you have a lot of users using your service at the same time, and speed is crucial. An example is Facebook's feed, which needs to recommend content almost instantly as you—and millions of people—are scrolling. In this case, software engineers become extremely important, as they are the ones who can build an infrastructure that can stand such loads.

To get a complete overview of these roles, see table 8.2, which highlights which types of tasks are most suited to each talent category.

Table 8.2 SW engineer, ML engineer, and AI researcher do their best work when the task matches their experience and background.

Software engineer	ML engineer	AI researcher
Usual background	Computer science	Computer science, statistics
Statistics, math, physics	Tasks	Implementing the application, integrating it with the existing infrastructure, building the database
Building and testing ML algorithms, developing a data strategy, monitoring the outcomes	Developing new algorithms, researching new solutions	Project fit
Complex IT infrastructure, very high performance required (for example, a self-driving car, or a service with a lot of traffic like Facebook), huge datasets (data engineers)	ML problem related to business problems solvable with state-of-the-art ML, like most of the examples discussed in this book	Complex—When the technology needed to solve a business problem isn't developed yet (for example, complex NLP tasks)

As always, keep in mind that the optimal skill set of the team will change as the project evolves over time, and even as different components of the project are completed. Factors like these will drive your decision to employ expert consultants or hire full-time team members. We advise against making the common mistake of hiring a hot-shot AI researcher without having a solid base of software engineering in place, as the new hire would likely be frustrated by the lack of proper infrastructure to move the work into production and would eventually leave. A common strategy is to start hiring for the more generalist roles first, so they gain experience with the broad context of the organization. It's easier to rely on consultants for niche knowledge like AI modeling, as their skills are more broadly transferable across multiple organizations (after all, image classification models are the same no matter whether you're trying to classify cucumbers or pedestrians).

Lastly, do not underestimate the importance of seniority. Although some tasks like data cleaning can be performed by junior figures, AI projects can get messy fast, and without the supervision of more senior persons, you risk ending up with unmaintainable code. Saving money now can lead to wasting even more money and time down the road.

This chapter introduced the main ingredients of any successful AI project: a data collection strategy, the software infrastructure and integration with existing processing, and a well-skilled team. We have also warned about many of the pitfalls troubling companies that are still inexperienced with AI. The next chapter provides the recipe for pulling these ingredients together into an AI project.

Summary

- The technical implementation of AI projects has three main components: data, model, and talent.
- A coherent data strategy takes into account the relative strengths and weaknesses of proprietary and external data.
- Besides quantity, other primary concerns about collecting data and labels are types of bias, coverage, and consistency.
- A good AI team includes people with different backgrounds and skills: software engineers, machine learning engineers (or data scientists), and researchers.

Go—AI
implementation strategy

This chapter covers

- The trade-offs in building an AI algorithm, buying from a provider, or using open source
- Developing a Lean AI Strategy to minimize risk
- Taking advantage of the virtuous cycle of AI
- Learning valuable lessons from AI failures

The previous two chapters gave you all the building blocks you need to define and implement an AI project. It's now time to put everything together. In this chapter, you'll learn how to decide which components to build in-house or buy from a third-party, and how to manage the implementation phase. You'll also become familiar with the most typical bumps in the road faced by inexperienced AI builders. By the time you reach the end of the chapter, you'll feel confident enough to kick-start your project *tomorrow*.

9.1   *Buying or building AI*

Paraphrasing what a wise man once said, sometimes the best way to successfully complete a project is never to start it in the first place. As an AI evangelist, one of the most impactful decisions you can make is to rely on products and services offered by AI providers and to avoid building some or all of the technology needed for an AI project. This decision applies to all three of the components of the project: data, model, and infrastructure.

This section will teach you how to think strategically about the *build or buy* question. Actually, we believe that the current status of the market for AI services calls us to add a third option: *borrow*. As we present each of these three options in the next sections, the fundamental concept to keep in mind is *implementation risk*. As you decide to buy or lease technology and infrastructure off the shelf, you give up flexibility and intellectual property, but obviously sidestep the risks connected to investing in the technology yourself.

Table 9.1 sums up the main differences between Buy, Borrow, and Build solutions. It's here for you to jump back to as needed, and we explain it in detail in the next three sections.

Table 9.1   Comparing Buy, Borrow, and Build strategies

	Buy	**Borrow**	**Build**
Need data	No	Yes	Yes
Need model development	No	No	Yes (potentially use open source models)
Need infrastructure	No	No	Yes (potentially use hosted infrastructure)
Risks	Low technological risk, but you're bound to the provider's agenda	Same as Buy for ML platforms, technological risk for open source	Highest technological risk
Team skill set required	Web development	Web development + minor data science	Web + ML
Up-front cost	None	Data collection	Data collection and model development
Variable cost	Little	Moderate	Amortized in the infrastructure/cloud investment

9.1.1   *The Buy option: Turnkey solutions*

The simplest option to implement AI technology is to use one of the turnkey solutions offered by tech providers like Google, Microsoft, or Amazon. These *Buy solutions* are also called *Machine Learning as a Service* (*MLaaS*).

In MLaaS services, tech companies build general-purpose ML algorithms, taking care of the data collection, training, and industrialization. You use their technology to interpret your data in exchange for money.

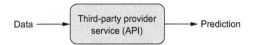

Figure 9.1 The provider you buy a turnkey solution from takes care of all the technical details: you need only to send requests with your data and get the response back.

As you can see in figure 9.1, all you have to do is send the data you want to analyze, and you get a prediction from their ML model. In technical terms, you'd be using an application programming interface (API) to send your data to a provider and get an answer. For example, almost every tech giant (Microsoft, Google, IBM) offers a computer vision API: you send them an image, and they send you back its content. Some computer vision APIs are particularly fancy and can give you interesting information like the estimation of the mood of a person in an image based on their facial expression.

One of our ML-based side projects from a few years ago was a voice transcription service for journalists and students who wanted transcripts of interviews or lectures. After we implemented the web application and confirmed demand for the product, we were spoiled by the number of choices when it came to finding an AI provider that could run the actual transcriptions. Google, Amazon, and Microsoft all offer a voice transcription service in dozens of languages, as well as several smaller providers that focus on specific niches.

Unfortunately, when using an MLaaS solution, you're dealing with the proverbial *black box*: you have no control over how the model is built, its performance, and the infrastructure that serves it. The good news is that you almost don't have to do anything in this case, as the provider has already done all the hard work of collecting data, training a model, and setting up the infrastructure to serve it (figure 9.2). All that's left to do is to integrate the solution into your product, a task that any web developer can sort out. This allows you to potentially get a first, quick prototype of your AI application in hours instead of weeks or months.

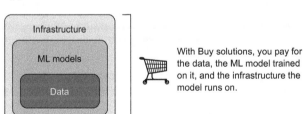

With Buy solutions, you pay for the data, the ML model trained on it, and the infrastructure the model runs on.

Figure 9.2 When buying a solution, the provider takes care of all three components (data, model, and infrastructure).

To give you an idea of the types of services offered as turnkey solutions, let's have a (nonexhaustive) look at Google's price list at the time of this writing:

- 2 cents per minute for transcribing speech into text
- $1 per document for natural language understanding: extracting structured data from documents and performing sentiment analysis

- $20 per million characters for translation
- $1 per image for detecting logos or faces on pictures

There are two main takeaways here. First of all, all turnkey solutions are focused on solving generic problems. This makes sense, as polishing and marketing these products takes a lot of investment that providers will commit to only if they think there's going to be a broad interest in the market. For instance, Google is never going to offer "cucumber-sorting AI as a service" because market demand would never be high enough to recoup development costs. Instead, it makes more sense for them to offer a service with broader interest that can recognize everyday objects like cats, dogs, or cars.

Second, from a financial perspective, Buy solutions have nearly zero fixed costs and higher variable costs than other strategies. In fact, with these solutions, there's no effort in data collection, data cleaning, ML engineering, and deployment. All you have to do is integrate an API: a task that takes the average web developer just a few hours. As you've seen in the previous price list, the costs are all pay-per-use.

From a technical standpoint, the level of risk associated with these solutions is extremely low. Because you're using products built by renowned tech companies, you can be fairly sure that you'll get state-of-the-art performance. Of course, this is true only as long as your application fits the task for which the service was engineered.

Beware: the fact that you're outsourcing all the technical risks doesn't mean that Buy solutions are risk-free. All Buy solutions have a major threat in common: because you don't own the underlying technology, you're beholden to someone else's agenda. They might decide to discontinue the product you're using and leave you to fend for yourself.

Our favorite cautionary tale involves San Francisco-based startup Smyte. The company developed ML models and a platform to help online communities fight spam, fraud, and harassment by proactively identifying malicious trends in comments and interactions. When Smyte was acquired by Twitter in 2018, customers woke up to find that the platform had been shut down, as Twitter decided it would focus on serving its internal needs only. High-profile customers like Meetup and Zendesk were left scrambling for a replacement as the turnkey solution they had been relying on simply stopped responding to their queries.

The risks of providers shutting down or changing their products creates *lock-in* toward their services. Lock-in effects also extend to security and privacy, as turnkey solutions are limited to running within the provider's network and cloud infrastructure, which might not be acceptable in security-minded industries like health care and defense.

However, the incredible speed and low fixed cost of these solutions makes a perfect case for using them for quick prototypes that can validate the market demand for your products.

9.1.2 *The Borrow option: ML platforms*

As you have seen, turnkey solutions all but guarantee state-of-the-art performance on many generic AI tasks. What about situations where your needs are more specific? For example, what about the cucumber classification task described in chapter 4? As we said, you won't find a "cucumber quality classification" product on Amazon's AI platform, because the market for it would be vanishingly small.

Instead, you can choose to use an *ML platform* product. Compared to turnkey solutions, ML platforms allow you to upload your own training data to optimize a ready-made model for your specific needs. In the case of cucumber classification, you would be able to take advantage of Google's image classification models, and fine-tune them with a labeled dataset of cucumbers. From the AI point of view, ML platforms often take advantage of the strengths of transfer learning to allow customers like you to use the provider's massive investments in modeling while adapting to niche needs (like cucumber classification).

From the point of the integration, ML platforms are just like Buy solutions: the model is hosted in the provider's cloud, and you just submit requests to it (figure 9.3). Prices for ML platforms are two to four times higher than for turnkey solutions to account for the added complexity. But the pricing model is the same: you pay only a small fee for each request, and a token amount based on the amount of custom data you want to train on.

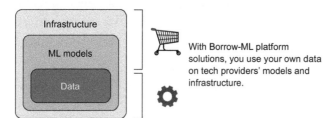

With Borrow-ML platform solutions, you use your own data on tech providers' models and infrastructure.

Figure 9.3 When borrowing a solution, the provider takes care of the model and the infrastructure, and you provide the data.

While ML platforms require no up-front investments per se, you'll need to budget for collecting and potentially labeling data, so you can take advantage of their customizability. ML platform products generally solve the same broad classes of problems as turnkey solutions; for example, you can upload your own text database to improve sentiment analysis, or submit a multilanguage corpus to improve translation accuracy.

We created a *Borrow* category for ML platforms because you're investing in a "borrowed" platform: you still don't own the IP for the model. However, you do own the training data that in many cases constitutes your real asset.

That being said, the lock-in effect for ML platforms might be even stronger than for turnkey solutions. The latter are so generic that, even if your provider shuts down, you're likely to find a similar offering from a competitor. On the other hand, the interactions between the secret sauce in the ML platform and your training data can be harder to replicate.

AI providers often advertise ML platforms as a great fit for projects using the structured business data described in chapters 2 and 3. Because the computational needs of these models are often modest, ML platforms offer *automatic ML* products that try multiple models on your data and automatically choose the best one. It's worth mentioning that, if a problem is simple enough to be solved by these automatic tools, the average ML engineer is likely to get similar performance with limited effort.

In our time helping companies with their projects, we found that for problems dealing with structured data (typically marketing, sales, or core business data), the biggest effort by far is in cleaning and preparing the data.

In one case, we needed to build an algorithm working with the call center data of a pharmaceutical company. This data had been collected for 14 years, but no one had put any effort into trying to get value out of it: it was a sunk cost used just for reporting. When an enlightened manager proposed building an AI algorithm, the first challenge we faced was trying to go through 14 years of history in order to understand the logic behind the data, and to clean outliers and potential data entry errors. If this wasn't enough of a challenge, over the years the company used two CRM providers, and therefore had inconsistencies in the formats and fields of data collected. Long story short, getting the data ready to be used took us three months. Once we had the data ready, building a model that performed well took roughly two weeks.

Finding the right model and tweaking it can be surprisingly quick. ML platforms won't spare you from the initial effort of getting your data ready to be used for an ML application, and thus provide only minor savings in terms of time and up-front costs. However, they do add variable costs as their business model is pay-per-use.

9.1.3 *The Build option: Roll up your sleeves*

If neither Buy nor Borrow solutions are a good fit for your project, you're going to have to go the *Build* route. By building your own model, you gain complete flexibility and control over your technology. In general, building your own model means you need to take care of all three components: data, model, and infrastructure (figure 9.4).

These are the two most common situations for which it's impossible to find Buy or Borrow solutions:

- *You use domain-specific data*—For example, if you're working on a 3-D MRI or other medical diagnostic tools, you'll work with three-dimensional black-and-white images. It's unlikely that you'll ever find a turnkey or ML platform product that can support them.
- *You have very specific needs*—For instance, you may want to build an ML algorithm that identifies cancer from X-rays of lungs and highlights where the cancer is. This last bit is an object localization task, a relative niche application that's covered by few or no providers.

With Build solutions, you're on your own; you need to gather data, train your models, and deploy them.

Figure 9.4   When building a solution, your team has to take care of all three components: data, model, and infrastructure.

From the point of view of development risk, the Build choice is the riskiest, because your team has full responsibility for the product. Luckily, they're often not alone, and can rely on two important accelerators of progress: open source models and hosted infrastructure. Let's see how each can help you build your project.

Open source models are freely available software (and, often, training data) that solves a specific problem. As long as its license is compatible with your intended use (for example, commercial use), your engineers can simply copy the code, customize it as needed, and use it in your product. If you're not familiar with the open source world, you might be wondering why people would offer their work for free. Well, the two biggest contributors of open source models are large tech companies and academics. Tech providers like Google and Microsoft release cutting-edge products to strengthen their reputation as AI leaders and attract people to their turnkey products and ML platforms. Researchers in academia publish their software to increase awareness of their work, attracting funding and recognition. For more niche cases, you might not even find any open source code at all. Your best bet then is to get your researchers to dig up relevant scientific papers from the academic community. Often, the description of the model included in the paper is enough for your ML engineers to replicate it with little effort, and then you're off to collecting training data.

Open source code is usually a great way to jump-start your development efforts. Your team will be able to start from a working solution and iterate it to adapt to your specific problem. Compared to ML platforms, the ability to tweak the model enables the ML engineers in your team to debug problems and experiment with changes to improve its accuracy.

Generally speaking, if you build your own model, you'll also need to provide and maintain the infrastructure for it, often by managing your own cloud resources. *Hosted infrastructure* frees your software engineers from this burden by letting you run your custom models in the cloud of a provider. As long as your model fits the provider's technical requirements (for example, in terms of programming language), you can use their hardware and networks to run your models. This works because, as we explained in chapter 8, most of the magic in building AI lies in having the right data and creating a good model. The software to manage the execution has quickly been standardized and thus commoditized in the past few years.

Open source code and hosted infrastructure can do a lot to reduce the investment needed to build your own models, saving your team many man-years of work. Most importantly, they can also give you a confidence boost. At the beginning of the project, knowing that somebody else was able to crack the same problem will clear away many doubts about its feasibility. Toward the end of the project, having the option to offload much of the deployment work to a vendor makes the team run faster toward the finish line.

At the end of the day, which scenario (build, borrow, or buy) you land on depends on the specifics of each AI project you'll work on. The next section will guide you through this decision.

9.2   *Using the Lean Strategy*

How can you choose which of the Buy, Borrow, and Build strategies is the best fit for your team and the project you're working on? Is it even possible to find a single strategy that can fit a project at every stage? This section introduces our answer to this question: the *Lean AI Strategy*, a framework we developed to help you build your AI products incrementally.

The word *lean* comes from *lean manufacturing*, a philosophy born in the Japanese manufacturing industry (particularly in automotive companies like Toyota) that aims to minimize production waste without sacrificing efficiency. Eric Ries adapted the idea to the world of entrepreneurship in his landmark book *The Lean Startup* (Crown Business, 2011). Ries introduced a process to manage innovation that encourages testing market and technology assumptions through continuous experiments. The core insight behind this strategy is that even CEOs and founders have little information about what the marketplace truly values, so they'd better quickly build a first iteration of the product, see if customers like it, and then improve it based on their feedback.

The Lean AI Strategy has the same goals: it's a process to incrementally implement AI projects while minimizing risk and resource waste (time, money, and team morale). Following the Lean AI Strategy, you'll learn to choose the best implementation plan for a given project (build, buy, or borrow).

As you begin the project, the first step is understanding the technological risks associated with each AI development path. Each option has an associated complexity that comes with short-term risks, while giving you a degree of flexibility that is related to long-term liabilities. The relationships between these risks and flexibilities are represented in figure 9.5.

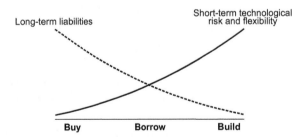

Figure 9.5   **Points on the Build versus Buy spectrum stack up when it comes to risk and flexibility.**

Now, imagine you're just starting the implementation of an AI project. This is the moment where uncertainty is highest, mainly because of three factors:

- *Business risk*—Does my solution hold business value?
- *Workflow risk*—Can I successfully integrate my solution in the current business?
- *Technological risk*—Will the technology work well enough?

The methodologies introduced in chapter 7 are meant to minimize business and workflow risks, but nothing compares to real-world testing with real people. To put your new product in front of real users, you'll often need to build at least some technology. *The Lean Startup* introduced the concept of *minimum viable product* (*MVP*): the smallest product you could possibly build while still delivering value to customers. In the world of AI projects, it is useful to think in terms of *minimum viable AI* (*MVAI*): the smallest and least risky technology that could possibly power your first MVP.

9.2.1 Starting from Buy solutions

The most important role of the Lean AI Strategy is getting you on the right path to build the MVAI. Given the high degree of uncertainty, it's a good idea to focus on a short-term strategy and defer long-term decisions to later, after the viability of the idea has been validated by customers. If you look at figure 9.6, this means starting from Buy solutions.

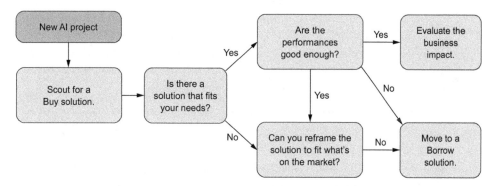

Figure 9.6   The first step when building the Lean AI Strategy for a new AI project is to start scouting for Buy solutions, and follow this decision tree.

The technical vocabulary we taught you in part 1 is enough to start scouting for Buy solutions on Google. For instance, let's assume you run a food-delivery startup and want to sort food reviews into positive and negative ones. As you recall from chapter 5, this application is called *sentiment analysis*. A good query to search for Buy solutions is "Sentiment Analysis API," which will return multiple results. In many cases, you'll find turnkey products from both large tech providers (such as Google, Amazon, or Microsoft) and smaller specialized companies. In the world of AI, you really should consider both. Large players have the advantage of scale, but small players might have the edge because their data collection and engineering efforts might be more closely aligned to the specific goals of your project.

If you find what you're looking for among the constantly growing offerings of AI providers, you're in luck. Adopting one of these is likely to be your best bet for developing the initial iteration of your AI project.

In other cases, you might not find a solution for the exact AI task your project needs. This isn't so uncommon; after all, providers invest resources into building only those products that have a large potential market. If this is the case for your project, you have two options:

- Reframe your AI project so it fits into an existing Buy offering.
- Move up the technological risk ladder and look for Borrow solutions.

You should begin by considering option 1 first. Is there any way you can rephrase your AI task so you can use what's on the market without compromising your value proposition? For instance, let's assume you are a telco company and want to test a super-fast customer support service: users write a message, and the AI automatically routes the customer to the best call center agent; for instance, "My internet isn't working" would be a technical issue, and "I'd like to activate the new offer" a commercial claim. Aside from specialized AI companies with a full-blown product for your specific project, it's unlikely that you'll find a turnkey product for this exact task.

On the other hand, you'll find several very accurate sentiment analysis algorithms on the market today. Although these algorithms wouldn't solve 100% of the task, what about using them to route angry customers to customer support directly, and neutral customers to manual sorting by a human operator? Obviously, this won't be the final solution, but it allows you to test basic assumptions:

- *Business assumptions*—Are users willing to engage with customer support through an automatic system, or do they ignore it completely?
- *Workflow assumptions*—Is the new system a time-saver for operators?

If you can't find a way to scale down your problem as we did in this example, it's time to consider switching to Borrow solutions.

You also might consider moving to a Borrow solution when you've tried a Buy solution and it didn't perform well enough for the project. But first, you should reconsider what it means to be "good enough": even if the AI isn't perfect and makes obvious mistakes from the point of view of a human, the project might still be a success for the organization. Even if that's not the case, take a second and pat yourself on the back. Thanks to the Lean AI Strategy and a focus on turnkey models, you've discovered important technical information about your project with little to no up-front investment in technology. Next, engage the ML engineers on your team to try to find out why exactly the Buy product doesn't work. Keep in mind that Buy products are the result of substantial engineering investments, and thus your team can hope to do better under only a single circumstance: lack of problem-specific training data (for example, cucumber classification, or a niche vocabulary in NLP tasks). For example, if you're finding that a Buy model has bad performance in translating documents from English to French, it's unlikely that you would be able to outdo Google and improve things by adding more training data. If you determine that the lack of task-specific training data is killing your project, Borrow models can be your way out of the problem.

9.2.2 Moving up to Borrow solutions

Remember that the power of Borrow models comes from allowing you to augment existing models from AI providers with your own training data. We called these customizable products *ML platforms*. If you do a good job of collecting (and potentially labeling) data that's a good fit for your project, you'll get the best of both worlds: using years of investment in precanned models while achieving good performance on your specific tasks. As a bonus, Borrow models free you from having to design, deploy, and maintain the infrastructure for your project. By using a Borrow solution, you'll also start to grow the in-house AI expertise that drives your data collection effort, and build up institutional knowledge about building, comparing, and evaluating the performance of various AI models.

In other words, stepping up from Buy to Borrow allows you to iterate on the AI components of the project while getting answers fast, since ML platforms are essentially a bolt-in replacement for turnkey models. To find a suitable Borrow solution, start from the search you've done for Buy solutions and take it from there. Keep in mind that the options for ML platforms might be even more limited than turnkey models, as adding the customization points for transfer learning is more work for the AI provider.

If you can't even find a Borrow solution for your AI project, you have to make the same decision you had to face when you were evaluating Buy options: Can you reframe your solution so it fits what's on the market? If not, your only option is to move up the technological risk ladder once again and start building your own model, as you can see in figure 9.7.

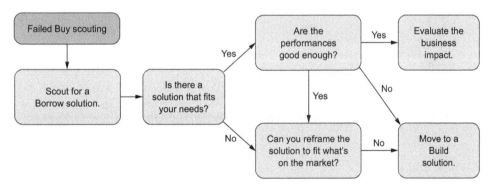

Figure 9.7 The same decision tree that we designed for Buy solutions works for Borrow ones, with different starting and end points (we start from a failed Buy scouting and end with moving to Buy solutions).

9.2.3 Doing things yourself: Build solutions

If you reach this stage of the Lean AI Strategy, there's not a lot left to decide. Your project doesn't fit any Buy or Borrow products on the market, and you can't reframe it to do so. This means that your team members are going to have to roll up their sleeves and start building the model themselves (likely taking advantage of the open source community and hosted infrastructure as described in chapter 8).

Because Buy is the "end of the road" for the Lean AI Strategy, we want to comment on each path that might lead your project here. The most typical situation occurs when the data that your project is using is uncommon or very specific. Think about an audio application that plans to classify bird species by their chirp. No ML platform product is likely to support transfer learning from animal sounds, and no turnkey solution is going to offer that either.

In other cases, we have seen teams with a working Borrow solution that want to try building their own model, expecting a cost reduction or an improvement in performance. Although it's true that building your own model (and managing all aspects of its operations) might have lower *variable* costs, many teams make the mistake of ignoring the substantial up-front investment that went into creating the Borrow solution they had been enjoying. Perceived performance benefits are often illusory as well: any Borrow model on the market went through extensive testing to verify its accuracy in a variety of scenarios. It's easy to get excited about positive early results and underestimate the amount of engineering effort needed to bring a Build solution up to scratch. The best way to approach a migration to a Build solution is to treat it like a side project, and not bet the entire AI strategy on it. This will help reduce the risk of the migration through constant monitoring of the in-house effort compared to the Borrow solution.

Besides these technical reasons, sometimes organizational or business issues make Build the only option. For example, both turnkey models and ML platforms generally run within the cloud resources of the AI provider. This factor makes them a no-no for privacy- or security-conscious industries like health or defense, because the potentially sensitive data must be shared with the provider in order for the system to work. Other organizations might decide to invest in creating a first-party IP even if this choice is not the cheapest or fastest way to implement a given project.

We can't really argue with a strategic point of view like this, but remember that you'll have plenty of time to develop your own IP *after* you've made a working prototype. Even if in the long run you'll want to develop your own model, we still encourage you to start by following the Lean AI Strategy and kick off your efforts with Buy solutions. This may be just a stepping stone, but it will still be invaluable to have a quick working prototype that you can use to test your most pressing business assumptions.

As a final word of caution, we warn you against going too deep into the R&D rabbit hole. After you've decided that you have to build your own model, it's easy to go overboard and become more and more ambitious. Experimenting with cutting-edge AI models is exciting and great for humanity. As a side bonus, your team is really energized and puts in its 110%. However, chances are that, if you're reading this book, you and your organization are not ready to embark on a multiyear R&D project to validate novel uses of AI or entirely new algorithms. Consider holding out on these "moon-shot" projects to pick them up after the AI culture in your organization is more mature.

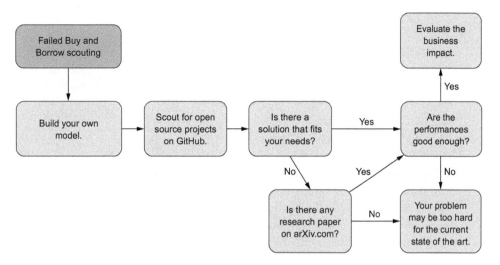

Figure 9.8   The Lean AI Strategy decision tree for Build solutions

The decision tree for the Build option is represented in figure 9.8.

In conclusion, the Lean AI Strategy encourages you to minimize implementation risk by delaying commitment to expensive and risky engineering tasks. Instead, it encourages you to kick-start the project by using Buy or Borrow solutions that enable you to take advantage of the economies of scale of large providers. As the project and your organization mature, you'll have plenty of opportunities to embark on technically more ambitious implementation plans.

As you jump from Buy, Borrow, and Build solutions following the Lean AI Strategy, you might have trouble deciding when to pull the trigger and deploy the project. Chapter 2 took a technical view of this aspect, and introduced the important measures of false positives and false negatives. The next section completes this discussion by telling you a more high-level story of how performance evolves through the life cycle of a typical AI project.

9.3   Understanding the virtuous cycle of AI

Let's rewind to the beginning of this book, when we first put ourselves in the shoes of the managers of a real estate website. We worked on a platform where homeowners could list their property for sale, and prospective buyers could look at the offers, schedule a visit, and finally buy one of the homes. We envisioned building a new feature enabling an AI model to automatically and instantaneously predict the best listing price for a home.

Our assumption was that users will like this feature, and it will give us a competitive advantage compared to other real estate platforms on the market. If we were right, people would start using our website more than those of our competitors, driving increased revenues, more users, and . . . more data.

What happens to ML algorithms when you have more data? Usually, their performance improves. Your product can become even better, and your predictions more accurate, making users happier and thus attracting more users. The result, again, is even more data.

What we just described is *the virtuous cycle of AI*: if AI improves your product, bringing more users and more utilization, you'll generate more data that you can use to feed back into the model, further improving it. It's a self-reinforcing loop that, potentially, never ends. You can visualize this loop in figure 9.9.

Let's see how the virtuous cycle of AI influences real-world products, using our real estate platform example. Before we got started with the first AI project, all we had was a standard website, probably similar to offerings by competitors in the same

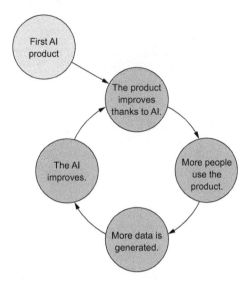

Figure 9.9   The AI virtuous cycle. As AI improves your product, more users want to use it. This leads to more data being generated, which improves your AI, which further improves your product, bringing even more users in.

space. The first AI product we decided to build was a home-price predictor: an ML algorithm that would learn from past property sales and automatically compute the most likely price for each property on the market.

This novel and curious feature generated press buzz and created a new advantage for our platform that differentiated us from the competition. Reasonably, we imagined that new customers would start to use our platform, attracted by our new house-price predictor. New customers don't just bring additional revenue, but also new data. When these new customers start selling their homes, the additional data we collect can be used to retrain our algorithms with even more data, improving its performance. Reasonably, an even better algorithm can bring us even more data, which brings us even more customers, and so on, as you can see in figure 9.10. The virtuous circle of AI can carry on forever, or until you start getting diminishing returns from your algorithms and reach a technology plateau.

You may ask, What if I don't have a lot of data, and my initial model can't match the standards of quality of my current product? We argue that in this situation, the virtuous cycle of AI is particularly important, and you should ship whatever brings *some* value to your customers, even if it's far from perfect.

To understand why, let's cover some basic concepts of how technological innovation is adopted and marketed. In 1962, communication studies professor Everett Rogers published *Diffusion of Innovations*, in which he presented a sociological model that describes the adoption or acceptance of a new product or innovation. The main

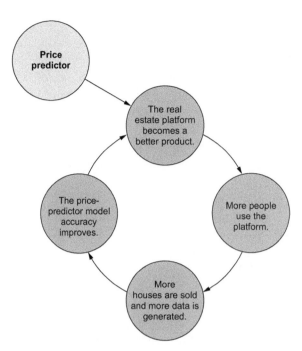

Figure 9.10   The AI virtuous cycle applied to the real estate example

insight is that a market is not made of one homogenous group of people; it's divided instead into groups of individuals who share similar characteristics:

- *Innovators*—These risk-takers have high social status, are social, and have financial liquidity. These are the people who line up in front of an Apple store the day before the release of a new iPhone.
- *Early adopters*—They are also risk-takers, are social, and have high purchasing power. Their choices are more conservative than innovators, so they may not line up the day before a new iPhone release, but you can be sure that they'll buy it the next day.
- *Early majority*—This is a large group of people with a mixed social status and purchasing power, who adopt an innovation after it has been released for some time. They value the improvement that technological advancements bring to their life but don't want to take risks. These are the people who either wait months after the release of a new phone to see what other people think, or can barely tell the difference from the older model.
- *Late majority*—Another large group of people, mainly skeptical and risk-averse. They value safety more than innovation, and don't want to switch to a new technology until they absolutely have no doubt about the return they'll get. These are the people with smartphones that are two to three generations behind.
- *Laggards*—The last ones to adopt an innovation. These are the people who still use a mechanical keyboard phone, and replace it with the cheapest model on sale when it breaks.

In 1991, Geoffrey A. Moore published *Crossing the Chasm: Marketing and Selling High-Tech Products to Mainstream Customers*, which built on the preceding theory and added a simple yet crucial insight: when introducing a technological innovation, passing from early adopters to early majority is not trivial, and many innovations fail at doing so. Moore introduced the concept of a *chasm*: a tough period of uncertainty when a company has reached all the innovators and early adopters in its market and needs to reach the early majority, as you can see in figure 9.11. This chasm exists because the early market (innovators and early adopters) and the late market (early majority, late majority, and laggards) are driven by completely different goals. Whereas the former value innovation and the worth that it brings, the latter value safety and are risk-averse, and it's hard to make them see the worth of your innovative product.

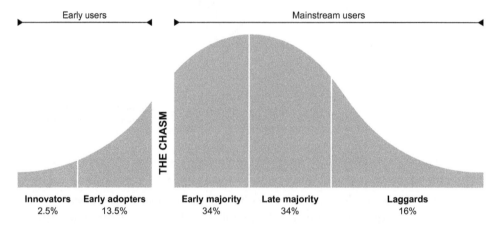

Figure 9.11   **The market for a technological innovation divided into its five customer groups. After the early adopters, we reach a chasm: a moment of high uncertainty when switching from early to mainstream users.**

Now, let's go back to our real estate platform and see how our ML-based innovation relates to the five groups we've introduced. Imagine that your first algorithm is worse than a human broker: let's say that its predictions have a 10% margin of error, while human brokers have only a 5% error rate. Hurried homeowners won't be concerned about the increased error rate, and are more interested in getting a number right away without waiting for a visit by a human broker. Or maybe they're technology enthusiasts rushing to try the new AI-based features that you're offering. They're the innovators and early adopters who will kick-start the virtuous cycle.

After these people start using your product, you'll start getting more data. You can use this new data to train your AI algorithms again. Let's assume that the performance of your algorithm improves and gets closer to a flesh-and-blood broker, say with a 7% margin of error. Now that you started closing the accuracy gap with human brokers, even less-brave users will choose to trade off that 2% accuracy for increased speed. The result, again, will be more data that you can use to keep improving the model.

Now imagine that thanks to the new data you collected through the primitive ML model, you finally reach the crucial milestone of human-machine parity: your algorithms are as good as an expert broker. Using your product is a no-brainer at this stage; users get the same performance as an expert broker, but it takes just a second to get it, without having to schedule visits. This is the level of performance needed to attract the early majority: they're OK with using new technology as long as it doesn't come with any downside compared to the status quo.

As in any other business venture, it's crucial that you're able to correctly communicate the performance of your technology to people, and they're able to understand it. This isn't trivial, and you shouldn't take it for granted.

If you're successful at communicating the potential of your technology, home sellers will want to use your model to have an instant quote for their home. Can you guess what the result would be? You're correct: even more data. Now, your algorithms can benefit from this additional data to even surpass human accuracy. Congrats, you now have a superhuman AI home-price predictor. Figure 9.12 shows the self-reinforcing relationship between technology performance and adoption.

If you had not shipped the first primitive product, you would never have kicked off this process that led you to a superhuman AI price predictor. For this reason, it's important to account for the AI virtuous cycle and ship AI products even if they're not perfect.

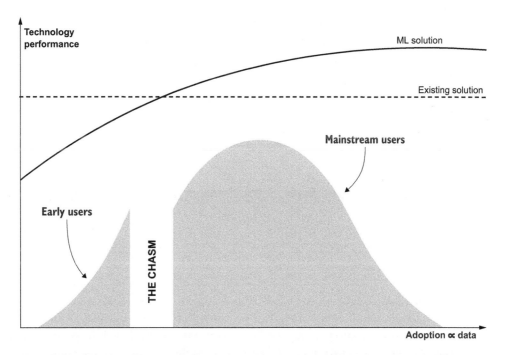

Figure 9.12 Because of the power of data, the performance of an ML-based problem depends on market adoption. Early users may be willing to compromise on performance, but as they use the product and data increases, you'll improve your technology until you can reach the mainstream market.

Ship early, and design your strategy so that each product iteration is functional to improving your algorithms, until your advantage is so big you can't be ignored.

If you're confident that acquiring more data is the key to allowing you to gain an advantage over your competition, you can consider unorthodox ways to get those first early adopters. An extreme strategy can be to heavily discount your new service or even give it away for free so you can quickly attract early adopters. Kicking off the AI virtuous cycle is so important that you may even plan to pay people to start using your product. You'll make up for these initial losses after the AI virtuous cycle kicks in, your technology starts improving rapidly, and the mainstream segment starts using your new service and paying for the value it brings them.

9.4   *Managing AI projects*

The Lean AI Strategy helps you decide whether to build, borrow, or buy a technological solution. No matter the option, you'll still have some development work to do. For example, even if you adopt a Borrow solution for the home-price prediction problem, the team will still have to write the plumbing code to connect the outputs of the model into the web application.

One of the worst-kept secrets in the industry is that managing engineers is like herding cats. This section is going to give you some inputs to lead the day-to-day operations during the implementation phase of an AI project. Even if you don't want to take on this responsibility personally, or decide to outsource the whole effort to consultants, it's still useful to know what modern software engineering practices look like.

The lean philosophy also extends to the implementation stage: it's best to break development into chunks that an individual team member can carry out in one or two weeks. Such a rapid iteration pace makes it possible to keep up with changing requirements from the organization, and even feedback from customers and users of the product.

Lean also means shipping software as soon as possible—in many cases, as soon as an MVP is ready. We have seen many teams endlessly strive for perfection, thus delaying the crucial moment when they can get meaningful information from their users.

The lean approach gives you a conceptual framework that emphasizes quick iteration, continuous improvement, and attention to feedback. But how does this work out in practice throughout the daily activities of your AI task force? This book is not about project management, but we feel it's useful for you to gain some knowledge about how the sausage is made.

A practice that aligns well with the tenets of the Lean AI Strategy and is used by most Silicon Valley companies today is Scrum, a flavor of Agile development. Think of Scrum as a practical implementation and rule book that helps teams put the concepts of the Lean AI Strategy into practice. Quick iteration is achieved by timeboxing work in periods of two weeks, called *sprints*. Progress toward the overall goal is decomposed in terms of *stories*, which represent a self-contained item of work that delivers a complete feature to the product. At the beginning of each sprint, the team decides which stories they're going to be working on during the next two weeks.

Because tasks are decided and allocated every two weeks, there's plenty of opportunity to align to changing requirements, or even failed attempts to implement models or data collection strategy. In many fields of AI, it's not uncommon to spend a few weeks developing a model, cleaning up the data, and doing the training, just to find out that the approach doesn't perform as well as expected. In those cases, keeping a quick iteration pace is critical to ensure that the team will eventually converge on a solution.

Lean is a general concept that works great for many types of software engineering projects, especially when technical uncertainty or changing requirements are involved. This also applies to AI projects, where in many cases you won't know how well your model performs until you've tried it on your task. However, for some aspects, AI changes the rules of the game, and this section tells you how. We have decided to focus on the two main aspects that are guilty of pushing AI projects off track:

- You're always worrying about data.
- AI projects are never really "done."

Let's talk about the first. Data collection (and cleaning) and model development are often carried out by different people within your team, just because the skill sets required are different. This creates a kind of chicken-and-egg problem: the software engineers depend on the ML engineers to make progress, and the ML engineers don't have data on hand for their experiments.

Following the principles of incremental iteration, a good way to break down this vicious cycle is to timebox multiple cycles of data collection and model development. As soon as software engineers have completed even a minimal portion of the training dataset, they can hand it off to ML engineers for them to develop and try models. In the meantime, they can move on to improve and extend the scale of their code to improve performance, while receiving feedback from ML people about the most important areas for improvement. The process starts over at the next cycle, giving you a good way to measure progress over time.

Let's cover the second problem now: AI projects are never really "done." If you're working on conventional software projects, clear requirements help you figure out when the product is "done." If you're leading a team that's making a home alarm system, you definitely need to make sure that opening a window will trigger the siren. As an AI evangelist, you don't have this luxury. This is because modern AI is based on machine learning, and thus will never reach the 100% perfection that we associate with conventional engineering.

In many projects, it's tricky to tie an organization-wide metric, like top-line growth, to the accuracy of the model. You'll know you're in one of those situations when you struggle to tell your team what level of performance you require out of the model. Once again, incremental iteration is the key to successfully get you out of these situations. The earlier you get a working prototype of the project out the door, the sooner you can get the organization to use it, and thus see how the accuracy of the model correlates with improvement in the organization (or happiness of the users). A great example that we have already discussed is churn prediction, as we can immediately see how improvements to the model increase retention. Even low-accuracy prototypes can be a great win for the organization and will undoubtedly help you get your message across.

We made sure to include several examples of failed AI projects and misunderstood technical points throughout the book. However, being the conscientious writers that we are, we couldn't end this chapter without a more complete discussion about what to do when things start to go awry.

9.5 When AI fails

Working in technology has taught us that if everything was working as advertised, many people would be out of a job. Building and maintaining software is hard, and AI is no exception. If anything, AI adds more challenges of its own. This entire section is devoted to stories of AI project failures. We have two good reasons for doing this:

- To warn that AI is not a silver bullet
- To prove that mistakes in AI strategy can be catastrophic

The goal is not to scare you away from tackling your projects, but rather to discover how some of the strategies we introduced in this book might have saved the protagonists of these stories. We decided to leave them for the end of part 2 so you can see how everything falls into place.

9.5.1 Anki

The first example is about Anki, a robotics startup that shut down in 2019 after receiving more than $200 million in funding. Back in 2013, Anki was so promising that it enjoyed the rare privilege of being invited onstage at the yearly Apple keynote. There, Apple CEO Tim Cook told thousands of technology enthusiasts that the budding company was going to "bring AI and robotics into our daily lives."

Fast-forward six years, and a company spokesperson told Recode this:

> Despite our past successes, we pursued every financial avenue to fund our future product development and expand on our platforms. We were left without significant funding to support a hardware and software business and bridge to our long-term product roadmap.

As the company was shutting down, its most advanced product on the market was Vector, a $250 robotic toy that pioneered Anki's flavor of "emotional intelligence," the ability to perceive the environment and express emotions to nearby humans. And yet, Anki was already advertising that it had more ambitious plans in the works, going as far as humanoid maids.

We don't want to indulge in armchair critique, but we do want to point out the potential imbalance we saw between short-term wins and long-term strategy. In this book, we've emphasized the importance of running timeboxed AI projects with quick returns for the organization. Instead, Anki was diverting resources from product development into "tomorrow's AI," the master plan for world domination that never actually came true. The AI-based vision of the "everyday robot" was in place, but it had never been broken into smaller bits that could be implemented over time.

9.5.2 *Lighthouse AI*

Another failure story comes from Lighthouse AI, a company that raised $17 million in funding to build an AI-powered home-security camera. The camera used AI to extract useful information from recorded video, and allowed you to ask about what happened while you were away, in natural language. For instance, you could ask, "What time did the kids get home yesterday?" and get video footage as an answer.

 Sounds useful, right? The market didn't agree. As CEO Alex Teichman wrote on the company's website:

> *I am incredibly proud of the groundbreaking work the Lighthouse team accomplished—delivering useful and accessible intelligence for our homes via advanced AI and 3-D sensing. . . . Unfortunately, we did not achieve the commercial success we were looking for and will be shutting down operations in the near future.*

Although the product was definitely impressive from a technical standpoint, it looks like the company didn't do enough market research and experimentation before jumping into the venture. You can use different strategies to test market interest before committing millions of dollars in R&D; for instance, running a crowdfunding campaign or collecting preorders. It's hard to say whether this strategy would have been a definitive fix, but you surely can learn from this example that even the coolest technology won't be enough to create a market. Instead, identify the biggest business threats to your project (first of all, people not bothering to buy it) and design creative strategies to manage them.

9.5.3 *IBM Watson in Oncology*

Now let's talk about another grandiose case of AI failure: the debacle of IBM Watson in Oncology. In 2013, IBM issued a press release boasting its involvement with one of the leading medical centers in the world:

> *The University of Texas MD Anderson Cancer Center and IBM today announced that MD Anderson is using the IBM Watson cognitive computing system for its mission to eradicate cancer.*

Just five short years later, *STAT* (a journal focused on the health industry) reviewed IBM's internal documents about the MD Anderson project and shared a quote by one of the doctors who took part in the pilot:

> *This product is a piece of s**t. We bought it for marketing and with hopes that you would achieve the vision. We can't use it for most cases.*

What happened here? This time, market demand was definitely strong: everyone on earth wants to see cancer eradicated. The first issue we see with this case is an unjustified focus on long-term AI vision. "Eradicating cancer" is as desirable as it is unlikely to be solved single-handedly by one tech company just because it closed a deal with a hospital.

On top of this, you'll be able to spot a whole series of technical mistakes as we shed some light on the inner workings of IBM Watson for Oncology. The medical technology was built on top of what IBM had developed to play the US game show *Jeopardy* and attracted some attention after winning against two human champions in 2011.

Jeopardy is a quiz show in which participants receive answers that they need to guess the questions for (basically, a reverse quiz). How did IBM transform the Jeopardy model to help oncologists? It started by finding suitable datasets. One of them was a set of 5,000 medical questions from the American College of Physicians (ACP). The following are examples of question/answer pairs in the dataset:

Q: The colorectal cancer screening test associated with highest patient adherence

A: Fecal immunochemical testing

Q: Non-Hodgkin lymphoma characterized by extranodal involvement and overexpression of cyclin D1

A: Mantle cell lymphoma

Q: Mechanism of acute varicocele associated with renal carcinoma

A: Obstruction of the testicular vein

Basically, IBM Watson was using text data as input and output of the model. Since you learned in chapter 4 that text data is still the trickiest sector for AI, let's see what specific issues IBM had to face when transferring its technology into hospitals. At MD Anderson, both "acute lymphoblastic leukemia," a kind of blood cell cancer, and "allergy" were often referred to with the acronym "ALL". Obviously, cancer and allergies are two very different medical conditions, but Watson couldn't distinguish between the two because they used the same acronym.

Another issue is that Watson struggled to consider multiple aspects of a patient, leading to potential disasters. For example, it suggested that a 65-year-old man with diagnosed lung cancer and evidence of severe bleeding should be treated with a combination of chemotherapy and a drug called bevacizumab, which can cause "severe or fatal hemorrhage" and shouldn't be administered to patients experiencing serious bleeding.

What can we learn from this? We already knew some of the things that emerge from this article: text data is hard to deal with, especially when you're working in an extremely complicated context. In the width-depth framework we introduced to describe the complexity of an AI application (chapter 4), Watson would score extremely high in both width and depth. Width is high because the model needs to understand a vast spectrum of words coming from different branches of the medical field, and all the potential acronyms and abbreviations as well. Depth is also extremely high, as we're asking our algorithm to come up with a sentence that describes a potentially complex combinations of drugs.

The challenges in working with this kind of data were recognized by Dr. Amy Abernethy, chief medical officer at Flatiron Health and former director of cancer research at the Duke Cancer Institute. In an interview for a paper published in the 2017 *Journal of the National Cancer Institute*, she stated, "The MD Anderson experience is telling us that solving data quality problems in unstructured data is a much bigger challenge for artificial intelligence than was first anticipated."

One way to simplify things is to reduce depth by posing the problem as a classification task dealing with structured data. Another is to reduce width by limiting the application to a specific kind of cancer. By applying both measures, instead of feeding the algorithm with wordy sentences filled with medical jargon, they would have used a table with patient information expressed in values (for example, "blood pressure = 110mm Hg"). The algorithm would have responded by choosing one out of a number of suggested therapies known in advance. A project like this is certainly less cool than an all-knowing AI that responds in natural language, but we argue that it's better to have something simple that works than something complex that doesn't.

9.5.4 *Emotional diary*

Finally, let's cover two examples from our consulting work that you won't find in the news. We changed some details to protect the privacy of our clients and respect our confidentiality agreements, but the lessons are still valid.

The first example is actually more of an averted disaster. A health-care company wanted to build an app to give emotional support to couples undergoing fertility treatment. Not only are these couples stressed out because they have difficulty conceiving, but the woman is also prescribed hormones that can have a strong impact on her mood.

The original idea was to build an "emotional diary" app for the couple. Every day, it would ping them to upload a selfie with a smile or a sad face. An algorithm would recognize their mood and answer with an appropriate motivating sentence. At the end of the therapy, the app would have created a "diary" of the emotional journey that the couple went through, hopefully ending with the beautiful gift of a child.

The company had already started to collect quotes from various technological providers and had come up with a marketing plan to promote the app across treatment centers. One morning, we discovered that Microsoft offers an "emotional detection API": a simple service that allows you to send a selfie to Microsoft's servers, which run an AI algorithm and return their evaluation of the emotion expressed by the person. We asked to pause the strategy for a day. The day after, we came back with a prototype app linked to Microsoft's service, which already included a few sentences to encourage the couple.

We took our bare-bones prototype and went to a fertility center to talk to some users. The verdict was unanimous: the women wanted to throw that phone at a wall. What we thought would be a supportive tool was instead seen as a disrespectful invasion of their privacy and intimacy. They were already stressed and doubtful they would ever become mothers; the last thing they wanted was an app that wanted selfies to send cheeky motivational quotes.

We canceled the program and went back to the drawing board. Fast prototyping and the use of APIs allowed us to find out early in the process that we were about to go full speed right into a wall.

9.5.5 *Angry phone calls*

Another example is a company that needed an AI algorithm that could identify emotions from voice recordings. During a phone call, the app should indicate when either speaker is angry, sad, happy, or neutral and provide suggestions to deal with the negative feelings. Our client came to us claiming that they had already found a technology provider that was reliable, and we dove head-down into execution without questioning the technology. Together, we drafted a comprehensive strategy, a business plan, and designed a minimum viable product (MVP) that integrated the third-party technology. Once we shipped the MVP, we found out that the performance of the tech provider was nowhere close to what they claimed (and we expected).

Apparently, the software was designed around a dataset of German speakers. We needed to apply it to the Italian market, and it turns out that an angry German and an angry Italian sound quite different. After acknowledging that the vendor was underperforming, we dug into the scientific literature to learn about the state-of-the-art performance in this task. We found out that even the state of the art was far away from the 90%-plus accuracy achieved in other AI tasks. Lesson learned? Test, test, test. Always question and validate what you read. Even if a technology provider claims to have a great product, spend one or two days to research the state of the art and to test whether it can reach the performance you need.

9.5.6 *Underperforming sales*

In another example, a large corporation asked us to cluster its sales data to spot underperforming customer accounts. The request came from the IT department, which managed large amounts of data and wanted to prove the value of that data collection effort. We ran our analysis and found a bunch of underperforming stores through which the company could have made $8.5 million more per year by changing the sales strategy! Everyone was excited, so we crafted a beautiful presentation for the CEO. He interrupted us after just a few minutes saying: "Guys, you're not telling me anything new. We made a special deal 10 years ago with these stores you call underperforming; I can tell you that the profit is very high with them. You're looking at the wrong metrics."

It turned out that the stores in question had custom volume discounts that were booked differently, and therefore didn't show up in the database we used. What do we learn from this story? Always include the business perspective when designing an AI project. Don't fall into the trap of designing AI projects with a tech-first approach: make sure the business value is there before thinking about algorithms.

You probably noticed that none of the solutions to these fledgling projects was to invest in better technology. The hero they needed is not a super-skilled data scientist, but an enlightened leader who understands the principles we covered in this book and has the domain knowledge, critical spirit, and drive to bring AI into an organization.

Congratulations! You basically (almost) made it to the end of the book! Part 2 covered a lot of material with real-life situations and stories that will help you find and complete impactful AI projects in your organization. Together with the groundwork that we laid down in part 1, you're now ready to think critically about how AI can benefit your organization. Take a deep breath and get ready for the last chapter, where we take a step back and discuss how the AI tools you've been learning about will shape society in the future.

Summary

- When building an AI project, you must decide whether to build technology, buy it from tech providers, or borrow it by using a mixture of third-party technology and your data.
- The Lean AI Strategy helps you minimize implementation risk by guiding you in the build/buy/borrow decision-making process.
- The AI virtuous cycle allows you to continuously improve your AI models by exploiting the new data you're collecting with your product.
- AI isn't a silver bullet. Countless companies have failed at AI, often because of poor strategy or lack of market interest in their AI-based products.

What lies ahead

This chapter covers

- Possible negative implications of AI on society
- The most promising ways in which AI can reshape humanity
- The potential for disruption by AI in specific industries

This is the last chapter of the book. By now, you have all the tools to understand what AI is and what the most important families of algorithms can be useful for. We also shared with you the lessons we and industry leaders have learned through building AI projects. However, just as no mountain ascent is complete without stopping to look over the landscape, our journey wouldn't be complete without a broader look at the future of AI. Thanks to your newfound knowledge about the technical and organizational aspects of AI, you now have the mindset you need to break through the hype and think critically about how this technology is going to shape society in the next 5 to 10 years.

The book focused on what AI can do within the boundaries of organizations. For this final chapter, please allow us to be a bit more philosophical as we broaden the horizons of our discussion to society as a whole. To give as balanced an outlook as possible, we decided to frame our discussion in terms of threats and opportunities. We also included a review of several industry-specific trends that you should be aware of. Keep in mind that the ideas we'll discuss are our own: we encourage you to challenge them and think critically.

10.1 How AI threatens society

Anytime we humans have developed groundbreaking technology, it has taken some time before we've also realized its potential risks and downsides. Have you ever seen one of those overly optimistic post-WW2 era advertisements about nuclear energy? Supposedly, we were all going to use atomic light bulbs and Uranium-enriched breakfast meals. The first jet airplanes in the 40s had square windows because they were easier to manufacture. It took a few crashes before engineers realized that the sharp corners often caused fatal cracks in the fuselage. It seems that some physiological bias pushes us to overlook the downsides of new technologies.

We shouldn't make the same mistake with AI. One of the most important properties of today's software products is that they're incredibly easy to scale and serve to millions or even billions of people. Imagine what would happen if a misleading, flawed, or downright dangerous AI application were distributed to billions of people. The outcome would be catastrophic.

We already have some (fortunately) limited examples of this. In 2016, Microsoft released a chatbot that could learn to tweet based on the tweets that people sent it. After less than a day, it grew into a full-blown racist. If there's something that this experiment can teach us, it is that AI can go really wrong really fast, which is the reason it's important to know the technologies' weaknesses and design products with them in mind.

In this section, we'll highlight what we believe are the main threats that society and organizations will have to face when AI-based products and services start gaining critical mass. As technologists and optimists, we're not trying to cry wolf here: our goal is to give you knowledge and perspective to form your own opinions.

10.1.1 Bias and fairness

In chapter 8, we warned you about the dangers of biased (or unbalanced) data, and how it often leads to the development of similarly biased machine learning models. This section rounds off that technical coverage with a deeper discussion about the social and ethical implications of this issue.

In general, you should be aware of two types of bias:

- Training distribution bias
- Labeling bias

You saw an example of *training distribution bias* in chapter 8, where we discussed a computer vision model that had trouble telling sheep apart from green fields. Because most of its sheep examples had a grass background, the model learned to hallucinate sheep even in pictures of fields that had none. You may think that this kind of bias isn't that big of a deal. The worst it can do is annoy users and reduce the accuracy of the model, right? Think again.

Amazon developed an AI model to help its HR department automatically select job candidates. The training set was obtained by matching the resumes of current employees with the results of on-the-job performance reviews. Unfortunately, it's well-known that tech companies have a gender gap problem. According to a 2018 study by McKinsey & Company and Pivotal Ventures, "Rebooting Representation: Using CSR and Philanthropy to Close the Gender Gap in Tech," only 26% of the tech workforce is female. The number drops to 11% for senior executive roles.

Now that you know more about ML, you can probably guess what happened when the HR data was fed into an ML algorithm. Since most "positive" examples in the current workforce (and thus in the training dataset) are male, the model will pick up that being male is a predictor of good job performance. Even blanking out first names in the hopes of gender-balancing the algorithm will not help solve the problem, because AI models are really good at picking up subtle hints. For example, only 5.6% of soccer club members in England are women. This means that a model can easily pick up on the fact that anybody who lists soccer on their resume is disproportionately likely to be male.

Speech recognition is another area where training biases can ruin the day. Captioned movies are a great source of data to train algorithms to transcribe spoken dialogue into written words. However, it turns out that most Hollywood actors have flawless pronunciation. Immigrants and people for whom English is a second language will find that models have trouble recognizing their voices because their accents weren't well represented in the training dataset. As long as these systems are deployed on superfluous products, like the Siri voice assistant, it's not such a big deal. But what happens when they start becoming an essential part of our life, like cars or government offices? If these algorithms fail to understand an immigrant's accented English, they're bound to be discriminated against and lose access to information.

The second type of bias that can affect an AI system is *labeling bias*. Part of the everyday narrative about AI is that machines are going to be more impartial and therefore less discriminative than human decision-makers. Instead, what happens is that ML models simply learn to reproduce the same biases that appeared in their training datasets.

A glaring example of this issue is the Correctional Offender Management Profiling for Alternative Sanctions (COMPAS) system used by some US courts to help judges decide on criminal sentences. The ML-based system supposedly estimates the "risk" that the defendant will commit crimes again in the future and recommends harsher sentences to those more likely to do so. In principle, COMPAS is a good idea that could reduce racial and social biases in the judiciary system. However, "Machine Bias," a 2016 piece by independent nonprofit ProPublica, reported that the system is highly skewed against people of color. Although we have no direct insight on how COMPAS is designed or implemented, it seems likely that the dataset used for training the models was itself biased against people of color because it was based on previous judicial decisions. In other words, models built using training data derived from human decisions are every bit as biased as the humans who made those decisions in the first place.

Bias and fairness often appear together in discussions about the ethical implications of AI, and are therefore easily confused. You can think of *bias* as a mathematical problem. A dataset or algorithm could be biased toward specific features and tend to favor them, but this is not necessarily a problem. *Fairness*, on the other hand, is a social construct.

Let's imagine we're building an algorithm to help a football team select its players based on the best performers of the previous season. It's likely that the algorithm will favor young and muscular players over older, overweight ones. This behavior would definitely be biased toward fit, young men. Would we say it's unfair, though? Most people wouldn't. Society accepts that football players have to be young and fit, and an algorithm with this behavior would be considered effective and not particularly unfair. Now imagine a similar algorithm tasked with making hiring decisions for the HR department of a tech company. We definitely wouldn't consider it fair if it kept selecting young and fit men over other demographics.

Not all hope is lost, though. By choosing how to assign labels, we're indirectly deciding the kind of behavior we want to encourage in our algorithm. If we are building algorithms for HR and we assign our labels based on previous HR decisions, we're promoting a simple automation of human decisions, which may be biased by previous HR managers. On the other hand, if we find a way to assign labels based on employees' performance, we are promoting the selection of high-performing employees. The same approach can be replicated for other delicate and potentially life-changing decisions:

- Making loan eligibility decisions based on how people actually repay their loans, instead of the previous decisions of bank officers
- Making health insurance decisions based on people's actual health, instead of past decisions by insurance companies
- Assessing the risk of an inmate committing crimes after being released from prison based on the historical behavior of previously released inmates, instead of past parole decisions by judges

Keep in mind that smarter design choices and bias-aware labeling might not be a complete solution. Many other forms of discrimination could affect one's life and thus inject biases into the data in subtle ways. For instance, even if we account for actual employee performance, but women nonetheless get fewer promotions due to a biased culture, this bias would leak into the data and the algorithm would learn it.

The solution to this problem is, perhaps unsurprisingly, to accurately analyze the data before using it to build and deploy AI applications. Researchers are working hard to build complex mechanical models that can automatically spot data biases. In the meantime, we need to be the ones asking the right questions and developing a sensitivity to the potential social bias that our data can hide.

Bias and fairness are one of the most important reasons we invested so much effort in helping you understand how data influences ML algorithms. Because we hope you'll become a protagonist of the AI era, it's important that you are aware of these threats and put forth effort to build technology that serves all people.

10.1.2 AI and jobs

The impact of AI on jobs is a topic that has filled entire books and yet still leaves us with untested hypotheses and unanswered questions. This short section is far from a complete answer, but we nonetheless wanted to offer some food for thought to help you develop your own thinking around this complex topic.

First of all, notice that throughout this book, we've talked about *tasks*. As you have learned, modern ML is perfectly suited to solve problems that are extremely well-defined, with very specific inputs and a very specific output. This means that we should change our narrative from "AI will replace human jobs" to "AI will replace human *tasks*."

Now, some jobs are so simple that they can be reduced to a single task: these are the ones at risk of disappearing completely. One example is truck drivers, who spend most of their time on the sole task of driving. As you're aware, self-driving technology has seen some amazing developments over the last few years, and it's likely that it will soon be able to entirely replace humans at the wheel. This means that one day, machines will be able to do the task that truck drivers spend 90% of their time on. It's needless to say what the implications will be for their jobs.

A question that we should ask ourselves is this: If a job can be reduced to performing a single task and is therefore amenable to today's AI, are we sure it's a good fit for a human in the first place? We don't think twice about deploying machines to take over dangerous jobs, such as inspecting nuclear power plants or monitoring offshore oil rigs. And yet, some jobs destroy people's souls without putting them at physical risk. In 2010, 14 workers jumped out of a window in a Foxconn electronics factory in Shenzhen, China. We argue that no job should be so soul-crushing as to push humans to take their lives, and we're probably better off if these jobs are taken over by machines that have no soul to be crushed.

After all, history is rife with stories of manual labor being replaced by machines. One could easily make the case that past technological revolutions, like the steam engine or the copying machine, nevertheless ended up igniting economic growth and raising the standards of living for many people on the planet.

And yet these hand-wavy arguments don't seem to convince the workers whose jobs are on the line. Supposedly, AI will replace some jobs but create some new ones. This is true, and not just for highly skilled positions like data scientists and ML engineers. Indeed, a new, growing trend is to train people to perform the task of labeling data for ML tasks. For instance, for every self-driving car company with hundreds of engineers in Silicon Valley, thousands of human labelers are looking through recorded footage and creating training datasets. We need to be honest, though: it's unlikely that these new jobs will be as plentiful or well-paid as those swept away by AI.

Our opinion is that we need to look at other industries that can absorb the jobs lost in other more automation-prone ones. Specifically, health care and education are the two important industries where costs have kept rising in the last decade, even in the face of increased digitalization and more-efficient processes. For example, according to the Federal Reserve Bank of St. Louis, the cost to attend a university increased nearly eight times faster than wages. Things don't seem better on the health-care side: the *Journal of the American Medical Association* (JAMA) reports that health-care spending in the United States rose nearly a trillion dollars from 1996 to 2015. Our hope is that the jobs lost because of automation in industries like transportation and manufacturing can be absorbed by those that need a "human touch" and will never be a good fit for complete automation. However, ours is just an educated hope because the dynamics behind these phenomena are incredibly complex.

We started this conversation emphasizing that AI will replace tasks, and not jobs. The majority of jobs will be impacted in a more subtle way than by being completely replaced. We look forward to the growth of *AI-augmented* or *AI-assisted* jobs: professions for which AI helps people do their job faster, better, or more pleasantly.

We saw two examples of this in the case study about Translated in chapter 5. The company uses AI to help project managers pick the best translator for a translation task by ranking thousands of resumes according to specific job requirements. It also offers professional translators a first translation attempt, leaving them free to correct it and focus their efforts on picking just the right word. According to Marco Trombetti, Translated's cofounder, the technology is really appreciated by translators:

> *Our technology is creating a lot of opportunities not just for us but also for the translators, that are finally not working on correcting again and again the same tedious stuff but are spending their time being more human, communicating what the text actually means and being more persuasive and creative.*

The truth is that at the moment, AI is improving the way we work and not throwing humans in the streets. It's easy to envision the latter happening in the near future, but we've provided more than one argument to support the idea that reality is not so clear-cut.

10.1.3 *The AI filter bubble*

Online platforms like YouTube and Facebook have become a primary medium for receiving news and commentary about the world. Given the essentially unlimited amount of content available on each of these platforms, their algorithms are what defines what we see and what we don't. In a sense, recommender systems have assumed the role of primary gatekeepers of information. Just think about it: What are the chances that you'll see a video on the 10th page of YouTube results? For better or worse, algorithms decide which content we get to consume.

In fact, personalization can become so extreme that media consumers are trapped inside a *filter bubble*, in which all of the content they consume is selected to match their beliefs and worldview. The term was coined by internet activist Eli Pariser in 2010 when he noticed that his friends' social media feeds showed either pro-Democratic or pro-Republican content, but rarely both. More generally, filter bubbles describe recommender systems that have tuned so accurately to the preferences of the user that they stop presenting any counterfactual content at all. Imagine joining several Flat Earth groups on Facebook, and seeing your news feed populate with Flat Earth–related content and enthusiastic comments. It wouldn't take long before our bias-prone brains would start to grossly exaggerate the number of Flat Earthers in the community. In fact, another common idiom for the filter bubble is *echo chamber*, because content and social interactions recommended automatically tend to reinforce the existing mindset, rather than challenge you with opposing views.

Something similar is happening with YouTube, whose recommendation engine is accused of nurturing extremism by focusing on increasingly extreme videos. *The New York Times* famously reported that starting to watch videos about vegetarianism would produce recommendations about veganism, just like videos about jogging would lead to recommendations about marathon running. More worryingly, the same dynamics also apply to more sensitive domains, like misinformation or fake news about politics, human rights, or violence. And indeed, many communities have started to voice their concerns to YouTube (and the government), demanding more oversight of what happens on the site.

From a technical point of view, you should realize that none of these issues are intrinsic to the technology itself. Many recommendation algorithms are based on similarity, either across different items or other users in the community. There's no "hate speech" knob that YouTube engineers tweak to increase engagement on the site. Instead, these extremist dynamics are a direct consequence of the business objectives that drove the adoption of recommender systems in the first place. These algorithms are designed to provide us with content that we're likely to engage with, and whether we like it or not, we want to see stuff that we agree with. As our interests start drifting toward one topic, any further recommendations will start to focus on that one topic, leading us to consume more of that content, leading to even more tailored recommendations, and so on. Figure 10.1 depicts this vicious cycle.

Recommender systems just don't have the abstraction ability to understand that recommending dentures to twenty-something customers is a dumb business idea, but showing both sides of a political debate is critical for a healthy society. Instead, they treat the latter just like the former, drawing people inside a thicker and thicker filter bubble.

In the aftermath of the 2016 presidential election in the United States and the Brexit referendum in the United Kingdom (also in 2016), the major social media platforms have strengthened their efforts against radicalization and extremism. And the solution might well be adding *more* AI into the mix. Relying on humans for the policing of abusive and unethical behavior is not really feasible at the massive operation scale of today's major social media networks. Instead, natural language processing and visual AI models can be used to automatically process and block forbidden content.

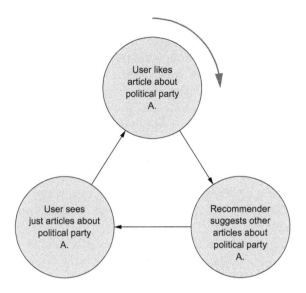

Figure 10.1 Recommender systems have so much power in determining our daily media consumption that they can create extremism bubbles in social media.

The core issue still stands: to provide a healthy information diet to the public, you need people to read both what they agree with and the opposite. Unfortunately, showing people content they don't agree with is not good for business, so the issue is still open.

10.1.4 When AI fails: Corner cases and adversarial attacks

When the first airlines opened up to civil transport after World War II, airplanes were unreliable and, frankly, dangerous beasts. With only limited experience with military aircraft (whose life was not that long for obvious reasons), engineers didn't have a good understanding of how the aircraft would fail during operation: misfiring engines, cracks in the fuselage, and so on. Over the following decades, they put together enough knowledge, theory, and experience to make air travel the extremely safe form of transportation that we enjoy today. As humanity starts relying on AI for life-or-death situations, such as health care or autonomous transportation, our understanding of its limits needs to grow accordingly. This section will teach you about two important failure modes of AI: *corner cases* and *adversarial attacks.*

Today's AI, based on machine learning, draws its power from its ability to learn shallow statistical correlations from massive amounts of data. Unfortunately, no algorithm or system known today shows the generalization and logical inference capabilities that humans have. In descriptive words, one could say that AI algorithms are extremely attentive to detail, but are "dumb" when it comes to drawing obvious conclusions from their knowledge or dealing with atypical situations. Take Tesla's autopilot, which can seamlessly drive for hundreds of miles on the highway, and yet had a crash in 2017 as it mistook a lightly painted truck for a patch of blue sky and drove right through it. No human would mistake a picture of the sky on a truck for the actual sky, yet one of the most sophisticated technologies of today still does. These are *corner cases*: rare situations that are hard to find in training data and that models can interpret in stupid ways.

There's really not a lot we can do about corner cases besides collecting more extensive and exhaustive datasets, and developing more robust models. However, when it comes to disasters brought about by AI models, corner cases are not the only issue we should look out for. Another, subtler, risk exists: *adversarial attacks*. It turns out that enterprising researchers have found ways to "confuse" neural networks, and generate visual noise (see figure 10.2) that neural networks misclassify almost 100% of the time. In other words, they've found ways to generate a seemingly random splash of color that models consistently classify as real objects, like a car or pizza. One could imagine taping printouts of figure 10.2 to paralyze self-driving cars in the area. More subtly, seemingly innocuous adversarial images can be injected into online content, forcing it to be classified as malicious.

Research on both creating and defending against adversarial attacks is still ongoing. Corner cases and adversarial attacks are two sides of the same coin, where we can't trust the output of ML models and need to find ways to protect society from their mistakes.

A patch to protect ourselves from these problems is to use redundant systems that are not based on AI. For instance, in the context of self-driving cars, many companies

Figure 10.2   Object detection models can correctly identify Gianluca on the left. However, the colorful image held by Nico is specially engineered to confuse the model so it that it can't detect him.

use traditional radar to check for physical obstructions to the car's path. It doesn't matter whether the car's AI interprets the signal from the cameras as a blue sky: if the radar detects an object, you'd better stop. Although these solutions can provide some reassurance, they are still patches. At their core, some applications of AI are still not robust enough to be deployed in potentially dangerous applications.

10.1.5 When the artificial looks real: AI-generated fake content

Both chapters 4 and 5 started with AI models that could understand media and language, but also showed algorithms that could *create* both—for example, by turning photos of zebras into photos of horses. This is exciting, because it rounds off AI abilities, allowing us to build creative, and not only analytical, applications. However, these creations are now so realistic and convincing that they're a powerful new weapon for malicious actors who want to manufacture and spread their own reality.

Stalin's regime in the Soviet Union of the 1930s famously altered photographs to remove political opponents and generally support the prevailing views of the government. At the time, those techniques were effective precisely because very few people even knew that altering photos was possible. As Photoshop and special effects in movies made the general public aware of these manipulation techniques, they lost some of their power. It might well be that the only reason we think pictures or videos are authentic is that we know that it takes a certain amount of effort and care to alter them. With the advent of generative networks, this barrier to entry is quickly dropping to zero.

In other words, this is another situation in which AI brings a *scale* advantage: it's now so easy and cheap to produce fake content that society needs to face the risk of it being used for unethical purposes. What we didn't tell you in chapter 5 is that GPT-2, OpenAI's most advanced model for text generation, was initially not released to the public. The researchers' concern was that the text produced by the model was so convincing that they were worried about bad actors using it to spam the internet with meaningless but enticing content (click bait). They decided to release a less powerful version of their model and wait for the NLP community to catch up and develop models capable of distinguishing this fake content.

Other players have not been so conscientious. Indeed, one of the early claims to fame of generative networks came in 2017, when anonymous Reddit user Deepfakes posted several pornographic videos featuring famous celebrities. It turned out that those stars never starred in any of those videos. Instead, Deepfakes used generative networks to apply the facial traits of famous actresses into existing material, roughly copying and pasting their faces and expressions. Deepfakes focused on celebrities because of the availability of training data (it's easy to find thousands of pictures of a celebrity), but the same technology would work with our loved ones or even politicians.

What is the solution to avoid the spread of fake content? Well, because scale is the problem, scale can be also the solution. As algorithms get better at producing fake text and fake images, so do algorithms that can spot them. It's an arms race between who wants to trick us and who wants to protect us, and the weapons in this fight are sophisticated algorithms. As our senses stop discerning what's real and what's not, the only thing we can do is ask algorithms for help.

10.2 Opportunities for AI in society

In a sense, this whole book is dedicated to the power and potential of AI, so we won't repeat ourselves in this section. Instead, we'll take a broader view and focus on the higher-level impact of AI on society rather than on individual organizations.

10.2.1 Democratization of technology

The recent uptick in AI technology has been largely fueled by the democratization of technologies and knowledge. Chapter 1 already presented the factors that drove the last 20 years of AI development: availability of large amounts of data and cheap computing power.

On top of that, it's important to mention the role that open research and open source software have played in the last few years. The AI community is incredibly open, and as you've seen in chapter 8, it's possible to find state-of-the-art research published for free on platforms like arXiv (https://arxiv.org). Open research is an incredible catalyst for the development of AI. Just put yourself in the shoes of a researcher who needs to solve a complicated ML problem: they can get access, for free, to a vast amount of research papers published by leading AI teams. Often, these papers come with code and data so everyone can try the algorithms by themselves and adapt them (or improve them) to match their own needs.

Just as open research allowed everyone to have free access to knowledge, open source tools enabled free access to state-of-the-art tools. Large tech companies like Google and Facebook rushed to build their own ML frameworks: software libraries that enable developers to build ML algorithms fast and efficiently. These organizations have a large interest in making their own framework a standard, in order to more easily attract talent. Google, for instance, has invested heavily in marketing its own ML framework called TensorFlow, so much that we've often heard business executives refer to it as a "must-have" technology in their stack.

If availability of data, cheap computing power, and open source research and tools have been the factors pushing AI forward in the past 20 years, what will push AI forward in the next 20?

The surge in data availability and computing power is not exhausted yet: they will keep driving AI innovation forward in the years to come. However, we are already starting to see the first instances of companies and research groups taking a step back from their openness. In the previous section, we mentioned OpenAI delaying the release of its language-generation model because of concerns about malicious actors.

Even if the release of open research could slow down, other factors are coming into play. One of the bottlenecks of AI has always been the scarcity of talent: it's hard to find people with the right skill set to work on AI. Thankfully, a growing number of freely available, high-quality online AI courses have already helped tens of thousands of people get up to speed with AI. This trend will keep going and inject much needed talent into the world of AI.

We're also excited by the development of ML tools for nontechnical people. For instance, Google has introduced a tool called Cloud AutoML to expand the pool of customers who can benefit from ML algorithms. It boasts a simpler user experience thanks to automation of the trickiest tasks in the development of an ML model. Think about it this way: before Microsoft Excel came out, the only way you could use computers was to learn a programming language and write code. With Excel, suddenly many more people had the skills to create a workbook for accounting, time tracking, or a thousand other uses. The same is happening with AI and products like Cloud AutoML.

It's not hard to imagine a future when you'll be able to build a whole ML product without having to write any lines of code. The whole premise of this book is that your job is to envision new AI-based products and let data scientists take over, but you may well be empowered to take care of the whole process soon with better, simpler tools. If we get there, the barrier to entry for AI projects would basically go to zero, and the only bottleneck would be your creativity and inspiration for new projects.

10.2.2 *Massive scale*

One of the most intriguing promises of AI is that it will drive the marginal cost of knowledge and expertise very close to zero, opening up products and services to audiences that could not afford them beforehand. They're so cheap that Google even translates web pages for free anytime you want. Just as the $10 smartphone allowed a billion people to go on the internet for the first time, imagine what $1 AI-based doctors, teachers, or lawyers could do for the world. As you have seen in the second part of this book, when the investment in collecting data and developing a model has been made, the variable costs of continuing to run it are really low (basically just computing power, which is getting cheaper all the time).

If Google democratized knowledge and search, and made them available to any internet-connected human on the planet for free, more-advanced AI technologies promise to do the same with insight and intelligence. Many of the economies of the world are being held back by a lack of knowledge and skilled labor, which can't easily be exported or trained. Instead, think about preschoolers in poor countries having access to AI-based tools that can teach them to read and write when there aren't enough skilled teachers to go around. What about self-adapting industrial control algorithms that allow industrialization in undeveloped areas with a scarcity of skilled line workers?

The potential for scale is not limited to developing economies, either. In most countries around the world, many knowledge-based products and services have a limited reach because of their price structure. How many cancer patients are not being diagnosed and treated early enough because they visit a doctor only once a year? What about giving them a preliminary AI-based checkup every day (or even every hour, using wearable sensors)? How many more lives could we save if everybody had access to such a service?

Closely connected to the concept of scale is the virtuous cycle of AI. AI-based products are cheaper, and so can be deployed and sold on a larger scale, leading to the accumulation of more data that can further improve the quality of the product, making it more appealing for users.

10.3   *Opportunities for AI in industries*

In this section, we single out the industries that we believe have the strongest potential for change and disruption by AI in the near future. Of course, this list is by no means exhaustive: it's designed to give you the pulse of what's happening in different sectors, and some elements to develop your own critical thinking. We encourage you not to take this section as gospel truth, but to use it as a starting point you can build on thanks to your background and your newfound AI knowledge.

In chapter 7, we tried to find objective criteria to assess the potential of an AI project. We concluded that the potential is directly correlated with how much it takes advantage of the two main strengths of AI: scale and accuracy. We can easily adapt the same criteria to whole industries. After all, an industry disruption may be seen as the compound effect of a multitude of AI projects from one or more companies.

In the context of an AI project, *accuracy* is a measure of how much your business would benefit from an increase in the accuracy of a certain task. To apply the accuracy factor to an entire industry, extend its meaning to the set of core processes that make up the industry. For example, a sector that is largely digitized and already efficient will probably gain little benefit from an increase in accuracy brought about by AI. On the other hand, industries that are still characterized by inefficient and ineffective technology can be heavily influenced by AI.

The same goes for *scale*. When talking about individual AI projects, the scale factor measures the positive impact brought about when a task is automated through AI. The same applies now that we're analyzing whole industries. If an industry frequently operates through "crufty" processes carried out by hand, there's a high potential for disruption by AI.

In the context of AI projects, we also evaluated and prioritized projects based on an organization's readiness. The same concept is valid for entire industries. As you now know, modern AI is largely dependent on the existence of large datasets to train ML models. If an industry is still powered by analog processes (aka pen and paper), it will have to go through painful digitalization work before AI can make a dent. On the other hand, industries that have already invested in digitalization and data management can start applying AI right away. Beware: this doesn't mean that industries with low technological readiness have low potential for AI. What low technological readiness tells us is simply that disruption will take longer to happen.

10.3.1 *Social media networks*

In a sense, we could say that social media networks were the Big Bang behind today's surge in AI investments. By putting billions of people online, they allowed researchers to collect the massive datasets required for the development of advanced AI models. The same huge population of users also provided a large pool for low-risk experimentation with new AI-based products, like automated face recognition and recommendation systems.

Social media users generate a large chunk of all the kinds of data that we explored in this book: from core business data about advertisements, user churn, and activation, to gigantic datasets of text and images. We can separate two main categories of applications:

- To deliver the main purpose of social media platforms: allowing advertisers to reach the right users
- To deliver services

Chapter 5 already covered sentiment analysis, one of the most basic tools in the NLP toolbox. Social media provides the ideal platforms to deploy sentiment analysis at scale, because interactions with the general public hold great value for companies. And yet, this is old news. Today's social platforms use AI algorithms to model user behavior and interests to personalize marketing messages and optimize advertising campaigns. In this context, AI's accuracy will keep on pushing the efficacy of content recommendation and ad placement.

We already talked about the threats of personalization at scale previously in this chapter. In this context, we want to focus on the opportunities that AI's scale potential provides. A first application is automated abuse prevention and detection: Facebook and other social media giants have already deployed models that can detect unethical and abusive content and prevent it from being shared on their networks.

For instance, every major social network uses AI to automatically spot violent or pornographic material *before* it's uploaded to the platform and served to their billions of users. Imagine a world without AI, where anytime you post a picture or a video, some person sitting in an office has to check whether it's appropriate. Social networks simply wouldn't exist (or they would, but they'd be filled with all kinds of human degeneration). Computer vision algorithms enable this kind of check at scale, and they're doing a very good job of keeping communities safe; for instance, it's extremely rare to find violent or pornographic material on Facebook.

While content personalization and moderation are old news, we turned to an expert to envision the future relationship between AI and social media. We asked Luca La Mesa, a social media marketer in Italy who has worked with many prominent organizations, about the trends he sees coming. He highlighted a positive story, Facebook's Safety Check feature that uses NLP models to scan messages and detect the early signs of a suicidal tendency. Human experts manually review cases that have been flagged by the algorithm, alerting authorities when appropriate.

But he also cited a more sinister episode, as reported by Gillian Brockell of the *Washington Post*. While pregnant, she posted on social media using hashtags like #30weekspregnant or #babybump. The algorithms picked up on her posts and targeted her with ads for baby products. Unfortunately, Brockell lost her child, but even as she was searching on Google for terms like "Braxton Hicks contractions" or "baby does not move," she kept being targeted with baby product ads that did nothing but inflict sadness. The only way she had to make it stop was to write an open letter to Twitter.

From what La Mesa has told us, it seems that AI is always bringing its scale advantage deeper into human interactions. If blocking violent material is a "must have" feature that we all expect from these platforms, Facebook's Safety Check is a beautiful addition that caught many people off guard. No one expected social media platforms to be able to provide such a service, and the only reason it's possible is that AI dramatically improved its capabilities in processing textual data. The negative example that La Mesa mentioned is once again proof that AI is simply not fit for corner cases. Hopefully, the depth at which these algorithms understand text will keep improving, and there will always be fewer and fewer cases like Brockell's.

10.3.2 Health care

Health care is an incredibly complex sector with many specific challenges, multiple stakeholders, and a complex regulatory environment. In such a broad industry, it's helpful to break down individual applications. AI will be impacting health care in three main areas:

- Diagnostics
- Drug discovery
- Operational efficiency and new care models

Table 10.1 lists how the three areas stack up in terms of the accuracy, scale, and technological readiness.

Table 10.1 Analysis of potential and technological readiness for AI applications in health care

	Accuracy factor	Scale factor	Technological readiness
Diagnosis	High	High	Low
Drug discovery	High	High	Exponentially increasing
Value-based care	High	High	Low

Using AI to improve the way doctors diagnose diseases is probably one of the most desirable applications of AI. The world has a limited supply of doctors, and they're all humans. Like all humans, doctors rely on the limited number of examples that they've seen in their lives, fuzzy data, and quite a lot of gut feelings.

Try thinking about this: every time Netflix recommends you a movie, it's using millions of data points and state-of-the-art technology that's been refined for years by world-class data scientists. Every time your doctor prescribes you a therapy, their decision is based on several years of training, maybe hundreds of people they've treated with similar symptoms, and a very limited set of data (assuming you haven't spent weeks locked up in a clinic doing medical tests). Netflix is much more sophisticated at recommending movies than your doctor is at recommending drugs. It's clear that a more data-driven approach to diagnosis and prescription can go a long way.

Using AI to improve diagnoses definitely has a high accuracy factor. We can all agree that if we had the opportunity to improve its accuracy, humanity would benefit. This specific application can also have a large scale factor. While AI would most likely be used to support doctors, not to replace them, some areas of the world simply don't have any doctors to go around. In these cases, an AI doctor could go a long way in providing simple healthcare at scale.

This is also true for the richest countries of the world, but for diseases that are not commonly treated by a doctor. An example is dermatological conditions. Let's take the case of acne: as the startup MD Algorithms reports, 90% of people with acne never see a dermatologist. This was an opportunity that the company exploited by building computer vision algorithms that can diagnose which kind of acne a patient has based on a selfie.

Unfortunately, access to data is probably the main factor holding these applications back. Most health-care processes are still analog (how many times have you seen a doctor walking into a hospital holding paper reports and a pen?). Even if the recent push toward electronic health records (EHRs) has somewhat improved the situation, the industry still has to come to grips with the impact of a digitized pipeline.

On top of that, what little data is available is fragmented, as different stakeholders including hospitals, payers, national health-care services, and pharmaceutical companies each own but a fragment of the clinical history of a patient. In other words, there's huge potential, but it's going to be hard to get all the players to collaborate.

The second big area for disruption in health care is drug discovery. The main trigger for disruption in this case is the observation that the price to discover a new drug is exponentially increasing. The R&D costs of the pharmaceutical industry have skyrocketed nearly a hundredfold between 1950 and 2010.

On the other hand, the cost for sequencing DNA is exponentially decreasing. The first whole human genome sequencing cost roughly $2.7 billion in 2003. By 2006, the cost had decreased to $300,000. The 2016 cost was around $1,000, and still shows no sign of stopping its fall. This means that it's now possible to generate massive amounts of genome data for cheap.

The widespread availability of biological data is the first step toward enabling AI to peek into the human genome and help design new drugs. Both small startups and large organizations are jumping on this train, often collaborating together. In 2018, Pfizer entered into a strategic partnership with an AI startup backed by tech giants like Tencent and Google called XtalPi. The goal was to predict pharmaceutical properties of small molecules and develop "computation-based rational drug design." Pfizer is not alone: other large organizations like Novartis, GSK, Sanofi, Amgen, and Merck have announced their own partnerships with AI startups. The aim is to combine their domain knowledge, data, and resources with the AI skills of smaller startups to discover new drug candidates for a range of diseases.

AI-aided drug discovery is still at an early stage, but the returns are extremely promising. Its accuracy and scale factors are both extremely high, as being able to develop more-effective drugs cheaper and faster will have an enormous effect on public health. Technological readiness is also improving quickly, as shown by the constant drop in DNA sequencing costs.

Finally, AI can also address the business side of health care, not just the medicine side. Health care is notoriously an inefficient sector, with many stakeholders with different incentives and practices that are not always in the best interest of patients.

With the aging of the population and increasing costs, government efforts are shifting toward a value-based service model: a system focused on the patient, where health-care providers are incentivized to provide the best care at the lowest cost. This is in contrast to the fee-for-service model, where providers are paid in proportion to the number of services performed, creating incentives that lead to waste and not always to the best outcomes for patients.

Think about it this way: when you see a doctor, most of the time they prescribe you a bunch of tests that you, your insurance, or your national health-care service will pay for. Often, the results of these tests do little more than lead you to . . . more tests.

Now, every time you see a doctor and describe your symptoms, it's likely that someone else in the world has had a very similar clinical history and very similar symptoms and has gone through a series of tests. If you recall our discussion about recommender systems in chapter 6, it looks like a potential application for AI, which could help doctors steer toward the best possible diagnosis or test path, saving money, time, and arguably improving the quality of care for patients.

Obviously, some pretty deep system-wide changes are necessary before we can go this route. This shift will probably be far down the line, not so much because of technological limitations but because of the readiness of the entire system. Yet, the potential is so high that we are confident this shift will happen anyway.

10.3.3 *Energy*

Energy production and distribution is undergoing a substantial transformation driven by a convergence of technological, economical, and environmental factors. Sustainable energy is finally starting to make business sense, as economies of scale bring prices down without the need for subsidies. At the same time, electric vehicles are becoming more widespread in many countries, and smart sensors are getting cheaper and being used more often in buildings and factories.

Table 10.2 presents the scale, accuracy, and technological readiness factors for the two key applications of AI in the energy sector: load balancing and energy consumption optimization.

Table 10.2 Analysis of AI potential and technological readiness for AI in energy

	Renewables production forecasting		
	Accuracy factor	**Scale factor**	**Technological readiness**
Load balancing	High	High	High
Energy consumption optimization	High	High	High

If you're not familiar with how the energy market works, here's a two-minute primer. Electrical energy is still difficult and expensive to store and stockpile for later use (even though new battery technology has started to change this). This means that energy companies have to produce exactly the energy that the grid demands at each moment of the day. If you turn on the AC in your room, a power plant somewhere starts burning more gas to fulfill the additional energy demand from your home. If energy companies don't produce enough, a blackout could occur. Excess production can damage the grid too. *Load balancing* is the key activity to run our society: at any moment in time, the demand and supply of energy need to be balanced.

Energy companies have become fairly good at predicting energy demand, modeling how families use their TVs and microwaves at night, or turn on the AC in the summer. Controlling production has not been a problem historically because fossil-fuel-based power plants can be adjusted up or down as needed. However, energy produced from renewable sources is much harder to control, or even predict, because it depends on fickle factors like wind or sun. At the same time, market deregulation pushes energy companies to solve these challenges without investing in additional infrastructure.

Luckily, along with challenges, opportunities are brought by new technologies like AI. Investments in digital technologies by energy companies have risen sharply over the last few years, with global investment in digital electricity infrastructure and software rising 20% annually since 2014, reaching $47 billion in 2016. This push is enabling us to build the underlying asset needed to power any AI: data.

Notice that everything we talked about earlier can be seen as a prediction/optimization challenge rather than an engineering one. For instance, we can use weather data to predict the energy that will be produced by renewable resources. Since we're able to get data from wind turbines, solar panels, and so forth along with weather data, we can use this information to forecast the production from renewables with higher accuracy and make utilities' lives easier.

Optimizing energy consumption is another use case that's generally a great fit for AI capabilities. In chapter 2, you saw how Google automated its data center operations to save energy. This was made possible in large part because Google had already installed many sensors and had invested in data collection and automation. As these enabling technologies spread to other buildings, factories, and infrastructure, AI-enabled optimization will also become more prevalent. Similar technologies can also be applied for residential housing, where they can help families reduce energy consumption too.

The realm of energy optimization is not limited to reducing the total amount of energy used. Energy companies, and thus the environment, also benefit when loads are distributed throughout the day according to the production patterns of renewable energy sources. For example, this might mean setting up electric vehicles to charge during the day, when solar power is plentiful.

In a world where climate change is increasingly—and rightfully—worrying the public, AI can and must be one of the weapons in energy companies' arsenals. With the right mindset, this technology can work as a layer that controls both the generation and production of energy, achieving new levels of efficiency and contributing to our fight against climate change.

10.3.4 Manufacturing

Ever since the lean manufacturing revolution of the 80s, the manufacturing sector has been heavily data-driven. Our capitalistic world pushes for constant improvement and optimization, and you can't improve what you can't measure. For this reason, factories were one of the first locations where data in a digital format started being collected for computers to analyze.

As you've learned in the book, anytime there's a treasure trove of data, the potential for AI projects follows, as the readiness is high and the barriers to entry low. The most familiar examples revolve around improving production efficiency, as you saw in the Google data-centers case study. A single production-line machine might have dozens or hundreds of temperature, pressure, and vibration sensors that produce a constant stream of data.

One of the oldest and most established applications of ML in manufacturing is *fault prediction*: using sensor data to get an early warning when a piece of equipment is about to break down. More-advanced efforts have helped users to understand whether it's possible to model the effect of key production parameters (such as pressure or cycle speed) on production quality. Just as in the Google data center case study, such a *digital twin* enables engineers to tweak and optimize the industrial process digitally, transferring the accumulated experience into the physical plant after they're confident with their results.

All these applications we have discussed so far use structured data, like sensor time-series. However, image-based AI models like the ones we talked about in chapter 4 have the potential to bring factory-floor automation to the next level. A prime candidate for this evolution is quality control, just as in the cucumber classification case study in chapter 4. Object classification and detection models based on deep networks are versatile and can be used to find occlusions or defects in the finished product simply by adding cameras to the production line.

More-powerful AI algorithms will also improve robotics and automation on the factory floor. A big limitation that is holding up increased use of robotics in manufacturing is the large amount of time and effort needed to program them to build new products. If you recall our discussion in chapter 7, you'll recognize that repetitive, narrow tasks like this are an ideal candidate for solutions based on machine learning.

It's clear that manufacturing is hungry for scalable technology that allows it to produce goods cheaper and faster. AI is the ultimate tool for this purpose, whether we're trying to predict faults or automate quality control. On the accuracy side, we know that AI is extremely narrow, and can't possibly reach human capabilities in handling exceptions in the near future. This means that humans will keep owning the realm of luxury and tailored goods for quite some time. After all, *handmade* is already a free pass to a higher ticket price, and the gap will probably increase as mass production becomes more standardized and cheaper.

10.3.5 *Finance*

When it comes to the applications of AI in finance, we need to distinguish between two separate worlds: commercial banking and trading. *Commercial banks* are the banks that we all deal with in our daily lives: they cash checks, mortgage homes, and so on. *Trading companies* buy and sell stocks and bonds on financial markets, trying to outsmart other investors to make money. Because banking and finance are heavily based on data and numbers, both of these have been early adopters of machine learning technologies. Chapter 2 presented an example of this when we discussed Square's merchant loans.

Commercial banks already make heavy use of AI tools for several of their core competencies, like fraud prevention and risk assessment. In the coming years, improvements to these models will filter down from other areas of AI to create healthier financial markets and thus reduce costs for borrowers and companies. In many core activities of the banking industry, profit is directly correlated with decision-making accuracy, and therefore the fit for AI is quite evident.

On the other hand, there's also great potential for using AI in entirely new ways, using its scale. Automating internal processes with AI tools like visual recognition and NLP is neither fancy nor a new idea, but will be important to reducing costs throughout the organization. As with any other customer-facing organizations, AI holds great potential for disrupting and improving the customer service relationships that are mostly taken care of by flesh-and-blood employees today. The same goes for the curated and personalized marketing offerings that can be created by tools like recommendation systems.

The same considerations also apply to a related industry: insurance. As AI models improve their ability to understand and structure information about the world, insurance companies can have a better idea of what risks they're insuring their customers against, and thus offer more adequate and personalized rates. Think about automated analysis of health data to provide personalized health insurance, or real-time intelligence about the types of roads that you usually drive on. While all of these ideas are possible today, AI will provide the scaling secret sauce that will allow insurance companies to extend them more broadly to their customer base.

Finally, financial trading is a bit of an odd duck, and we won't spend much time talking about it. Wall Street is a secretive and specialized world in which some of the nerdiest minds try their best to extract proprietary information that they can use to inform their trading decisions and "beat the market" with superior returns for their investment. This means that many of the AI tools that we have described in the book can in one way or another be used to make money on the financial markets. A familiar example is using visual object classification models on satellite data to count the number of cars leaving Ford factories, and thus predict how the automaker is doing *before* it releases its reports. This proprietary information can then be used to bet on the stock price going up or down, pocketing any profits. The same idea also applies to many of the other models we have presented in the book; for example, sentiment analysis on social media to understand how a company is perceived by its customers, and thus whether its future prospects are good.

Wall Street has already been using these tools for a decade or more, so what's going to happen in the next few years? We don't know! There is so much money at stake that these trading companies keep all their AI advances close to their chests. Two things are certain: the more accurate you are at making decisions and the faster you can make them, the more money you'll make. For these reasons, AI and trading will always be best friends.

10.3.6 *Education*

Of all the industries we have analyzed so far in this section, education is probably the furthest behind in AI usage. In our opinion, the most exciting potential for their intersection lies in *personalization*: the ability to customize the learning itinerary of each student based on their strengths and weaknesses. Some massive open online courses (MOOCs) have been pioneering in this area just because of the incredible challenges arising out of the need to mentor and grade tens of thousands of students with limited budgets.

It turns out that constant and personalized feedback is the most important component of an effective learning strategy. Luckily, many of the AI models that we have discussed in this book are actually very good at classifying inputs as "good" or "bad." Going beyond classic automatic grading systems, we can imagine vision-based models that can automatically grade painting techniques based on their similarity with the work of great artists of the past. Or even NLP-based models that can assess the vocabulary of young writers by comparing their homework with great literary masterpieces.

Of course, a lot of work remains to be done before AI-based models can provide the backbone of the school system as we know it today. However, several specific education segments are already taking advantage of AI tools. We already have automated music teachers that can alert students when they're playing out of tune, or language-learning tools that can help eliminate accents. These niche sectors play to the strengths of especially advanced AI algorithms, like those in media, and are pushing education to be more friendly for "trial-and-error" learners. In other words, ultimate personalization becomes *gamification*, providing each student instant feedback.

One of the most exciting promises about AI in education is that it's going to help provide the next billion students in the developing world with the same level of education that the developed world is enjoying today.

10.4   *What about general AI?*

Ever since the term *artificial intelligence* came up, people enjoyed betting on how long it would take before AI could match the performance of the human brain. As you will recall from our brief history lesson in chapter 1, this majestic goal is called *general AI*, exactly because it can tackle any task. Unsurprisingly, the recent spate of successes by deep learning has fueled optimistic guesses, with prominent people in the community suggesting we will reach human-machine parity as soon as 2030.

Entire books have been written on artificial general intelligence (AGI), so we don't dare try to cover the topic exhaustively. (We can recommend *Superintelligence* by Nick Bostrom, Oxford University Press, 2014.) Our goal for this section is to get you thinking about the most realistic and immediate opportunities for AGI.

After reading this book, we hope you realize that we're still far away from the versatile, fast-learning marvel that is human intelligence. Modern AI is based on machine learning, and modern ML is basically still pattern-matching on steroids, even if it allows us to build valuable products. Many people believe (and we tend to agree) that the technology used to build the narrow AI applications described in this book is unsuitable for AGI.

This opinion is shared even by some of the godfathers of AI. For instance, Geoffrey Hinton, one of the fathers of deep learning, confessed in an interview that he's "deeply suspicious" of the underlying principles that currently allow neural networks to learn, and doesn't believe they'll ever scale to true intelligence. Judea Pearl, another AI pioneer, argues that current machine learning is stuck at fitting curves, without understanding what the world around us means. In other words, we're still busy teaching computers "what" is happening in the world, but we haven't even started tackling the "why."

The knowledge you received from this book likely brought you to the same conclusions about the future of AGI. In any case, we don't think you should despair. We certainly don't. An incredible number of real-world applications can be built with the ML and narrow AI tools that we already know how to use.

We reached out to Denis Rothman, AI expert and author of three successful books, and asked him for his opinion on AGI. We couldn't phrase it better:

Artificial intelligence as some super consciousness is not only a mirage, for the moment, but most importantly, AGI is useless.

Automation, with AI agents or not, will continue to increase exponentially in the years to come. AI agents that specialize in a variety of domains will provide increasing power to IoT.

If we now put this together, we get a network of connected automated agents enhanced with AI that will transform the world as it is today. This is not any better or worse than the first cars, trains, airplanes, and telephones.

Now, some prominent names are still warning us about the danger of superintelligent AI. One of them is Elon Musk, who has often warned us about the dangers of a super-human AI, going as far as speculating about its potential to end civilization. We're so early in the development of AI that it's difficult to foresee whether this apocalyptic scenario will actually happen. For now, the dangers seem focused on structural societal change and loss of jobs, as we discussed earlier. You can relax for now: Terminator is still nowhere to be seen.

10.5 *Closing thoughts*

Our goal for this book was to give you the knowledge and tools you need to bring the benefits of AI into your organization, even without technical skills. We worked hard to coach you into a leader who could begin and direct the discussion about finding the most promising areas for using AI in your organization. In the first part of the book, you learned the more technical information about the AI toolbox: various types of algorithms for working with the types of data you're likely to encounter in today's organizations. The industry case studies and examples scattered throughout the material have shown you how tech leaders think and plan their AI goals.

In the second part of the book, you learned how to roll up your sleeves. We showed you how to find and understand the most promising opportunities for using AI in your business, recruit the right team, and get started with the implementation.

Some of you already had an AI project in mind when you picked up the book. For you, we hope the book has given substance to your plans by teaching you the actual capabilities of today's AI in a hype-free way. For those of you who did not have a project in mind, we hope that we inspired you with the latest from industry and academia, and that your plans are now more concrete.

Either way, our best wish is that you feel confident and energized to jump back into your team, organization, or startup, and start working toward your first AI project. We wish you the best of luck.

Summary

- Several unsolved ethical challenges remain around the role of AI in society—most importantly, fairness, safety, and dependability.
- AI is unique in that large amounts of knowledge, software, and data have been freely available since the start of its development, making it easier for everybody to participate in its growth.
- AI can push the variable cost of expertise and knowledge close to zero, making it possible to create new products and services that operate at massive scale with little capital.
- Because of their massive scale, many of the biggest sectors of the economy (like energy and health care) stand to benefit the most from developments in AI.

index

A

A/B testing 164
abuse prevention and detection, automated 223
accuracy 52, 55, 129, 148–149, 222
actionable results 55
adversarial attacks 218–219
agents. *See* chatbots
AGI (artificial general intelligence) 2, 231–232
agriculture, optimizing with deep learning 85–90
AI (artificial intelligence) 1–9
    data science vs. 7
    defining 6–7
    explainable 83
    for media 176
    history behind 2–4
    machine learning and 4–6
    origin of term 2
    overview 6–8
    virtuous cycle of 198–202
AI spring 3
AI vision 142–143
AI winter 3–4
ALPAC (Automatic Language Processing Advisory
    Committee) report 3
Amazon
    label collection by 172
    Mechanical Turk 173
    training bias and 212
ancillary data 169
Andrieu, Isabelle 113–118
Anki 204–205
APIs (application programming interfaces) 187
artificial general intelligence (AGI) 2
artificial intelligence. *See* AI
arXiv platform 170, 220

audio 84–85
automated abuse prevention and detection 223
automated customer segmentation 44–52
automation, of industrial processes 163

B

backpropagation 75
banking 229
"Better Data Centers Through Machine Learning"
    (Kava) 27
biased data 177–179, 211–214
big data 173
binary classification model 58
binary classification tasks 53
black box
    DL models as 83
    machine learning as 35, 187
borrowing solutions 186, 188–190, 195
Bostrom, Nick 231
bots. *See* chatbots
Box, George 34
brittleness, of expert systems 4
Brockell, Gillian 224
brokerbot 96, 99
building solutions 186, 190–191, 195–197
business goals 159
business outcomes, tying metrics to 56–58
business risk 192
business threats 150
buyer persona 50
buying solutions 186–188, 193–194

C

chasm 200
chatbots
  goals for 91
  past failure of 92, 211
  query example 94
churning customers, predicting 38–41
classes, number of examples per 176
classification algorithms 52–55
cleaning data 190, 203
Cloud AutoML 221
cloud resources 191
clustering algorithms 55–56
collaborative filtering 127–129
commercial banking 229
COMPAS (Correctional Offender Management
    Profiling for Alternative Sanctions)
    system 212
computer vision 69–70, 72
  APIs for 187
  huskies vs. wolves identification example 83
computing power, machine learning and 5
content curation and community building 136
  collaborative filtering 127–129
  Netflix case study 131–136
    business value of recommendations 134–135
    recommendations and user experience
      133–134
    recommender system 131–133
  recommender systems 120–127
    content-based systems beyond simple
      features 124–126
    limitations of features and similarity 126–127
    pitfalls of 129–131
content generation 81–82
content, fake 219–220
Continue Watching Ranker, Netflix's 132–133
contrarian examples in datasets 178
conversion rates and upselling, boosting 42–44
Cook, Tim 204
core business data 35, 169
  case studies 25–33
    Google' energy bill 25–29
    lessons learned 32–33
    Square 29–33
  defined 14
  evaluating performance and risk 33–35
  FutureHouse example 18–22
  machine learning advantage 22–23
  overview 14–15
  real estate marketplace example 16–18
corner cases and adversarial attacks 217–219
Crossing the Chasm (Moore) 200
crowdsourcing, labeling of data 173

customers
  churning, predicting 41
  classification of support tickets for 95
  helping choose content 164–166
  targeting of, improving 161–162

D

data
  biased 177–179
  cleaning 190, 203
  dollar density of 14, 17
  domain-specific 190
  preparing 190
  quality of 177–180
  structured 15, 174
  time-series data 175–176
data engineers 181
data science 7
data sources 160
data strategy 168–177
  amount of data needed 173–177
  where to get data 169–173
datasets
  contrarian examples in 178
  third-party 170–171
  using transfer learning with small datasets
    76–78
deconstructing AI products 152–157
deep learning
  costs of 76
  optimizing agriculture with 85–90
deep neural networks 73–76
Deepfakes (anonymous Reddit user) 219
DeepMind 27, 143
democratization of technology 220–221
depth metric, in NLP 93–96
  in text classification 102
  sentiment analysis and 98
diagnosis, in health care 224
Diffusion of Innovations (Rogers) 198
DL (deep learning), algorithms in 73
DL models
  as black box 83
  in NLP 104
DNA sequencing 225–226
doctors, AI 224–225
document search 106–108
dollar density of data 14, 17
domain-specific data 190
drug discovery 224–226
DS (data science) 7

E

early adopters 199
early majority 199
ECS (effective catalog size) metric 134
education 230–231
embeddings 80, 154
    in content-based systems 125–126
    in document search 107
    in text classification 103
emotional diary example 207–208
emotional glossaries 100
encodings. *See* embeddings
energy consumption optimization 226–228
Excel, number of columns vs. rows in 174
expert systems 3–4
    brittleness of 4
    maintainability of 4
explainable AI 83
explicitly programming computers 4
extremism, recommender engines and 216–217

F

face recognition 78–81
FaceApp 146
Facebook
    feed of 182
    label collection by 172
    Safety Check feature 223–224
failure of AI 204–209
    angry phone calls 208
    Anki 204–205
    emotional diary 207–208
    IBM Watson in Oncology 205–207
    Lighthouse Artificial intelligence (AI) 205
    underperforming sales 208–209
fairness 211, 213–214
fake content 219–220
false negatives. *See* FNs
false positives. *See* FPs
fault prediction 228
features 19–20, 160
    defined 21
    in customer churn prediction 39
    in image classification 70, 75
    in sentiment analysis 101
    in structured data 174
    in supervised learning 21, 172
    in web-based subscription business example 44
    number of 174
    recommender systems and 121–124
filter bubbles 215–217
filtering, collaborative 127–129
filters 71

finance 229–230
financial trading 230
first AI winter 3
FNs (false negatives) 52–53
    costs of 57
    implications of 57, 159–160
FPs (false positives) 52–54
    costs of 57
    implications of 57, 159–160
    recall metric and 57
Framing Canvas 158–161
    for automating industrial processes
        exercise 163
    for helping customers choose content
        exercise 164–165
    for improving customer targeting exercise
        161–162
freemium model 44
From Zero to AI (Valigi, Mauro) 110
future of AI 233
    AI as threat to society 211–220
        bias and fairness 211–214
        corner cases and adversarial attacks 217–219
        fake content 219–220
        filter bubbles 215–217
        jobs 214–215
    general AI 231–232
    opportunities in industries 222–231
        education 230–231
        energy 226–228
        finance 229–230
        health care 224–226
        manufacturing 228–229
        social media networks 223–224
    opportunities in society 220–222
        democratization of technology 220–221
        massive scale 221–222

G

gamification 231
Gao, Jim 14, 25, 28–29, 32, 142, 175
general AI. *See* AGI
genome sequencing 225
GitHub 170
Gomez-Uribe, Carlos 134–135
Google
    energy bill 25–29
    involvement in XtalPi 226
    label collection by 172
    reCAPTCHA 172
GPT-2 model 108–111, 219
Graham, Paul 101

H

health care 224–226
Hinton, Geoffrey 231
hosted infrastructure 191
human genome sequencing 225
Hunt, Neil 134–135

I

IBM Watson in Oncology 205–207
if-then rules 3
image classification 73–76
    face recognition 78–81
    features in 70, 75
    inputs and outputs of 69
    number of examples per class 176
    overview 69
ImageNet dataset 72, 176
implementation risk 186
implementation strategy 209
    building solutions 190–191
    failure of AI 204–209
        angry phone calls 208
        Anki 204–205
        emotional diary 207–208
        IBM Watson in Oncology 205–207
        Lighthouse Artificial 205
        underperforming sales 208–209
    Lean Strategy 192–197
        borrowing solutions 195
        building solutions 195–197
        buying solutions 193–194
    managing AI projects 202–204
    ML platforms 188–190
    turnkey solutions 186–188
    virtuous cycle of AI 197–202
incomplete training sets 178
industries, AI opportunities in 163, 222–231
inference 20
    defined 21
    in web-based subscription business example 43
    training vs. 20
initiators 141
innovation 140–144
innovators 199
inputs. See features
insurance industry 229
intelligence, defining 6
internal data 169
interpretable results 55

J

jobs 214–215
Jun-Yan Zhu 82

K

Kaggle website 170
Kava, Joe 27
known unknowns 34
Koike, Makoto 85
KPIs (key performance indicators) 28–29, 159–161
    for automating industrial processes 163
    for helping customers choose content 164–166
    for improving customer targeting 161–162

L

La Mesa, Luca 223
labels 19–20
    collecting 172–173
    defined 21
    hacked 173
    in customer churn prediction 38–39
    in sentiment analysis 101
    in supervised learning 172–173
    in unsupervised learning 48
    in web-based subscription business example 44
    labeling bias 212–214
    natural 172–173
    paid 173
laggards 199
late majority 199
leaders 141
Lean Startup, The (Ries) 192
Lean Strategy 192–197
    borrowing solutions 195
    building solutions 195–197
    buying solutions 193–194
load balancing 227
lock-in effect 188–189

M

M (Facebook Messenger's personal assistant) 92
"Machine Bias" 212
Machine Learning as a Service (MLaaS) 186
machine learning engineers 181–183
machine learning. *See* ML
maintainability, of expert systems 4
manufacturing 228–229
marketing. *See* sales and marketing
massive open online courses (MOOCs) 230
Matecat translation system 114

mathematics skills 180
McCarthy, John 2
Mechanical Turk 173
media 90
  AI for 176
  audio 84–85
  computer vision 69–72
  content generation and style transfer 81–82
  face recognition 78–81
  image classification 73–76
  optimizing agriculture with deep learning 85–90
  precautions 83–84
  transfer learning, using with small datasets 76–78
metrics, tying to business outcomes and risks 56–58
minimum viable AI (MVAI) 193
ML (machine learning)
  algorithms 21
    defined 19
    supervised learning and 21
  as black box 35
  defined 4
  frameworks for 220
  overview 4–6
  platforms for 188–190, 195
  problems, defined 19
  skills needed for 180
  See also features
ML inputs. *See* features
MLaaS (Machine Learning as a Service) 186–187
models
  defined 19, 21
  machine learning engineers and 181
  open source 191
  researchers and 181
ModernMT 115
MOOCs (massive open online courses) 230
Moore, Geoffrey A. 200
Musk, Elon 232
MVAI (minimum viable AI) 193

N

narrow AI 2
natural conversation 108–111
natural labels 172–173
Netflix 131–136
  business value of recommendations 134–135
  Continue Watching Ranker 132–133
  Page Generation algorithm 133
  Personalized Video Ranker algorithm 133
  PVR (Personalized Video Ranker) 131, 134
  recommender system of 131–133, 225

  Top N Video Ranker algorithm 132–133
  Trending Now algorithm 132–133
  Video-Video Similarity algorithm 133
"Netflix Recommender System, The" 134
neurons, artificial 73
NLP (natural language processing) 118
  adding NLP capabilities to organization 96–112
    designing products that overcome technology limitations 111–112
    document search 106–108
    natural conversation 108–111
    scoping NLP classification project 105–106
    sentiment analysis 99–101
    text classification 102–105
  complexity, measuring 93–96
  overview 92–93
  Translated case study 113–118

O

object classification 86
one-shot learning 80
open research 220–221
open source models 191
open source software 220–221
OpenAI 108–111, 220
Opower case study 58–64
opportunities for AI in industries
  education 230–231
  energy 226–228
  finance 229–230
  health care 224–226
  manufacturing 228–229
  social media networks 223–224
output. *See* labels

P

Page Generation algorithm, Netflix's 133
Pariser, Eli 215
Pearl, Judea 231
performance in sales and marketing, measuring 52–56
  classification algorithms 52–55
  clustering algorithms 55–56
performance, evaluating 33–35
personalization
  for business 38
  of educational content 230
Personalized Video Ranker (PVR), Netflix's 131, 133
Pfizer 225
photographs, AI-generated 219–220
Pole, Andrew 64

precautions 83–84
precision 54–56
predictions 19, 155
preparing data 190
Prisma app 82
profiling 50
projects
    AI 142
        breaking down into minimal technological
            components 157–161
        evaluating 146–150
        managing 202–204
        threats to 150, 152
    data science 7

R

readiness 147, 149–150, 222
real estate marketplace example 16–18
recall 54–57
reCAPTCHA 172
recommender systems 120–127, 215–217
    content-based systems beyond simple
        features 124–126
    limitations of features and similarity 126–127
    Netflix case study 131–133
    pitfalls of 129–131
redundant systems 218
research, open 220–221
researchers 181–183
return on investment (ROI) 146
reviews. See user reviews
Ribeiro, Marco 83
risks
    analyzing 150–152
    buy solutions and 188
    evaluating 33–35
    flexibilty and 192
    of implementation 186
    tying metrics to 56–58
Rogers, Everett 198
ROI (return on investment) 146
Rothman, Denis 231

S

SaaS (Software as a Service) business model 42
Safety Check feature, Facebook 223–224
sales and marketing 67
    automated customer segmentation 44–52
    boosting conversion rates and upselling 42–44
    case studies 58–67
        Opower 58–64
        Target 64–67

marketing segmentation 37–38, 44
measuring performance 52–56
    classification algorithms 52–55
    clustering algorithms 55–56
predicting churning customers 38–41
reasons to apply AI to 37–38
tying ML metrics to business outcomes and
    risks 56–58
Samuel, Arthur 4
scale 148–149, 221–222
scoping NLP classification project 105–106
Scrum 202
second AI winter 4
sentiment analysis 99–101, 223
    algorithms for 99
    buying solutions for 193
    example of 111
    number of examples per class 176
    on tweets 95
    social media and 223
skeptics 141
skills, needed for AI team 180
Smyte (company) 188
social media
    as source of data 223–224
    filter bubbles in 215–217
software engineering skills 180
software engineers 181–183
spam filtering 101
speech generation 85
speech recognition 84–85, 212
sprints 202
Square 29–33
stories 202
strong AI. See AGI
structured data 15, 174
style transfer 81–82
Superintelligence (Bostrom) 231
supervised classification 89, 153
supervised learning
    algorithms used with 21, 24
    features and 21
    labels and 24
    overview 21
    targets and 21
    unsupervised learning vs. 48
survivorship bias 179

T

take-rate 134
Target case study 64–67
targets. See labels
tasks, humans replaced by AI for 214–215
team, recruiting 180–184

technological risk 192
technological threats 150
technologists 141
technology, democratization of 220–221
Teichman, Alex 205
Tencent 226
TensorFlow framework 220
Tesla's autopilot 217
text classification 102–105, 154
text generation 219
text to speech 85
threat to society, AI as 211–220
    bias and fairness 211–214
    corner cases and adversarial attacks 217–219
    fake content 219–220
    filter bubbles 215–217
    jobs 214–215
threats to AI projects 150–152
time-series data 175–176
timeboxing 202
TNs (true negatives) 53, 57
Top N Video Ranker algorithm, Netflix's 132–133
topic classification 176
TPs (true positives) 53, 57
training 19
    defined 21
    incomplete training sets 178
    inference vs. 20
training distribution bias 211–212
transfer learning
    in NLP 103
    using with small datasets 76–78
Translated case study 113–118, 215
Trending Now algorithm, Netflix's 132–133
trigger word detection 85
Trombetti, Marco 113–118
turnkey solutions 186–188
tweets, sentiment analysis on 95

U

underperforming sales example 208–209
unknown unknowns 34
unsupervised learning 45–49
    in energy company case study 62
    supervised learning vs. 48
upselling 42–44
user experience 130
user reviews
    overview 97
    sentiment analysis of 99–101
    text classification and 102–105

V

value-based health care 224
Vector (robotic toy) 204
Video-Video Similarity algorithm, Netflix's 133
violent material 223
virtuous cycle of AI 198–202

W

Waibel, Alex 5
wide approach, to data collection 179
width metric, in NLP 93–96
    in text classification 102
    sentiment analysis and 98
word embeddings, in document search 107

X

XtalPi 226

Y

YouTube, recommender engine of 216